TROPICAL FLOWERS
of Southeast Asia

Text by
William Warren

Photos by
Luca Invernizzi Tettoni

PERIPLUS

EDITIONS

Published by Periplus Editions (HK) Ltd.

Copyright © 1996 Periplus Editions (HK) Ltd. All rights reserved.
Printed in the Republic of Singapore.
ISBN 962-593-134-1

Publisher: Eric M. Oey
Design: Peter Ivey
Editors: Thomas G. Oey, Berenice Braislin Oey
Production: Mary Chia, Su T. C.

Distributors

Benelux Countries
Nilsson & Lamm
Postbus 195, 1380 AD Weesp, The Netherlands

Germany
Brettschneider Fernreisebedurf GMBH
Hauptstrasse 5, D-85586 Poing

Indonesia
C. V. Java Books
P.O. Box 55 JKCP, Jakarta 10510

Japan
Charles E. Tuttle Inc.
21-13, Seki 1-Chome, Tama-ku, Kawasaki, Kanagawa 214

Malaysia and Singapore
Berkeley Books Pte. Ltd.
5 Little Rd, #08-01, Cemtex Industrial Building, Singapore 536983

Scandinavia
Platypus Förlag
Inspekrörsgatan 4, 252 27 Helsingborg, Sweden

Introduction

The first Southeast Asian gardens, in the Western sense of the term, were those planted around royal palaces and Buddhist or Hindu temples. From written accounts, we know that these included trees and shrubs sometimes selected purely for their ornamental qualities but more often because of their symbolic associations and use in ceremonies. In the earliest days the plants were nearly all native to the region, but these were later joined by countless introduced specimens, to such an extent that few, if any, of the surviving landscapes bear much resemblance to their original composition.

The gardens of ordinary homes were similarly prescribed by tradition, serving utilitarian rather than decorative aims. The overwhelming majority of the specimens produced edible fruits or leaves and roots that could be used in cooking or traditional medicine.

All this began to change with the arrival of outsiders, mainly Europeans, who brought with them not only new concepts of garden design (and purpose) but also new ornamentals to enhance them. The movement of plant materials around the world during the past 500 years is an extraordinary story, nowhere more so than in tropical regions where the climate enabled introduced species to become established within a short time.

Take, for instance, the now ubiquitous chilli pepper, essential to a dozen or so cuisines. This pungent little fruit was unknown outside its native tropical America before Columbus made his historic voyage toward the end of the 15th century, one of his objectives being to discover the source of the black pepper then so coveted in Europe. Precisely how and when chillies made their way to Asia is unknown, but they were almost certainly brought by some of the Western explorers who came in the next century and rapidly became such an integral part of various cultures it is difficult to imagine their absence.

The same thing happened with countless ornamental plants. These came primarily from Central and South America, but also from Africa, remote islands like Madagascar, and arid Australia. Every Southeast Asian garden today displays evidence of this great botanical migration through such now common species as the Acacia and the Flame Tree, the Allamanda and the Bougainvillea, the Canna and the Heliconia, to select but a few at random.

Some came early and haphazardly. Others were introduced more systematically through the great 19th-century botanical gardens. With few exceptions, they adapted quickly, and many soon could be found growing as wild as real natives. The process still continues. Visit any nursery plant market in Jakarta, Singapore, or Bangkok today, and you will find specimens that have yet to acquire local cultural associations, sometimes even local names. Come back in a few years, though and they may well be relatively commonplace.

Adenium

ADENIUM OBESUM (A. COETANEUM)

Botanical Family:
Apocynaceae
Thai name:
Chuan-chom
Malay name:
Adenium merah
Indonesian name:
Adenium merah

A member of the same botanical family as the Frangipani—it is, in fact, sometimes called the Japanese Frangipani—Adenium is a small treelet native to arid East Africa and Arabia, reaching a height of about 1 m. It has pale-grey succulent stems that produce a white, poisonous latex when cut, glossy club-shaped leaves at the branch ends, and, unlike most succulents, an almost continuous display of large, trumpet-shaped flowers that range in color from pink to crimson. The leaves often fall during wet weather or when the plant is in flower.

Intolerant of damp conditions, Adenium is usually seen grown as a pot plant in Southeast Asia, preferring a sunny location on a balcony or terrace and a well-drained potting soil mixture. It may also be used in rock gardens. Propagation is most often by cuttings, though old plants may produce seeds. Frequent applications of liquid manure increases flowering, which in the right location is more or less continuous.

African Tulip Tree

SPATHODEA CAMPANULATA

The main attraction of this ornamental tree is its large, tulip-shaped, orange-red flowers, sometime 3 inches in diameter, which appear several times a year in clusters at the ends of its higher branches. Each flower lasts for several days before it falls and is replaced by another; a cluster may thus continue to bloom for a month or more. The flowers are followed by long, boat-shaped pods which eventually split open to release masses of winged seeds. A rare variety has pure yellow flowers, but seeds rarely breed true and the only certain method of propagating these is by root cuttings.

A native of Uganda, *Spathodea* grows into an upright tree up to 10 m. high with dark-green compound leaves. Because of its rapid growth—as much as 6 feet in a year—the wood tends to be soft and brittle; branches are likely to break in high winds, making it unsuitable for planting near a house. It thrives in almost any kind of soil but needs full sun to bloom well.

Botanical Family: *Bignonia*

Thai name: *Khae sad*

Malay names: *Sepatu diat, Pancut-pancut*

Indonesian names: *Sepatu diat, Ki engsrot*

Allamanda

ALLAMANDA CATHARTICA

Botanical Family:
Apocynaceae

Thai name:
Ban buree

Malay name:
Alamanda kuning

Indonesian names
*Alamanda kuning;
Lame aruey (Sunda)*

Originally from Central and South America and named after the Brazilian naturalist Allamand, the bright yellow-flowering Allamanda has become a garden staple in most parts of the tropics, usually as a woody climber but often, too, as a bushy shrub in a variety called *A. schotti*. One variety known as *A. grandiflora* has particularly large funnel-shaped flowers up to 10 cm. in diameter, while another, *A. violacea*, has pale mauve blooms. There is also a dwarf cultivar increasingly seen in low plantings. Given a sunny location, it flowers continuously and requires little attention; it is often used in seaside gardens. All varieties can be propagated easily by cuttings.

As with other members of the *Apocyaceae* family, such as the Frangipani, all parts of the plant, including its milky sap, are poisonous, but the leaves, made into an infusion, are used in traditional medicine in South America as a purgative and vapor produced by boiling the leaves is said to be a remedy for coughs.

Angel's Trumpet

DATURA SUAVEOLENS

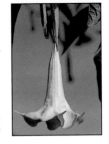

There are several varieties of *Datura*, most of which become small trees several meters high and have very large white, trumpet-shaped flowers that hang like bells from the branches; on some the flowers may be pink or mauve. In Indonesia, the shape of the flower has inspired the name kecubung, (also used for the loudspeakers on old phonographs.) The leaves are greyish-green and spear-shaped and the wood is quite brittle. The plant grows best at slightly higher altitudes.

Daturas belong to the same family as the Deadly Nightshade (which also includes the familiar tomato) and contains the poisonous alkaloid scopolamine, though in some varieties like *D. metel* it is more concentrated than in others. In properly controlled quantities the chemical produces hallucinations, which has resulted in its use in religious rituals both in its native tropical America and also in some parts of Southeast Asia; a miscalculation, however, can be fatal.

Botanical Family:
Solanaceae

Thai names: *Datura suaveolens*, *Lam-pong*

Malay name:
Kecubong

Indonesian name:
Kecubung

Balsam

IMPATIENS BALSAMINA

Botanical Family:
Balsaminaceae

Thai name:
Thian

Malay names:
Pacar air, Balsam,
Keembung, Inai ayam

Indonesian names:
Pacar air, Balsem,
Keembung, Inai ayam

There are numerous varieties of *Impatiens*, a number of which are native to Southeast Asia. *I. balsamina*, commonly known as the Annual or Garden Balsam, produces white, pink, red or purple flowers on a fleshy stem and is grown commercially in some places for the production of fingernail dye. The flower petals are sometimes used as offerings in Bali. One variety, *I. oncidiodes*, has yellow flowers and is native to the highland areas of Malaysia.

More ornamental varieties, called Busy Lizzies, are usually grown as decorative pot plants on verandas and terraces or in moist, semi-shaded locations beside ponds and waterfalls. They can be found in a wide range of flower colors, from white to bright crimson, some with double blossoms and others with dark purple leaves. These hybrids require intensive manuring and seeds of the double-flowering types do not always breed true. At higher altitudes, *Impatiens* become quite sizeable shrubs several feet high and can be used in massed plantings.

Banana

MUSA SP.

In addition to the dozen or so edible bananas found in every Southeast Asian country, there are a number of varieties grown as ornamental plants in gardens. These are generally smaller than the commercial bananas, with either attractively patterned leaves or, more often, striking flowers—actually bracts—that shoot up prominently from the crown; the fruits are small and usually inedible.

On *M. coccinea*, native to tropical Southeast Asia, the bracts are a brilliant red-orange, while on another variety they are pale lavender. *M. sumatrana*, popularly known as the Sumatran Banana, grows to several meters in height and has leaves that are beautifully patterned with purple markings when they are young. *M. velutina* not only has decorative pink bracts but also small bright-pink, velvety fruits full of seeds; as they ripen, the fruit peels gradually fold back, hence its popular name the "self-peeling banana."

In a garden, these ornamental bananas need protection from strong wind and moist, jungle conditions.

Botanical Family:
Musacae

Thai name: *Kluay*

Malay name:
Pisang

Indonesian name:
Pisang

9

Bat Lily

TACCA INTEGREFOLIA (T. CRISTATA)

Botanical Family:
Taccaceae

Thai name:
Niam ruesee

Malay name:
Keladi murai

Indonesian name:
Keladi murai

The Bat Lily, sometimes also called the Black Lily, is one of the most unusual plants found growing in the jungles of Southeast Asia and, increasingly, as an oddity in many gardens. From its rosette of handsome, glossy-green leaves emerges a series of purplish-black flowers that do indeed resemble rather fanciful bats with their strange, outwardly curving petals and sepals and long, whiskery appendages. This is one of the very few black-flowering plants in the world. To be grown successfully in a garden, it requires protection from the sun, ample moisture, and rich, well-drained soil. In the wild, the Bat Lily dies down in the dry season and returns with the rains.

There are about 60 species of *Tacca*, most of which originate in Southeast Asia, and some produce different-colored flowers—green and brown, for example, or green with yellow and purple markings. A member of the same family is *T. leontopetaloides*, the arrowroot, which is an important source of starch in its native South Pacific.

Bottlebrush

CALLISTEMON

Native to Australia, *Callistemon* is a family that consists of some 30 species, most of which are distinguished by their drooping spikes of bright red flowers that appear on young twigs and do indeed resemble the brushes that give the small tree its popular name. The tree can attain a height of several meters but is usually less, taking an attractive, willow-like form with small, greyish green leaves along branches that sway pendulously in a breeze. Leafy sections on the branches alternate with the flowering sections.

Not surprisingly in view of its homeland, the Bottlebrush prefers a dry location—it does well in seaside gardens—and flowering is reduced in wet soil or during prolonged rain. Pruning will also reduce flowering but is sometimes necessary to achieve a denser crown and a more attractive shape.

In Australia there are many other varieties of *Callistemon*, including one with creamy white flowers, but these are not yet common to Southeast Asian gardens.

Botanical Family: *Myrtaceae*

Thai name: *Liew dok*

Malay names: *Berus botol, Kalistemom*

Indonesian names: *Berus botol, Kalistemom*

Bougainvillea

BOUGAINVILLEA SP.

Botanical Family:
Nyctaginaceae

Thai name:
Fuang fah

Malay names:
Buganvil, Buginvila,
Bunga kertas

Indonesian names:
Buganvil, Kembang
kertas, Bunga kertas

Named after Louis de Bougainville, a French navigator who first came across it in Brazil during the 18th century, Bougainvillea now lends brilliant splashes of color throughout the tropical and sub-tropical world, from the beaches of Bali to the Mediterranean. The "flowers" are actually colored bracts, each of which carries an insignificant true white flower at its base.

There are two main groups, *B. glabra* and *B. spectabilis*, which have been cross-bred and hybridized into numerous varieties that vary widely in color, form, and size of bract. Those belonging to the *glabra* group tend to flower year-round in Southeast Asia, while those of the *spectabilis* group are at their best only in the dry season; since they require plenty of sunlight and well-drained soil, both are ideal for seaside gardens. Another group, known as Mrs. Butt, consists of seasonal bloomers and are often grown as potted specimens on terraces.

Purple or magenta are the most common Bougainvillea colors, but other hues may range from pure white to orange to rich crimson. Some hybrids have two colors on the same plant—pink and white, for instance, or pink and orange—and are known as "rainbow" Bougainvilleas. There is also a variety with huge double bracts, whose principal disadvantage as an ornamental is the fact that the bracts remain on the plant after turning brown and must be removed by hand to prevent the plant from looking unsightly.

Though by nature a scandent shrub, Bougainvillea can be grown on supports as a vine, clipped into a hedge, or trained to make a free-standing standard. (The latter has become popular among wealthy Thais in recent years, probably because of its resemblence to the old topiary plants that were once commonly used in local gardens.) Propagation is by woody cuttings, and the plants should be pruned after flowering to ensure abundant new growth.

12

Canna

CANNA SP.

Botanical Family:
Cannaceae

Thai name:
Buddha-raksa

Malay names:
Bunga tasbih, Kana

Indonesian names:
Bunga tasbih, Kana
Ganyong, Puspa

Native to tropical America and the Caribbean, Cannas in numerous hybrid forms have long been popular in Southeast Asian gardens, where they were one of the earliest foreign introductions, often grown along drives or in large, massed beds The commonest flower colors are yellow and red, but they are also found in pink, orange, cream, and mixtures; similarly, some of the hybrids have handsome dark purple or variegated leaves rather than the usual pale green.

Cannas require full sunlight, rich soil, and plenty of water to flower well. Propagation is by root division, and the stalk should be cut back to the ground or pulled out after blooming; many gardeners believe the entire bed should be dug up after a year and replanted.

Ripe Canna seeds are strung into prayer beads by both Buddhists and Muslims, while in Hawaii they are made into ornamental leis. The rhizomes of some species are also cooked and eaten or made into an arrowroot starch.

Champak

MICHELIA CHAMPACA

Native to the region and belonging to the same family as the much larger Magnolia, Champak produces rather inconspicuous but intensely fragrant flowers that are used extensively in floral decorations and as religious offerings in Thailand, Bali, and the Indian communities in Malaysia. *M. champaca*, most commonly seen in gardens, is a small tree with glossy leaves and yellow or orange flowers; *M. alba*, which has white flowers, is much larger, growing up to 40 feet. The flowers of both have 12 narrow, waxy petals in three series, the inner series being the smallest, that radiate around a greenish pistil. The larger flowers can be up to 10 cm. in diameter, while smaller ones are only about 1 cm. Flowering is year-round.

Oil extracted from the flowers can be used in the production of perfumes, and a preparation made from the bark is used in traditional medicine to reduce fever.

Champak trees do best in sandy soil or high ground with good drainage and no flooding.

Botanical Family:
Magnoliaceae

Thai name:
Champi

Malay name:
Cempaka kuning

Indonesian names:
Kantil; Locari (Java),

Chenille Plant

ACALYPHA HISPIDA

Botanical Family:
Euphorbiaceae

Thai name:
Hang ka-rok

Malay names:
Ekor kera, Akalifa ekor kucing

Indonesian names:
Ekor kucing; Tali anjing (Sunda), Wunga tambang (Java)

Also popularly known as Cat's Tail, this bushy shrub with bright-green oblong leaves is striking because of its prominent display of hanging inflorescences, each up to 50 cm. long and carrying numerous small flowers. Those usually seen in gardens have dark red flowers, but there is one variety with deep purple flowers and another with white. The plant may grow as high as 2 m. and flowers year round but requires considerable pruning to keep it from becoming too tall and untidy.

The *Acalypha* family also includes a number of popular foliage plants which enliven gardens with their brightly-colored leaves rather than their flowers. These include *A. wilkesiana*, sometimes called the Beefsteak Plant, on which the leaves are red or copper colored, and *A. godsefiana*, on which the leaves are ruffled and grow tightly together. All Acalyphas require a location with plenty of sun. In many gardens, they are prone to attack by insects and thus require regular spraying to look their best.

Copperpod Tree

PELTOPHORUM PTEROCARPUM (P. INERME)

This popular garden tree, grown both for its shade and its flowers, is also sometimes called the Yellow Flame Tree or the Yellow Poinciana since its umbrella shape and small, doubly-compound fern-like leaves are similar to those of *Delonix regia*. The bright-yellow flowers which appear in erect clusters are smaller and different in shape, however, and the tree as a whole is denser.

The leaves fall for a short time during the dry season and the velvety-brown flower buds appear along with new growth; the flowers continue after the tree is fully leafed, creating an attractive mixture of yellow and green. Flowering is followed by masses of thin, flat copper-colored pods, each holding three or four seeds, which give the tree its other popular name.

Native to coastal Malaysia and tolerant of most conditions, the tree is often planted along avenues and in parks for shade. The bark is used in Java to make a dark brown color for dyeing batik cloth.

Botanical Family:
Caesalpiniaceae

English name:
Copperpod tree

Thai name: *Non-see*

Malay name:
Batai laut

Indonesian names:
Batai laut, Soga

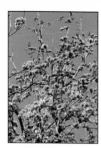

Coral Tree

ERYTHRINA SP.

Botanical Family:
Leguminosae

Thai name:
Thong-lang

Malay names:
Dadap, Dedap

Indonesian names:
*Dadap, Dadap ayam,
Dadap laut,
Cangkring*

There are around 65 species of *Erythrina*, some native to North and South America, others to Australia, Africa, and East Asia. The variety seen most often in Southeast Asian gardens is *E. variegata (indica)*, a fast-growing spiny tree with large three-parted leaves. In areas with a pronounced dry season such as Thailand, northern Malaysia, and most of Indonesia, the tree sheds its leaves for a short period and then, just as new growth starts, is covered with a mass of beautiful scarlet flowers. The tree is also known as the Dadap and the Tiger's Claw, the latter a reference to the shape of the flowers.

There is also a form with boldly patterned green and yellow leaves that makes a handsome foliage addition even when not in bloom and a small variety on which both leaves and flowers appear at the same time. Quite large cuttings, 2 m. or more in length, will easily root and become sizeable trees, which is perhaps why the Balinese regard it as a symbol of life-energy.

Crepe Ginger

COSTUS SPECIOSUS

Despite its popular name, this is only a rather distant relative of the edible ginger. Like many other members of the large *Costus* family its stalks tend to curve spirally from underground tubers to a height of up to 3 meters; these then produce large, brownish-red bracts, resembling small pineapples, from which emerge the delicate frilly white flowers. The three true petals of each flower are inconspicuous, almost hidden by the large crepy white stamen which takes a bell form with fluted edges and a yellow throat. The young shoots may be eaten as vegetables.

Botanical Family:
Zingiberaceae

Thai name:
Ueang-mai-na

Malay names:
Kostus setawar,
Pacing, Globa utan

Indonesian names:
Kostus setawar,
Pacing, Pacing tawar

The Crepe Ginger prefers a protected, jungle-like environment and can be found growing wild through much of Southeast Asia, its native region. It flowers most profusely during the rainy season.

Another *Costus* sometimes seen in gardens or as an ornametal pot plant is *C. malortieanus*, which is smaller and is grown less for its rather inconspicuous flowers than for its velvety, oval leaves, patterned with light and dark green.

Crown Flower

CALOTROPIS GIGANTEA

Botanical Family:
Asclepiadaceae

Thai name: *Dok rak*

Malay names:
Widuri, Reminggu

Indonesian names:
Biduri, Widuri

This large, rather sprawling shrub, which belongs to the milkweed family, grows wild along the shores of Southeast Asia and the Pacific and is also popular in dry gardens exposed to strong sea winds, where less hardy plants find it difficult to survive. It has oval, light-green leaves, milky stems, and almost continuous clusters of waxy flowers that are either lavender or white in color; each flower consists of five pointed petals in a star shape, from the center of which rises a small, elegant "crown" that holds the stamens.

In Thailand, the long-lasting flowers are often used in leis and other floral arrangements. In some parts of Bali the lavender flowers are used to make magic designs before a cremation ceremony, while the white ones are used in offerings. They were also reputedly popular with Hawaii's Queen Liliuokalani, who regarded them as emblems of royalty and wore them strung into leis. The flowers have also been imitated in carved ivory.

Cup of Gold

SOLANDRA NITIDA

This woody creeper, a native of Mexico, belongs to the same family as the Tomato and the Deadly Nightshade, though it bears little outward resemblance to either. It has large, fleshy, rather pointed leaves and very large, cup-like yellow-gold flowers, each about 20 to 22 cm. long; the interior petals are streaked with brown. Once the heavy buds begin to unfold, the process is so rapid it can be watched. In most parts of Southeast Asia it blooms profusely several times a year, though there are usually some flowers at almost any time. Given a strong support, it will climb quite rapidly and soon form a dense mass.

Another variety, *S. longifolia*, often seen in Singapore and Malaysian gardens, is more of a scandent shrub; it has oval leaves and creamy-white flowers and is popularly called the Chalice Vine. This can be grown in a large pot, clipped into a hedge, or in a bed of mixed species. Both varieties are easily propagated by cuttings and grow in sun or light shade.

Botanical Family:
Solanaceae

Thai name:
Tuay-thong

Malay name:
Solandra kuning emas

Indonesian name:
Solandra kuning emas

Firecracker Plant

RUSSELIA EQUISETIFORMIS (R. JUNCEA)

Botanical Family:
Scrophulariaceae

Thai name:
Russelia, prathat Chine

Malay name:
Ruselia letup-letup

Indonesian name:
Ruselia letup-letup

Also sometimes called the Coral Plant or the Fountain Plant, this native of Mexico is a scandent shrub with long drooping stems, tiny leaves, and small, bright-red tubular flowers that appear along the stems and that resemble tiny firecrackers. It prefers full sun and dry conditions for profuse flowering and is often seen used in a rock garden or a raised bed so that its hanging branches appear to maximum effect. *R. sarmentosa* is a more shrubby variety with smaller, less showy flowers, sometimes used in borders.

The plant needs to be pruned back hard at least once a year to make it bushier. The plants can be divided for propagation or cuttings can be used.

Another, very different shrub, *Hamelia patens*, is also called the Firecracker Plant in Thailand; the small tubular flowers on this are red-orange in color, it has pale green rounded leaves, and becomes a good-sized shrub when grown in the full sun.

Flame Tree

DELONIX REGIA

Discovered in the early 19th century in its native Madagascar by the botanist Wensel Bojer, the Flame Tree—also variously known as the Flamboyant, the Poinciana, and the Flame of the Forest—quickly spread throughout the tropics and became one of the most popular ornamental trees.

Growing rapidly from seed, the tree may reach a height of 5 to 8 m. and forms a dome of long, sweeping branches with attractive feathery, fern-like leaves. The most spectacular flowering occurs in places where there is a prolonged dry season; after a leaf drop, the tree remains bare for several months and then, just as the new leaves appear, it bursts into an almost solid mass of blossoms that vary in color from crimson and scarlet to orange and apricot, scarlet being the most common. Somewhat resembling a *Cattleya* orchid, each flower has five petals, one of which is erect and usually white streaked with red. The flowers are replaced by heavy brown seed pods that remain on the tree for months.

Botanical Family:
Leguminosae

Thai name:
Hang-nok-yung

Malay names:
Flamboyan, Merak, Semarak api, Sepanggil

Indonesian names:
Flamboyan, Merak

Frangipani

PLUMERIA SP.

Botanical Family:
Apocynaceae

Thai name: *Lan-tom*

Malay names:
Cempaka kubur,
Cempaka mulia,
Kamboja

Indonesian names:
Kemboja, Cempaka,
Bunga Jepun

The Frangipani is among the easiest of tropical trees to propagate from seeds, cuttings, and air-layering, which is perhaps one reason why this native of the New World quickly spread to other warm-weather regions. Another is the beauty of its fragrant, five-petalled flowers, which are used as offerings in both Buddhist and Hindu ceremonies; it is also seen planted in Muslim cemeteries in Malaysia and Indonesia.

The small to medium-sized tree was named after the French botanist Charles Plumier (1646-1706), who made three voyages to the Caribbean area in the 17th century. It has acquired an unusual range of popular names, among them Dead Man's Fingers (Australia), Jasmin de Cayenne (Brazil), and the Pagoda or Temple Tree (India). Two explanations have been given for Frangipani, the commonest. According to one, it was derived from a perfume created by an Italian family of the same name before the discovery of the Western Hemisphere; another claims that the thick white latex that flows from a cut in the tree reminded French settlers in the Caribbean of "frangipanier," or coagulated milk.

There are several distinct species, of which the most widely-cultivated is *P. rubra*, the progenitor of countless varieties. *P. rubra forma acutifolia*, for example, has very fragrant white flowers with yellow centers, while others come in varying shades of pink, yellow, red, and combinations. *P. obtusa* has somewhat larger white flowers and blunt-ended leaves. There are also dwarf varieties that are popular with container gardeners.

Except for *P. obtusa* and some of its varieties, all Plumerias have an annual dormant period in which they stop growing and flower less profusely; many shed their leaves at this time. They require good sun and well-drained soil to flower best. Cuttings root easily in a mixture of sand and light soil, as do even quite large branches; trees up to 7 meters high with almost no roots can be moved without any serious setback.

Gardenia

GARDENIA JASMINOIDES

Botanical Family:
Rubiaceae

Thai name: *Pud sorn*

Malay names: *Bunga cina, Gardenia jasmin*

Indonesian names: *Kaca piring, Gardenia jasmin*

Regarded almost as an emblem of the tropics, the intensely fragrant Gardenia is a native of South China, a bushy shrub that can grow up to 3 m. but is usually kept smaller by pruning. It has glossy green oval leaves and pure-white flowers, double in the variety most commonly seen in Southeast Asian gardens. One form has variegated, green-and-white leaves, and there is also a dwarf variety that is somewhat more temperamental and thus often grown as a pot plant.

Gardenia flowers are short-lived, soon turning yellow with a black center, which is probably why they are less commonly seen in offerings and floral arrangements than other fragrant blossoms.

Another species is G. *carinata*, the Malaysian Tree Gardenia, which can grow to 10 m. high and has fragrant flowers that are creamy white when they open but turn orange later. Flowering on this type is less frequent than on the shrub variety.

Globe Amaranth

GOMPHRENA GLOBOSA

Though native to more arid regions of the New World, this small, shrubby annual—also popularly called Batchelor's Buttons—is widely grown in most of Southeast Asia thanks to its profusion of long-lasting flowers. These are globular in shape and actually consist of numerous individual flowers, each enclosed by papery petals; the most common color is magenta, but there are also white and pale mauve varieties. Blooming occurs for around three months during the rainy season, inspiring one of its Indonesian names which translates as the "three-month flower." The flowers retain their color for more than a week.

The flowers are used in Bali in religious offerings (above right) and to decorate sacred flags, while in Thailand they form the most important component of a traditional floral arrangement in which blooms are imbedded in shaped mounds of damp sawdust. To the confusion of visiting plant collectors, Thais often dye the flowers, producing unusual colors never seen in nature.

Botanical Family:
Amaranthaceae

Thai name:
Ban-mai-ru-ruey

Malay names:
Ratnapakaya, Bunga kancing, Gomfrena

Indonesian names:
Ratnapakaya, Bunga kancing, Gomfrena

Golden Dewdrop

DURANTA REPENS

Botanical Family:
Verbenaceae

Thai name:
Tien thong

Malay name:
Duranta

Indonesian name:
Duranta

This tall shrub, seen in many gardens, receives its popular name from the small, yellow-orange berries that follow the flowers, in such quantities that they cause the slender branches to droop gracefully. The flowers are either white or a delicate lilac-blue and often appear in combination with the berries. A native of tropical America introduced to Southeast Asia in relatively recent years, the shrub may grow several meters tall but is generally smaller. Flowering and fruiting are almost continuous but the plant needs regular pruning to maintain an attractive shape.

There is another form of *Duranta* with variegated leaves, which blooms and fruits less profusely, as well as one in which the leaves are bright yellow in a sunny location. These are often kept sharply pruned and used as ground covers or as low hedges, though in Thailand they are sometimes trained into topiary-like standards. The yellow-leafed variety, which Thais call "Golden Tea" (*tien thong*) becomes a large shrub if not kept clipped back.

Golden Shower Tree

CASSIA FISTULA

This native of India, also known as the Indian Laburnum, is one of the most beautiful of all tropical trees when it sheds its leaves and bursts into a mass of long, pendulous yellow-gold flowers. This generally takes place at the height of the dry, hot season, but the tree also blooms well in damper places like Singapore. The flowers are followed by long black cylindrical seed pods which contain a pulp used in some places as a purgative. *C. fistula* is the national tree of Thailand, where it is often seen along roads and avenues.

Other *Cassia* varieties are also found in gardens and public plantings. *C. multijuga* and *C. siamea* are yellow-flowering, while *C. bakeriana*, a native of Thailand, has pink blooms. *C. javanica*, less commonly seen, has pink and white flowers; crosses between this and *C. fistula* have produced many hybrids called Rainbow Shower Trees, with blends of pink, yellow, and apricot, although these do not seem to do as well in Southeast Asia as in places like Hawaii.

Botanical Family:
Leguminosae

Thai name:
Raja-pruk

Malay names:
Tengguli, Kasia sena, Bereksa

Indonesian names:
Trangguli, Tengguli, Kasia sena, Bereksa

Heliconia

HELICONIA SP.

Heliconias are native to the American tropics, and while a few can be found in seasonally dry locations, most come from moist or wet regions. The genus belongs to a larger taxonomic category called the Zingiberales, which also includes *Musaseae* (bananas), *Strelitziaceae* (birds of paradise), *Zingiberaceae* (gingers), *Costaceae* (Costus), *Cannaceae* (Cannas), and *Marantaceae* (Marantas).

Growing from rhizomes, they have erect shoots, each composed of a stem and leaves and often (though not always) terminated by an inflorescense of frequently brilliant color which comes from the bracts rather than the actual flower. There are three basic leaf arrangements: those on which the leaves are oriented vertically and have long petioles, like bananas; those on which the leaves are more or less horizontally positioned and have short petioles, like gingers; and those on which the leaves stick out obliquely, like Cannas.

Botanical Family:
Heliconiaceae

Thai name:
Kam-pu

Malay name:
Helikonia

Indonesian name:
Helikonia

Flower bracts are usually bright red, yellow, or both, but may be green or pink. They may be smooth or covered with either short or long woolly hairs, and prominently erect, emerging from the base of the leaves, or pendant. On some, the main attraction is not the inflorescence but the coloration of the leaves. There are dwarf Heliconias, medium-sized ones, and giants that can reach several meters or more. Approximately 250 species and almost as many forms or cultivars have been identified.

Among the varieties often seen in Southeast Asian gardens are *H. bihai*, commonly called the Lobster Claw, which has bright red bracts; *H. striata*, which includes the low-growing Dwarf Jamaica; *H. psittacorum*, a large group of medium-sized Heliconias with orange, yellow, pink, or cream-colored bracts, often in combinations; and *H. caribaea*, giants with yellow or red bracts. Hanging Heliconias include *H. rostrata*, with red and yellow bracts and *H. chartacea* (popularly known as "Sexy Pink"), with spectacular pendulous red and pink bracts.

Hibiscus

HIBISCUS SP.

Botanical Family:
Malvaceae

Thai name: *Cha-ba*

Malay names:
*Kembang sepatu,
Bunga raya, Bebaru,
and others according
to species*

Indonesian names:
*Kembang sepatu,
Bunga raya, Bebaru,
and others according
to species*

There are few tropical gardens that do not contain at least one, and usually several, of the numerous varieties of Hibiscus. *H. rosa-sinensis*, the most common type, originated in South China, where it had much smaller flowers than the showy hybrids that have been developed over the years, particularly in Florida and Hawaii. Another variety, *H. schizopetalus*, native to East Africa, has pendulous flowers with lacy petals and a long pistil that hang from the shrub like small chandeliers. New hybrids are constantly being introduced, thus increasing the already extensive choice available to gardeners.

Hibiscus flowers range in size from small to enormous (some as much as 20 to 30 cm. in diameter), occur in both single and double forms, and come in almost every color, from pure white through yellow and pink to ruby-red. One species, *H. syriacus*, has bluish mauve flowers, though this does not grow as well in the tropics as in cooler climates. Some varieties also have attractive variegated foliage, green and white tinged with pink, which makes them useful in massed bed planting.

Though Hibiscus flowers last only one day, most varieties bloom so profusely there are nearly always several open at any time. The red Hibiscus is the national flower of Malaysia and is commonly seen in offerings and as decorations in Bali. In Indonesia it is called the "shoe flower," supposedly a reference to the fact that juice extracted from the petals was used to darken shoes. Both leaves and flowers are edible and sometimes used in traditional medicine.

Also seen in some gardens, though quite different in appearance from the usual Hibiscus, is *H. mutabilis*, popularly called the Rose of Sharon or the Changeable Rose. This is a very large shrub up to 5 m. high with greyish-green leaves; the large flowers, either single or double, are pure white in the morning but change to deep pink by late afternoon.

33

Honolulu Creeper

ANTIGONON LEPTOPUS

Botanical Family:
Polygonaceae

Thai name: *Puang chom-pu*

Malay name: *Bunga berteh*

Indonesian name: *Bunga berteh*

Also variously known as the Mexican Creeper, Bride's Tears, and the Coral Vine, this native of Mexico (where it is called *cadena de amor* or "chain of love") is a slender climber seen growing on many walls and fences. It has rough, heart-shaped leaves with wavy edges and almost continuous sprays of small flowers that are usually pink but also occur in white. The flowers have no petals, the colored part being the calyx; they last for some time in water and are thus useful in flower arrangements. The plant climbs by means of curling tendrils and grows quite rapidly, as high as 10 m. if provided with proper support. The lower parts, however, become rather bare after a time and the vine may have to be sharply pruned back if a thick screen is desired.

Propagation is by seed, but those from the white variety do not breed true and cuttings must be used. Honolulu Creepers need full sun to flower profusely and, as their place of origin suggests, do not like damp locations.

Ixora

IXORA SP.

A sturdy, free-flowering shrub that thrives under a variety of conditions, Ixora is one of the most popular garden plants all over Southeast Asia. Its flowers, which occur in clusters of as many as 60 at the ends of the branches, are found in a wide range of colors and its size may be either dwarf or quite large.

Botanical Family:
Rubiaceae

Thai name: *Khem*

Malay names:
Iksora, Soka, Kembang santen merah, Kembang asoka

Indonesian names:
Soka, Kembang asoka, Iksora

The most common is *I. javanica*, a medium to tall shrub with largish pointed leaves, on which the flower clusters are red or red-orange. *I. coccinea* is smaller with more rounded, glossy leaves and flowers that may be red (the usual color), yellow, or orange, while *I. chinensis*, still smaller, has white, yellow, pink, or orange blooms. *I. finlaysoniana*, native to Thailand, is quite large, almost a small tree, and has fragrant white flowers. A dwarf form of *I. coccinea*, which grows only to a height of around half a meter and has smaller leaves and flowers than the normal form, is popular for making low hedges or for use in a formal, European-style garden.

Jade Vine

STRONGYLODON MACROBOTRYS

Botanical Family:
Leguminosae

Thai name:
Puang yok

Malay name:
Strongilodon

Indonesian name:
Strongilodon

For sheer beauty, few other vines can equal this native of the Philippine jungle in full bloom. A rampant climber, it ascends high into trees or densely covers a pergola with its three-parted leaves that are brownish and limp when they first appear. The pea-type flowers, which hang down in spectacular clusters as much as a meter long, are a bluish jade-green, one of the rarest colors in the plant world. Each flower has long pointed keels and wings that curve back; long-lasting, they are used for leis in Hawaii.

The Jade Vine has a reputation among gardeners for being temperamental and seems to be more vigorous at slightly higher altitudes, such as in the Malaysian and Indonesian highlands and northern Thailand; for this reason, it is not commonly found in many private gardens. On the other hand, there is a well-established specimen in the Singapore Botanic Gardens and it has been grown succesfully in Bangkok as well. One requirement is well-drained soil but regular watering when flower buds appear.

Jasmine

JASMINUM SP.

Thanks to its potent fragrance, Jasmine is one of the most popular flowers throughout Southeast Asia, used for leis, religious offerings, and other floral decorations, as well as to flavor tea and food (a popular Thai hot-season delicacy is iced jasmine rice). Though there are several species, two are most frequently found in gardens and commercial nurseries, both with white flowers that may be single or double.

J. sambac, the most common, is an evergreen climber, sometimes kept clipped to form a low shrub; while not a particularly attractive plant, the flowers are strongly scented and continuous, thus making it popular with gardeners. This variety flowers best when kept dry, well fertilized, and frequently pruned. *J. rex,* sometimes called Royal Jasmine, is a handsome climber with much larger and more beautiful star-shaped flowers which are, however, only faintly fragrant. There are several other climbing varieties as well with small flowers.

Botanical Family:
Oleaceae

Thai name:
Buddha-chart

Malay name:
Melati

Indonesian name: ,
Melati

Lantana

LANTANA SP.

Botanical Family:
Verbenaceae

Thai name:
Puang pa-ka-krong

Malay names:
*Kembang tahi ayam,
Lantana*

Indonesian names:
*Kembang tahi ayam,
Lantana*

Almost as soon as it was introduced as an ornamental from its native South America, Lantana escaped the garden and is now found growing as a weed in most parts of Southeast Asia. *L. camera*, the most common variety, is a prickly shrub with white, yellow, orange, or red flowers, while *L. sellowiana* is a trailing plant with rosy lavender flowers, often seen as a ground cover. Each flower cluster is made up of florets, tiny tubes which have five lobes. Cultivars of *L. camera* with larger, more attractive flowers have been introduced, but all the shrub forms need frequent pruning to keep them from becoming leggy.

The hairy leaves of Lantana have a pungent smell when touched, which makes them unappealing to most animals and some people as well—the Indonesian name means "chicken droppings." Insects and birds, however, are attracted to the flowers, and the crushed leaves are used in traditional medicine for treating ulcers, wounds, and insect bites.

Lipstick Tree

BIXA ORELLANA

This small tree, which can reach a height of 3 to 4 m., is a native of tropical America. It has large green leaves, often tinged with red and prominently veined, and pale-pink flowers which last only for a day. Since the buds open in succession, there are usually a number of blooms. The attraction for most gardeners, however, is not the flowers but the masses of decorative seed pods that follow; these are red or reddish brown and covered with coarse, soft hairs, somewhat resembling the popular fruit rambutan. There is considerable variation in fruit color on different plants, and those with the brightest color—usually found at higher elevations—are most sought after.

The popular name derives from the fact that the orange-red material surrounding the seeds is used as a face paint by tribal people as well as to make a dye to color lipstick, oleomargarine, and cheese. The dried seed pods, which split open to reveal rows of seeds covered with the material, can be used in floral arrangements.

Botanical Family:
Bixaceae

Thai name:
Kham-ngo

Malay name:
Kesumba

Indonesian names:
Kesumba keling,
Kesumba

Lotus

NELUMBO NUCIFERA (NELUMBIAN NELUMBO)

Botanical Family:
Nymphaeceae

Thai name:
Bua luang

Malay names:
Teratai, Bunga padam

Indonesian names:
Seroja, Bunga padam, Teratai

No other plant figures so prominently in Asian religions as the Lotus. Both Hindus and Buddhists regard it as a sacred symbol and use it not only in offerings but also in countless art forms. Except for one yellow-flowering variety found in North America, the Lotus is native to Asia and flourishes in a wide range of climates from India to China.

Unlike other members of the water lily family, its large pink or white five-petalled flowers and leaf stalks rise above the water, sometimes for a considerable distance. The large, round leaves are covered with a network of microscopic hairs, which keeps them dry in a rain. When the flower petals fall, they are replaced by a flat-topped seed pod divided into compartments, resembling a wasp's nest.

The underground tubers of the Lotus are a source of vitamin C, protein, and starch, while the seeds, boiled in sugar, are a popular sweet. The leaves are used as a wrapping for steamed foods, to which they impart a delicate flavor. Even the pollen was used in ancient China to make a cosmetic.

Madagascar Periwinkle

CATHARANTHUS ROSEUS (VINCA ROSEA)

This shrubby plant, which grows about 60 cm. high on soft stems, is actually a perennial, though it looks like an annual and is often grown as such. The flowers, appearing in clusters at the branch tips, are white with a pink or yellow center or rosy pink with a red center and occur almost continually if the plant is given a sunny location. Despite its popular name, it is believed by some to actually be a native of the Caribbean. It can be seen growing wild in many places, especially along beaches, but is also used in gardens because of its dependable flowers and ability to survive in near-drought conditions.

Like other members of its botanical family, the Madagascar Periwinkle is poisonous. On the other hand, two of the many alkaloids it contains in minute quantities have medicinal properties and in recent years have been the subject of research into the treatment of certain cancers. It is also used in traditional medicine in some parts of the worl to treat various diseases, among them diabetes.

Botanical Family:
Apocynaceae

Thai name:
Pung puay

Malay names:
Kembang sari Cina,
Tapak dara

Indonesian name:
Tapak dara

Mickey Mouse

OCHNA SERRULATA

Botanical Family:
Ochnaceae

Thai name: Kamlang changsan, mick-ee

Malay name:
Okna kuning

Indonesian name:
Okna kuning

This native of tropical Africa is a woody shrub with glossy leaves that can grow to a height of two or more meters, though it is usually smaller. It has attractive yellow flowers, followed by jet-black seeds surrounded by bright red sepals; to the imaginative, the arrangement of the seeds and sepals suggests the face of Walt Disney's famous cartoon character and is responsible for the popular name. Often the flowers and seeds appear at the same time.

A comparatively recent introduction to Southeast Asian gardens, the shrub has become popular due to its frequent flowering and ability to withstand a variety of conditions. Another thing that recommends it to gardeners is the fact that except for an occasional stem-borer it is rarely attacked by insect pests and thus needs little or no spraying. It needs some pruning to maintain a good shape and does best in a sunny location. Propagation is by seeds, which sprout and grow quickly, or by cuttings from hard wood, which are slower.

Morning Glory

IPOMOEA SP.

The *Impomoea* genus includes not only the species popularly known as Morning Glory but also numerous others, one of them the familiar sweet potato.

Among the Morning Glory varieties that burst into bloom when the sun first strikes them are the pale-pink flowering *I. carnea*, the deep blue *I. learii*, the pale mauve *I. pulchella*, and the rich wine-red *I. horsfalliae*. *I. alba (Calonyction aculeatum)*, on the other hand, only opens after dark and for that reason is called the Moon Flower; the huge flowers are pure white and fragrant and open so rapidly one can watch them doing so.

Yet another species seen throughout Southeast Asia is *I. aquatica*, the Water Convolvulus, the leaves and stems of which are commonly used in Chinese cooking. The stems are hollow, and the plant is usually seen floating on ponds, though there is also a variety that grows on land; the trumpet-shaped flowers are pale pink with a dark-pink throat.

Botanical Family: *Convolvulaceae*

Thai name: *Pak-bung farang*

Malay name: *Sri pagi*

Indonesian names: *Sri pagi, Gamet*

New Guinea Creeper

MUCUNA BENNETTI

Botanical Family:
Leguminosae

Thai name:
Puang ko mane

Malay name:
Mukuna New Guinea

Indonesian name:
Mukuna New Guinea

"Probably the most showy of all tropical climbers" is the way one standard reference book describes this rampant creeper. The seeds were first collected in its native New Guinea shortly before the second world war and germinated at the Singapore Botanic Garden, where its brilliant display of bright orange-red flowers attracted much admiration.

The climber requires a good deal of space to grow properly and thus is usually seen in larger gardens, either twisting up into a tall tree or over a pergola so that its long flower clusters can hang down to maximum effect. The pea-type flowers are quite large and grow closely together on stems that emerge from the woody branches; flowering takes place once or twice a year. Fine hairs covering the flower calyx cause itching if brushed against the skin. Though the New Guinea Creeper belongs to the same botanical family as the celebrated Jade Vine and has similar leaf and flower forms, it is a different species.

Orchid Tree

BAUHINIA SP.

Named after two brothers, John and Casper Bauhin, the genus Bauhinia includes some 500 species. Most are identifiable by their two-lobed or twin leaves, but otherwise they vary greatly and include shrubs and vines as well as the small trees that are popular in gardens from their native India to Florida.

Two widely-grown tree varieties that are very similar as far as foliage is concerned are *B. variegata* and *B. purpurea*, both popularly called Orchid Trees. On the first the five-petaled flowers may be pure white, lavender, or purple, while on the second they are purple, though in a wide range of shades. One way to distinguish between the two is that the flower petals on *B. variegata* tend to overlap, while those on *B. purpurea* are narrower and separated. Another variety comes from Burma and has pink flowers. The Orchid Tree grows quickly from seeds and needs a sunny location to bloom well; it profits occasionally from hard pruning, which encourages a better shape.

Botanical Family:
Leguminosae

Thai name: *Chong-ko*

Malay names:
Orkid, Bauhinia

Indonesian names:
*Daun Lilin, Bauhinia,
Daun kupu-kupu*

Orchids

ORCHIDACEAE

Botanical Family:
Orchidaceae

Thai name: *Depends
on species*

Malay name: *Orkid*

Indonesian name:
Anggerek

Even if they are not serious collectors, most gardeners in Southeast Asia display at least a few pots of orchids, either hung from the eaves or in a proper lath-house. This is scarcely surprising in view of the wealth of specimens surrounding them: peninsular Malaysia alone has nearly 800 identified native species, not to mention the thousands of hybrids that have been produced. Both Singapore and Thailand are leading exporters of cut orchid flowers.

The following varieties are among the most frequently seen in gardens:

DENDROBIUM. One of the largest Asian orchid genera, Dendrobiums are also among the easiest for non-professionals to grow when conditions are favorable. Flowers usually appear in sprays at the end of long, cane-like structures called pseudobulbs and come in almost every color of the rainbow.

VANDA. Vanda are monopodial in growth, which means they have a central stem with one growing tip and flower stalks that emerge from the stem between the leaves in each row. The flowers are usually fairly large, from 5 to 10 cm across. One hybrid, *V. Miss Joaquim*, is the national flower of Singapore.

PHALAENOPSIS. Sometimes called Moon Orchids, these are monopodial with thick, leathery, dark-green leaves and long, arching sprays of large white, pink, or yellow flowers with different-colored lips.

CATTLEYA. Among the showiest of orchids, these are roughly divided into two groups: the one-leaved or labiate *Cattleya*, which have spectacular, broad-petalled flowers, and two-leaved or bifoliate kind which have smaller but more numerous flowers atop pseudobulbs.

PAPHIOPEDILUM. Popularly known as "lady's slippers" these are terrestrial orchids, some with mottled leaves and others plain green; the slipper-like flowers are often beautifully colored. They do best at cooler altitudes.

Pagoda Flower

CLERODENDRUM PANICULATUM

Botanical Family:
Verbenaceae

Thai name: *Chat faa*

Malay names:
Klerodendrum pegoda,
Senggugu

Indonesian names:
Klerodendrum pagoda,
Bunga pagoda

A native of Southeast Asia, this tall, woody shrub has very large, glossy, three-lobed leaves. The red-orange flowers appear at the top of the plant, each flower about 1.5 cm. in diameter with exceptionally long protruding stamens; they are arranged around a spike in a conspicuous conical form that has led to the popular name. The flowers are unscented but attract butterflies, particularly the beautiful Birdwing, during the several weeks they remain on the plant. The shrub grows up around 3 m. but is usually kept pruned to about half that height.

A number of other *Clerodendrum* varieties are also found in Southeast Asian gardens. C. *fallax (speciosissimum)* is similar to the one above but with larger flowers, while C. *fragrans (philippinum)* has very fragrant pinkish-white flowers that grow like an old-fashioned nosegay and C. *ugandense*, a scandent shrub, has flowers that are a blend of pale and dark blue and grows best at higher altitudes such as in northern Malaysia and Thailand.

Peacock Flower

CAESALPINIA PULCHERRIMA

This attractive treelet, which probably originated in South America, is sometimes called the Dwarf Poinciana or Dwarf Flame Tree due to the resemblence of its flowers and bipinnate leaves to those of *Delonix regia*. They are indeed related botanically, but *Caesalpinia* is a distinct species which grows only to a height of about 3 meters, retains its leaves year-round, and blooms almost continuously. The flowers, which appear in clusters on long, erect stems, are smaller than those of the Flame Tree and have exceptionally long stamens and a prominent pistil which projects from the center.

The most common flower color is red-orange, sometimes with a yellow margin, but one variety has pure yellow flowers and on another they are strawberry-colored; in Bali they are used in offerings and as table decorations. The flowers are followed by flat, black seed pods which remain on the plant for some time. *Caesalpinia* requires hard pruning, especially when young.

Botanical Family:
Caesalpiniacea

Thai name:
Nok-yung Thai

Malay name:
Bunga merak

Indonesian names:
Perdu menahun,
Kembang merak

Plumbago

PLUMBAGO AURICULATA
(FORMERLY P. CAPENSIS)

Botanical Family:
Plumbagicinaceae

Thai name:
Payup mawk

Malay name:
Ceraka biru

Indonesian name:
Ceraka biru

Plumbago is a native of South Africa and is found in both tropical and sub-tropical gardens. It does better at slightly higher altitudes where there is a prolonged dry season than in areas with heavy rainfall, which tends to beat down the flowers and leave them looking bedraggled.

By habit a woody, climbing shrub—in temperate countries it is often seen trained up walls in conservatories—it is usually kept pruned into a bushy shape in Southeast Asia. The small, five-petaled flowers that appear in clusters at the branch tips are baby blue, a relatively rare color in the tropics and the principal reason for Plumbago's popularity among gardeners; the intensity of the blue varies from bright to pale and there is also a white variety. Though they appear to be delicate, Plumbago flowers are surprisingly tough and in Hawaii are sometimes used in leis and flower arrangements. It requires full sun and a rich soil for profuse flowering and the plant should be cut back hard after each display.

Poinsettia

EUPHORBIA PULCHERRIMA

This native of Mexico has become world-famous as the "Christmas Plant," used in seasonal displays and offered as gifts in potted form. In tropical gardens, it is a sizeable shrub which can grow to a height of several meters and, moreover, its bright flowers appear not only at Christmas but at other times as well.

The "flowers" are actually bracts which surround the real ones, which are inconspicuous. Vivid red is the most common color, but there are also creamy white and rose pink varieties, as well as some with double bracts. The Poinsettia is a "short day" bloomer, which means that flowering is conditioned by the amount of daylight it receives; in most parts of the world, this accounts for its display of blooms in November and December, though in places like Singapore, where the days scarcely vary in length, it may have flowers at almost any time. A variety seen in northern Thai gardens has very small white bracts which entirely cover the plant during the winter months.

Botanical Family:
Euphorbiaceae

Thai name:
Ton Christmas

Malay names:
Kastuba, Poinsettia,
Eufobia Natal

Indonesian names:
Pohon merah,
Kastuba, Poinsettia,
Eufobia Natal

Pride of India

LAGERSTROEMIA SPECIOSA (L. FLOS-REGINAE)

Botanical Family:
Lythraceae

Thai name: *Ta-bak*

Malay names:
Bungur tekuyung,
Bungur raya

Indonesian names:
Bungur, Bungur raya;
Wungu, Ketangi,
Laban (Java)

Also popularly known as the Rose of India and the Crepe Myrtle, this native of India is one of the most popular flowering trees in the tropics. It can eventually reach a height of 30 m. but is slow growing and smaller specimens, which flower when relatively young, are usually seen in gardens; the tree is also used along avenues in several Southeast Asian capitals.

The rather long, pointed leaves drop during the dry season, turning red before they do so, and the tree blooms along with the appearance of new foliage. Really successful blooming takes place only in regions with pronounced wet and dry seasons. The flowers appear in prominent clusters at the branch-ends in colors that range from pale to deep lavender, with occasional white or pink varieties; each flower is made up of six or more ruffled petals and they make a very attractive display when seen in a mass. Since seeds do not breed true, the only way of ensuring a desired color is by propagation from cuttings or marcots.

Rangoon Creeper

QUISQUALIS INDICA

This vigorous climber, native to Southeast Asia, is most often seen growing over pergolas or walls. It is also sometimes popularly called Drunken Sailors, possibly a reference to the way the flowers bob up and down in a strong wind. Several times a year—in some places almost continuously—it produces clusters of small, fragrant flowers which start off white and then turn pink or crimson as they grow older. A double variety introduced in fairly recent years has unusually large clusters of frilly flowers.

The Rangoon Creeper grows so rapidly, especially during the rainy months, that it can quickly get out of hand and invade neighboring areas if not controlled by frequent pruning. Some growers believe it should be cut back hard every two or three years and substantially every year at the end of the rainy season. It also requires regular spraying since the leaves are prone to attack by a night beetle and may look unsightly. Propagation is by root suckers or by woody stem cuttings.

Botanical Family:
Combretaceae

Thai name:
Lep mue nang

Malay names:
Wudani, Kuikalis, Akar Dani

Indonesian names:
Ceguk, Wudani, Kuikalis, Akar Dani

Red Ginger

ALPINIA PURPURATA

Botanical Family:
Zingiberaceae

Thai name:
Khing daeng

Malay name:
Alpinia merah

Indonesian name:
Alpinia merah

This native of Melanesia and the Moluccas is not a true ginger of the edible type, though it belongs to the same botanical family and is somwhat similar in appearance. It has sturdy leaf stalks that rise from underground tubers with large leaves up to a foot long arranged along the upper stalks. The "flowers"—actually bright red bracts that cover the small inconspicuous true flowers—rise prominently from the tops of the stalks, often reaching a foot or more in length. Old stalks die back after flowering, but new rooted plants sprout among the withered bracts.

Thanks to its long-lasting flowers, which are widely used in arrangements, the Red Ginger is now seen in many tropical gardens. In some parts of the South Pacific, the flower bracts are sewn together into ceremonial dress or strung into leis. There is also a pink-flowering variety, as well as a relatively rare cultivar called "Jungle Queen" with large, rounded shell-pink or pure white inflorescences.

Sandpaper Vine

PETRAEA VOLUBILIS

The popular name of this woody climber from South America is derived from its pale-green leaves, which are very rough to the touch. Its widespread popularity with Southeast Asian gardeners, however, is due to the periodic appearance of cascading racemes of lavendar-blue flowers which occur in large numbers and give it the appearance of a tropical wisteria. What seems at a casual glance to be the flower is actually the calyx, five-pointed and pale blue; the true flower is a rich violet in color and grows at the center. The flower falls quickly, but the calyx remains for many days. Flowering is most profuse during the dry season.

There is a white-flowering variety in Central America but this does not seem to have been introduced to Southeast Asia. A shrub variety, *P. rugosa*, grows to about 2 meters high and has shorter flower sprays, though the flowers themselves are larger. Neither of these varieties is as yet common to gardens in the region.

Botanical Famly:
Verbenaceae

Thai name:
Puang kram

Malay name:
Petrea mera

Indonesian name:
Petrea mera

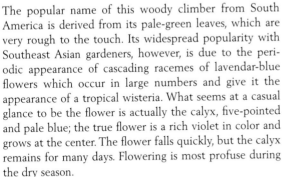

Scrambled Eggs

CASSIA SURATENSIS

Botanical Family:
Leguminosae

Thai name:
Song-ba-don

Malay name: Kasia

Indonesian name:
Kasia

This tall shrub, often a small tree, is very common in Southeast Asian gardens and often seen planted along city streets and roadsides. The common name derives from its continuous display of pale or bright yellow flowers that appear in quantity at the end of the branches. These have five petals and are similar in form to those of the Golden Shower tree but never look as spectacular since they do not hang and occur along with the leaves, which are compound and made up of about eight pairs of leaflets. The seeds occur in flat brown pods and germinate easily.

C. *suratensis* grows rapidly and tolerates a considerable degree of neglect as well as poor soil, and these characteristics, together with its dependable flowering, no doubt account for its popularity. There is considerable variation in flower color, ranging from bright to very pale yellow, which some believe is caused by the type of soil in which the tree is grown; in any event, seeds do not always breed true to color.

Sea Hibiscus

HIBISCUS TILIACEUS

This small tree, which comes from the tropical Orient and Pacific region, bears little outward resemblence to the popular shrub Hibiscus, though it is increasingly being used as an ornamental in seaside gardens. It has large heart-shaped leaves, downy underneath, and five-petaled, Hibiscus-type yellow flowers that turn a darker hue before they fall. The tree tends to creep and twist along the ground rather than growing upright, but old specimens can become quite large and have sizeable trunks. Hawaiians fashioned outriggers for canoes from the curved branches, and the Balinese also use the wood for carvings.

Botanical Family: *Malvaceae*

Thai name: *Po thalae*

Malay name: *Bebaru*

Indonesian name: *Waru*

Another tree that is sometimes given the same popular name and also grown in gardens is *Thespecia populnea*, which has similar leaves and flowers; though of the same general botanical family, it belongs to a different genus and grows to a considerably greater height. Both varieties can be seen in many resort landscapes, where they tolerate strong sea winds.

Spider Lily

CRINUM ASIATICUM

Botanical Family:
Amaryllidaceae

Thai name:
Plub-plueng

Malay name:
Krinum bakung

Indonesian name:
Krinum bakung

This handsome Crinum is native to Southeast Asia and is seen not only growing wild in swamps but also in many garden plantings, thanks to its willingness to tolerate a wide range of conditions, including strong sea winds. It has a massive, fleshy stem that grows to a height of about a meter and long, succulent, bright-green leaves. The flowers, which appear frequently on stalks in a sunburst arrangement, are white and fragrant. Another variety, C. *amabile*, is much larger and has pink flowers trimmed in wine-red; unlike C. *asiaticum*, this requires full sun to bloom well. The root is used as a poultice for treating wounds, while the poisonous juice acts as a purgative.

Another plant also often called a Spider Lily is *Hymenocallis littoralis*, which has somewhat similar flowers that are also different in that the star-shaped flowers have a membranous tissue connecting the petals at their base. *Hymenocallis* also has strap-shaped leaves that emerge straight from the underground tubers.

Torch Ginger

NICOLAIA ELATIOR (PHAEOMERIA SPECIOSA)

This spectacular member of the ginger family is native to Malaysia and Indonesia and is one of the most beautiful of all flowering tropical plants. Both leaf and flower stalks emerge separately from underground tubers. The leaf stalks grow as tall as 5 meters, while the pyramidal flower heads rise about a meter. Colored bracts protect the small tubular flowers and open outward to expose them, resulting in a rounded creation that at first glance looks artificial. The most common form has bright red flowers, though there is another with pink blossoms. Before the bracts begin to open, the flower heads are eaten raw in Malaysia. The leaves and stem of a close relative, *N. hemisphaerica*, can be processed into paper, while another, *N. heyneana* has medicinal properties and is used to treat ailing livestock in Java.

Named after Czar Nicholas I of Russia (1796-1855), the plant does best if given rich soil, plenty of water, and protection from strong winds.

Botanical Family: *Zingiberaceae*

Thai name: *Ka-la*

Malay name: *Nikolaia*

Indonesian name: *Nikolaia*

59

Trumpet Tree

TABEBUIA

Botanical Family:
Bignoniaceae

Thai name:
Chom phu pantip

Malay name:
Tabebuia

Indonesian name:
Tabebuia

A native of South America, this flowering tree was introduced to Southeast Asia in relatively recent years but is now often seen in gardens and along streets. Most varieties are deciduous, producing flowers after the leaves fall, and for this reason they do best in places where there is a prolonged dry season.

The most common variety is *T. rosea*, which has tubular, pale-pink flowers in small clusters and is sometimes called the Pink Trumpet Tree; this is planted along many streets in Bangkok, where it quickly attains a height of five to six meters and blooms during the dry season from January to March. Another pink-flowering species, *T. pentaphylla* is smaller, blooms more or less continually in smaller quantities, and does not shed its leaves.

Two other decorative members of the family are *T. donnell-smithii*, the Gold Tree, which once a year is entirely covered with bright yellow flowers, and *T. argentea*, which has silvery-grey leaves and yellow flowers.

Virgin Tree

MUSSAENDA SP.

There are about 60 species of *Mussaenda*, mostly from tropical Africa, but those that are seen in Southeast Asian gardens come from the Philippines. The most popular is *M. philippica*, also called *Dona Aurora*, a large shrub that can become a small tree. It has medium-sized oval leaves and very prominent displays of large, velvety sepals, leaf-like in shape, surrounding small star-shaped flowers. White or pink are the usual colors, but there is also a bright red variety as well as one developed in the Philippines on which the sepals are pale pink rimmed with rosy pink; the latter was named Sirikit in honor of Thailand's Queen. Another Mussaenda, *M. glabra*, is a small, scandent shrub and has only one large, creamy-white sepal instead of a cluster.

Mussaendas need frequent pruning to prevent them from becoming leggy and to encourage more blooms. They also require a sunny location. Flowering occurs throughout the year.

Botanical Family:
Rubiaceae

Thai name: *Don-ya*

Malay names:
Nusa indah, Musenda

Indonesian names:
Nusa indah, Musenda

Water Lily

NYMPHAEA SP.

Botanical Family:
Nymphaeceae

Thai name: *Bua*

Malay names:
Teratai, Seroja, Telipak

Indonesian names:
Padma, Teratai, Serojo

Almost every garden with a pond offers a display of Water Lilies, sometimes almost covering the entire surface with their round floating leaves and beautiful cup-like flowers. There are both day and night blooming varieties, large and small, in a wide range of rainbow colors.

Those most commonly seen in Southeast Asia are hybrids belonging to three groups. One is *N. lotus*, commonly called the Egyptian Lotus though it is a different plant from the true lotus; this has large white, pink, or crimson flowers. The others are *N. capensis*, the Cape Blue Water Lily, which has fragrant blue or mauve flowers, and *N. mexicana*, the Yellow Water Lily, on which the blooms are smaller but in a subtle mixture of colors.

A close relative is the spectacular *Victoria Amazonica* from Brazil, the largest of the water lilies, on which the ribbed leaves can be a meter or more in diameter; the huge, fragrant flowers are white when they open at dusk and turn pink as they age.

Yellow Oleander

THEVETIA PERUVIANA (T.NEREIFOLIA)

This tropical American native has narrow, light green leaves and a more or less continuous display of satiny yellow, funnel-shaped, slightly fragrant flowers; there are also varieties with apricot-colored or almost white flowers, though these are not as often seen. Flowers are followed by small, green, apple-like fruit which, like the leaves and the white latex the plant exudes, are extremely poisonous; it is said that a single fruit can be fatal and thus *Thevetia* should not be planted where it might tempt small children.

Thevetia belongs to the same botanical family as the Oleander and also has a similar growth pattern. It is bushier, however, and if not pruned fairly often can become a small tree up to four meters in height. It is thus a useful addition to small gardens and for screening purposes. It prefers a sandy soil and full sun is required for profuse flowering. Propagation is by cuttings or by seeds, though these are slow to germinate.

Botanical Family:
Apocynaceae

Thai names:
Thevetia Peruviana,
Rum-poey

Malay name:
Tevetia Peru

Indonesian names:
Ki hujan, Tevetia Peru

Index by Latin Name

CRUSADES AND CRINOLINES

Books by Ishbel Ross

CRUSADES AND CRINOLINES

GRACE COOLIDGE AND HER ERA

SILHOUETTE IN DIAMONDS
The Life of Mrs. Potter Palmer

THE GENERAL'S WIFE
The Life of Mrs. Ulysses S. Grant

FIRST LADY OF THE SOUTH
The Life of Mrs. Jefferson Davis

ANGEL OF THE BATTLEFIELD
The Life of Clara Barton

REBEL ROSE
Life of Rose O'Neal Greenbow, Confederate Spy

PROUD KATE
Portrait of an Ambitious Woman, Kate Chase

JOURNEY INTO LIGHT

CHILD OF DESTINY
The Life Story of the First Woman Doctor

ISLE OF ESCAPE

FIFTY YEARS A WOMAN

LADIES OF THE PRESS

HIGHLAND TWILIGHT

MARRIAGE IN GOTHAM

PROMENADE DECK

CRUSADES
and Crinolines

THE LIFE AND TIMES OF
ELLEN CURTIS DEMOREST
AND WILLIAM JENNINGS DEMOREST

ISHBEL ROSS

HARPER & ROW, PUBLISHERS
NEW YORK, EVANSTON, AND LONDON

LIBRARY OF CONGRESS CATALOG CARD NUMBER: 62-20116

Contents

(v)

Acknowledgments

In preparing this biography of Mr. and Mrs. William Jennings Demorest I have worked from the original and complete files of the Demorest publications from 1860 to 1898—*Mme. Demorest's Mirror of Fashions, Demorest's Illustrated Monthly Magazine* and *Mme. Demorest's Mirror of Fashions, Demorest's Monthly Magazine, Demorest's Family Magazine* and *Young America.* I have also used the files of *Godey's Lady's Book, Harper's Bazar, Harper's Magazine, Harper's Monthly Magazine, Harper's Weekly;* and *Frank Leslie's Ladies Gazette of Paris, London, and New York Fashions, Frank Leslie's Illustrated Weekly* and *Frank Leslie's Illustrated Newspaper.*

I am greatly indebted to William J. Demorest, grandson of Mr. and Mrs. Demorest, for the use of the family files, and for recollections and memorabilia of the family; and also to Henry Curtis Morris, of Washington, their nephew, for an important family scrapbook, letters and helpful reminiscences. Mrs. William G. Goodell, of Evanston, Illinois, a niece of the Demorests, was good enough to supply me with essential information on the Curtis sisters. I am grateful to Mrs. Elizabeth Bancroft Schlesinger, Mrs. Herma Briffault, Miss Hilda Couch and Dr. Edward T. James for courtesies in connection with this book, and to a number of residents of Saratoga Springs and Schuylerville who have specific knowledge of the Demorest and Curtis families. I owe special thanks to Frank Sullivan, Mrs. Mary E. Anthony, Mrs. Henry Foote, Mrs. Walter A. Britton, Miss Marjorie Riordan, John Youngflash, Miss Pearl Tolmie of Saratoga Springs, and to Mrs. W. Hayward of Ballston Spa. Clifford Rugg, County Historian of Schuylerville, was particularly helpful in my search for old records, and others who gave me special aid in this field were Mrs. Tsing Chu and Mrs. Blanche Sigsby, of the Saratoga Public Library, and Miss Fanny C. Howe, Miss Irene Van Horne and Miss Carol Dean, of the Troy Public Library.

Illustrations

The following are grouped in a separate section after page 148.

(ix)

CRUSADES AND CRINOLINES

CHAPTER I

Saratoga Fashions

A TALL GIRL of fifteen, dark-eyed and observant, watched the Broadway parade on a hot July morning in 1840. Carriages rolled past in clouds of dust that veiled the gowns, hats, parasols and assorted faces of Saratoga's summer visitors. But the carnival spirit eclipsed the fashion parade. Ellen Louise Curtis had driven in from the family homestead to watch the celebration for William Henry Harrison and to hear Daniel Webster speak on behalf of the Whigs.

Political feeling ran high in Saratoga at any time and the novel tactics of the "Tippecanoe and Tyler too" presidential campaign had whipped up a hot tide of local interest. The Whigs found a strong political issue in the hard times that prevailed. They staged the most spectacular campaign attempted up to that time in their determination to snatch the Presidency from the Democrats. President Van Buren, with his Dutch ancestry and local ties, was no stranger to the spa where political passions boiled and men of all types foregathered. The bland, smooth-visaged President was in disfavor after the panic of 1837.

The Seminole War still plagued the country and the echo of Andrew Jackson's policies lingered in the air.

Harrison did not visit Saratoga but he was not missed. In the words of the social historian Philip Hone: "All the world is here: politicians and dandies, cabinet ministers and ministers of the gospel; office holders and office seekers; humbuggers and humbugged; fortune hunters and hunters of woodcock; anxious mothers and lovely daughters." The spectators watched a log cabin being drawn along the street by sixteen gray horses. Flags, banners, mottoes and emblems danced before Ellen Curtis' eyes. A ball thirty feet in circumference hung suspended over a carrier loaded with fervent Whigs. "Keep the Ball Rolling" ran a passing sign. Campaign songs were hoarsely sung. There were shouts, cheers, jeers.

When Daniel Webster's leonine head came into view at Temple Grove fresh storms of applause broke forth. The heat and noise of the morning came to a climax with a sudden thunderstorm just as he was ready to speak. To add to the confusion the platform crashed. Planks splintered to the sound of screams. No one was hurt and the show went on. Webster's rolling tones kept the crowd spellbound for three hours as he spoke from a wagon.

The town, well used to celebrations, had spent itself two weeks earlier on a great Sunday-school pageant celebrating the Fourth of July on historic territory. Ellen, born on November 15, 1825, at old Saratoga, otherwise known as Schuylerville, had been hearing almost since infancy of the battles that had raged close to her home and had made history in the War of the Revolution. She knew that General Burgoyne's surrender at Schuylerville, where her father had his hat factory, was the turning point in the war and a decisive moment in American history. This knowledge was part of her heritage, for both her parents sprang from established families that had shared in the history of the region. In the year of her birth Joseph Bonaparte, whom Napoleon had made both King of Naples and King of Spain, had stopped at the United States Hotel as the Comte de

Survilliers. In the same year Lafayette, touring the country, had talked to Mrs. Harrison Gray Otis and the spectacular Mme. Jumel on the piazza, where all could see them.

When Ellen was fourteen Martin Van Buren, leader of the party opposing Governor De Witt Clinton, was cut dead by the stately Mrs. Clinton at a dance given in his honor in the same hotel. All Saratoga gossiped about this. So did the politically alert in Washington, Albany and New York. That same year Henry Clay, visiting Saratoga, was followed along Broadway by cheering crowds that unhitched the horses of his carriage and drew it by hand. He spoke beneath the spreading trees in front of the United States Hotel, and this time Mrs. Clinton, recognized as Queen of the Spa, swung down a garland of roses and hyacinths by a silken cord—a coronet for the South's great orator and gallant. It touched his brow and he brushed it lightly aside. Thus Ellen early in life was conscious of the larger world, of the comings and goings of distinguished travelers, of fashionable clothes and political schemers, of Washington Irving strolling along Broadway, and the wives of the Southern planters dazzling the town with their jewels, coaches and Paris gowns.

Her own life ran along simple lines, although her family were comfortably off and well entrenched as valued members of the local community. She was the second of eight children born to Henry D. Curtis and Electa (Abel) Curtis. Her sisters were Matilda (Till), Elizabeth (Lib), Katherine (Kate), Anna Mary and Teen. She was known from girlhood as Nell. Her two brothers were Zachariah and Edwin L. Curtis.

The Abel family had moved from Dutchess County into the Saratoga region at the time of the War of the Revolution and settled on the shores of Saratoga Lake. They became closely identified with community affairs and the first local school stood on their property. Zachariah and Henry Curtis left Stillwater to settle in Saratoga Springs around 1796, taking possession of three hundred acres of uncultivated land. Two years later Nell's father was born, one of the nineteen children of Zachariah and Sarah

(Moore) Curtis. He grew up to be a farmer and hatter. To the day of his death he was regarded as a sturdy figure of great integrity. His counsel was sought in community, church and school affairs and he kept abreast of political events, both local and national. There was an Irish strain in Nell's blood on the paternal side and the Abels were of French and Dutch ancestry.

The Curtis boys and girls led an outdoor life. They went on hay rides and joined in community sings. They learned to ride and drive and sometimes went into town in the farm wagon with their tall father when he sold milk, or visited him in the two-story building where the beaver toppers were made. They watched the swift slash of the razor across the beaver skins and the fashioning of the hats that townsmen would wear. George IV had popularized brown beaver by wearing it at Ascot but black and gray predominated at the Curtis factory. The high hats cost from $20 up and had considerable staying power.

The spa was still in its infancy at the time of Nell's birth. Broadway was an open country road. The thick woods covering the hillside to the west were not fully cleared until after 1840 and wild game still roamed there. Deer and bears were seen close to the farm, and foxes and wolves were heard of from time to time. All manner of birds haunted the woods. The rabbits were a plague. Fish and water fowl abounded in Lake Saratoga. The village of Saratoga Springs, breaking away from old Saratoga, was incorporated when Nell was a year old, although New Englanders had been settling there since 1790 and early in the nineteenth century it was already rated the most fashionable watering place in the country. A favorite country drive for visitors was from Saratoga Springs to Schuylerville, or old Saratoga, which with the opening of the Erie Canal in 1825 had changed from a tiny hamlet with little but the Schuyler mansion, some mills, a distillery, blacksmith shop and a few houses, to a flourishing community. Warehouses were built for grain and mercantile goods, and factories like the Curtis hat emporium flourished. New and robust elements came pouring in from all quarters with the opening of the canal, so that by the 1840's Saratoga was heading into an era of great prosperity.

Nell's parents had watched the quick growth of the community as the invasion set in—the settlers and then the summer visitors. They had seen Ballston Spa in its early glory, when the Sans-Souci Hotel, with its boast that it was modeled after Versailles, had been the scene of brilliant gatherings. The Curtises had also watched its decline as one large hotel after another was built at Saratoga Springs and the fashion focus shifted. In these earlier days coaches from three lines ran twice a day between Albany and Saratoga Springs and stages making connections with the canalboats at Fort Edward left the Springs for Boston three times a week. The spa was a regular stop on the summer circuit that linked New York with the Catskills, Glens Falls, Lake George, and even such distant points as Niagara Falls, the Great Lakes, Portland and Boston.

But by 1833 the railroad had been extended to Saratoga and a bell jangled from the old brick station as couriers led the passengers to omnibuses plastered with the signs of their hotels. The cholera blight of 1832 had led to a ban on the drinking of the mineral waters. This was a strange year all round. Meteors flashed across the skies and nightly the moon was a deep gold instead of being pale and silvery, a puzzle to little Nell Curtis, then seven years of age. The birds were silenced and the woods and groves were deathly still when lime was plastered over houses, trees, steeples and cupolas. Visitors shunned Saratoga that year and the residents went quietly on their way while tales of frightful havoc reached them from New York and all points between.

By the time Ellen attended Schuylerville Academy she was well aware of the resort world so close to her home. At the age of fifteen she was uncommonly tall, slender and arrow-straight. She was not a beauty but from adolescence on she moved with the kind of stately grace that was later to be remarked on in the world of fashion. Her pallor was smooth and exotic. Her features were sharp, almost aquiline, but her sparkling dark eyes softened her air of severity. She had a thoughtful face, strong in contour, already suggesting the calm judgment of her later years. Her hair was dark and abundant, done up in burnished braids.

Among the six sisters Nell and Kate, moving toward maturity, were particularly alive to the show of fashion that could scarcely be matched anywhere in the country in the 1840's. Their own simple voiles and muslins were made by local dressmakers or by themselves, but they early acquired a sense of style. They had watched the huge coaches rumbling in from the South with the planters' wives tricked out in Paris finery, their trunks filled with the gowns that later would liven up the spa. They had learned to separate the accents of Alabama from those of Mississippi; of South Carolina from the slurred note of Georgia. They had taken stock of the amiable Negro coachmen with their brass-buttoned coats, top boots and hats with softly curled brims, as they steered their horses through the maze of carriages on Broadway. Inside sat the Southern beauties with their tiny parasols, striped muslins with bishop sleeves, flowered bonnets and tasseled boots. It was a world of high style, easy frivolity and political intrigue quite manifest to the observer as these visitors strolled beneath the trees, drove over to Ballston, played bezique, or talked and flirted.

It all made its impression on the growing girl from the well-ordered and somewhat austere Curtis home. However, ambitious though Nell undoubtedly was from her earliest years, she could scarcely have dreamed in the 1840's that eventually she would became a noted fashion arbiter, outfitting many of the celebrities who later visited Saratoga, and smartening up mass fashions across the country. She never tired of strolling with Kate past the long wooden hotels of Broadway with their cupolas, balconies and cornices half hidden by the tall old elms that rustled softly and preserved the village air of simplicity. Woodbine draped the seventeen columns of the piazza of Congress Hall which, by the time of the Harrison campaign, had rooms for hundreds of guests. June roses rioted in pink and crimson clumps around the United States Hotel, with its row of columns and wide piazzas.

When night fell all was music and gaiety in the hotels that sprawled in ghostly outline among the trees, their windows throwing bright beams into the night. It was a different scene when Nell drove to town with her father in the morning as he delivered milk. Wan-faced women in shawls or light spring wraps went drowsily to the springs past flowering shrubs. By noon the gamblers were out after a night of poker, faro or monte. At this time Saratoga was catching the grafter, the corrupt politician, the gambler, the confidence man, as well as the conservatives. Outright crooks rubbed elbows with old Dutch families, with the Southern hierachy, celebrities from abroad, the nation's leading political figures, the poets, dreamers, publishers and preachers of the hour. To promenade, to share in a quadrille at a champagne ball, to cast their chips in the gaming rooms, to buy diamonds for a Broadway beauty, resulted in some odd combinations of saints and sinners.

The Curtis girls were still too unworldly to catch the undercurrents of life at the spa, but they were keenly aware of the fashions, the music, the glamour and the elaborate equipages that they passed on their visits to town. They had moved from Schuylerville to the old family property in Saratoga while Nell was still in school. There was constant discussion among the natives of the fast and evil life that was also part of Saratoga Springs. In particular, there were whispers about Mme. Jumel, blonde, showy, always dressed in the latest style, pushing her way quite militantly to the lead of the daily coach procession, never forgetting that she had once been married to Aaron Burr. She was not particularly beloved at Saratoga but she rarely missed a season during the 1830's and 1840's. She had a house of her own on Circular Street but often stayed at the Pavilion or the United States Hotel and never failed to draw attention to herself.

Nell and her sisters matter-of-factly tested the cosmorama, the solar telescope, the swing boats and the circular railroad. As they grew older they strolled past the shops and commented on the bonnets and gowns on display. They discussed their hopes for the future. Finally, when she was eighteen and newly graduated from the Academy, Nell astonished her family by announcing that she planned to become a milliner. Hats were a family tradition and she and Kate had always liked to sew, design and run up dresses and bonnets for themselves. She had often copied the bonnets she saw in the Broadway parade. Her mother, a woman of character, had no wish to thwart her independent daughter but she did not want her to become an apprentice in this burgeoning trade. Mr. Curtis came to the rescue with funds that enabled Nell to buy some goods and employ an experienced milliner to help her run a little business of her own in Saratoga. She was full of creative ideas and at the end of the year she decided to move on to Troy, then a leading millinery center. In a short time she became superintendent of a millinery establishment that brought her into touch with the merchandising markets of New York and Philadelphia.

She studied dressmaking as well as hats, and picked up valuable experience in both fields. Soon she was watching what the Liverpool packets brought in from abroad in the way of flannels, cashmere shawls, tartans, Norwich crapes, cambric muslins, calico and bobbinet laces. Near her own establishment was George E. Webber & Company, advertising the "cheapest bonnets in America." In fact, they cost six cents. Real French flowers, mantillas and parasols helped to bolster up this widely advertised millinery establishment. But bonnets were under medical fire at the moment. The tiny oyster shell designs, small and tight, hugging the cheeks and neck, were giving women neuralgia, tic doloreux, loss of sight and ear trouble, or so the medical men maintained.

Inevitably Nell's next step was to New York. By this time she felt that she had had enough experience to tackle the metropolis of the 1850's. Her work eventually brought her into touch with William Jennings Demorest, a spirited figure in the merchandising world who was suffering at the time from the business depression that stretched like a blanket over the tip of Manhattan Island. Their meeting was to have much significance for the fashion and magazine world of the mid-nineteenth century. Their history would be closely tied to the growth and development of New York from the time of the Civil War to the Golden Nineties, and their impact on fashion and temperance reform would be international in scope.

When Nell Curtis first encountered Mr. Demorest through a business transaction, he already had a career in merchandising behind him and had abandoned all thought of the ministry, his first goal in life. He had come to New York in his late teens from Brighton, a hamlet on the outskirts of Rochester, where he was born on June 10, 1822. At first he lived with relatives. He joined the Spring Street Presbyterian Church when he was twenty, worked in a dry goods store and studied arduously in the hope of becoming a divinity student. He was secretary of the Christian Union connected with his church, an energetic society of young men training for the missionary field, and he identified himself with church activities in general. While studying for the ministry he got up at unearthly hours to read, because the shop where he worked opened at seven in the morning and did not close until ten at night. His employer, noticing that his attention was often focused on a book, told him one day that he had better make up his mind whether he wished to preach or to stay in commerce.

Young Demorest consulted his tutor, who was also his pastor, and was advised to stick to his bread and butter. If the Lord wanted him in the ministry he would open the way, said the good divine. But the way did not open and he chose the worldly route that led eventually to great prosperity. He was spurred on by the fact that he soon had a family to support, for in 1845 he married twenty-two-year-old Margaret Willamina Poole, the daughter of Joseph and Jeannette Poole. At first the Demorests lived on Varick Street, where their two children were born— Vienna Willamina in 1847 and Henry Clay Demorest in 1850. Family responsibilities drove young Demorest into strenuous efforts to make a living, so he decided to advance himself in the merchandising field. He was an active, imaginative young man with great physical energy and an inventive turn of mind. He was of Huguenot ancestry, and was of the eighth generation descended from David des Marest and Marie Sohier, who arrived in New Amsterdam in 1663. After two years on Staten Island they moved to New Harlem where Mr. Demarest, as he came to be known in the new land, served as overseer and constable. In 1677 he bought a large tract of land on the Hackensack River from Sir George Carteret. It was known as the "French Patent" and became a family stronghold for the Demarest family.

The spelling of the name as Demorest showed up for the first time with William Jennings Demorest's grandfather, Cornelius, who served with the Bergen County militia during the War of the Revolution. He lived for a quarter of a century in New York and was licensed in the early part of the nineteenth century to keep a cart. He married a girl named Ann Ekkeson and they had a son Peter, who was Mr. Demorest's father. Peter married Jane Brouwer in 1810 at Newton in Sussex County, but they moved eventually to Brighton. They had seven children and William Jennings Demorest was the oldest. William was staying with his uncle Michael Dealing at Nyack when his home in Brighton burned down in 1837. His father died trying to save one of the little sisters. She was afraid to jump from the window as the other children had done and she, too, died in the flames.

The memory of this family catastrophe was still fresh in his mind when young Demorest settled in New York in the early 1840's. There was plenty to engage his interest in what he saw around him. Horace Greeley had just founded the New York *Tribune* and Charles Dickens was turning a critical eye on America as he toured the country in 1842 and attended the Boz ball at the Park Theatre in New York. The Croton Reservoir had been opened and its ramparts were already a popular parading ground. Young Demorest, like other New Yorkers, took his wife far north for Sunday afternoon strolls around the reservoir.

At this time the Demorests lived in a modest way on Varick Street, and everything that had to do with trade or church affairs enlisted the merchant's interest. In the year before their marriage President Tyler had made Julia Gardiner, the Rose of Long Island, his bride in the Church of the Ascension. The dry goods men were particularly interested in this event for the new First Lady had shown them all four years earlier how to popularize a merchant's wares. Elaborately gowned in a flounced dress and long black velvet cloak, with a huge bonnet framing her face, she walked along swinging over her arm a decorative placard proclaiming: "I'll Purchase at Bogert & Mecamly's, No. 86, 9th Avenue. Their Goods are Beautiful & Astonishingly Cheap."

The trade center of the city had shifted abruptly after the great fire of 1835. The wholesale dry goods merchants who had been burned out left Pearl Street forever and opened farther north. Within a year the devastated area had been rebuilt. New methods of merchandising were employed. Three years after the fire the *Sirius* and then the *Great Western* arrived on successive days, the first ships to cross the Atlantic under steam. In themselves they heralded a new era in commerce and speeded up the imports that supported the native trade at this time. Most fine materials came from abroad—silks from Italy, France, India and China; woolens, calicoes and cassimeres from Britain; feathers and artificial flowers from France. There were only ten native manufacturers of flowers and a vast demand for their wares as bonnet trimmings. The choice grades were imported. Most of the ready-made clothes for men came from New Bedford, long accustomed to outfitting sailors home from their whaling expeditions. The drapers of New York and Boston traded in these suits and the earliest shirts came from a factory at Cherry and Market Streets.

But Henry Sands Brooks was already catering to the custom trade from his establishment at Catherine and Cherry Streets.

A dandy himself, he often wrapped his packages in black silk handkerchiefs for which he did not charge, and he kept sherry and Medford rum under the counter to hand out nips along with his wares. His bolts of cassimere, osnaburg, doeskin, velvet, silk and satin were the finest to be had. In 1850 the firm name of H. and D. H. Brooks & Company was changed to Brooks Brothers, and the familiar Golden Fleece trademark came into use. Eight years later a larger store opened at Broadway and Grand Street with a four-dialed globe clock, illuminated from the inside by gaslight. And here Abraham Lincoln bought the overcoat for his second inauguration and the Prince Albert coat, waistcoat and trousers that he wore on the night of his death.

George Opdyke, who later became mayor of New York, was one of the first citizens to engage in the dry goods business. In the early 1830's he manufactured clothing in New Orleans. Manufacturers were divided into 363 categories when Mr. Demorest came to New York and much of the distribution was done by mail and express systems. The village merchant who visited New York from two to four times a year and returned home laden with goods was a link with the larger world of commerce. But it was not until 1850 that the dry goods men in New York took firm hold of the domestic market. Until then Boston, Philadelphia and Baltimore had been the domestic commission centers and Boston controlled most of the output of the New England mills. Philadelphia had more than a score of commission houses selling all manner of domestic goods, notably the denims, checks and stripes then so popular. Hartford had a brisk dry goods trade, but New York was recognized chiefly as the market for imports. However, the evolution of the clothing trade, the influx of immigrants who turned to the garment industry, the growth of small towns and cities across the country, vitalized the industry as a whole and gave it national scope. In 1850 America's cotton and woolen products aggregated $112 million in value, and its textile output was estimated at $129 million. Imports in the same year totaled $59 million, ten times what they had been in 1795.

The prince of merchants in the growing city was A. T. Stewart, the lean, sandy-haired Irishman who called no man his friend but scattered millions. His fellow merchants feared and disliked him. He gave them no quarter, but H. B. Claflin, a bald, rubicund merchant from Massachusetts stood up to him and ran an establishment that he called the "grandest dry goods house in the world." Firms from other cities kept agents on the Claflin premises with the names of their houses conspicuously displayed. The big manufacturers and the trade in general preferred him to Stewart, but Claflin could not cope with the "corners" established by his rival in quality goods. Stewart corralled the best silks and the finest carpets, and the manufacturers were forced to deal with him. He frowned on employees who drank or gambled, while Claflin was genial and humorous, generous with credit and tolerant in his dealings with his staff.

Although Stewart was recognized as omnipotent, many merchants whose names would live on in New York history already had a firm foothold in city commerce. When Mr. Demorest bought out his employer and embarked on a dry goods business of his own on Broadway, close to Canal Street, a near neighbor was Aaron Arnold who had opened originally on Pine Street in 1825 to deal in imported goods and had then moved to Front Street and again to Canal, where his tiny panes of glass were typical of the period. In the year that young Demorest married, so did an Englishman named James Mansell Constable, who had arrived with a cargo of woolens. He joined forces with Arnold along the street, married his daughter Henrietta and the firm of Arnold Constable thus came into being. By 1849 its annual sales amounted to $250,000 and its "Marble House," with horsehair chairs for the customers and porters in blue uniforms with red bindings, gave dash to the place. Real lace at this time sold at $1,000 a yard and a camel's-hair shawl cost $1,200.

Lord & Taylor had been moving uptown since 1826, when water was still being drawn from the public pump and pigs were the town's garbage collectors. Samuel Lord and George Washington Taylor prospered and in 1853 opened a store at Grand and Chrystie Streets with a central rotunda, a dome and Gothic windows. But this did not suffice for the fashionable trade that flowed in, and six years later they opened magnificently at Broadway and Grand Street with a store billed as looking "more like an Italian palace than a place for the sale of broadcloth." Awed customers paused to admire its steam elevator and Tiffany chandeliers. Shopkeepers by this time were catching on to the fact that flattering lighting was helpful to sales. Things obviously had moved ahead from the 1830's, when porters went around carrying goods in their hands and the land above Fourteenth Street lacked both lighting and police protection. In 1839, when New York covered an area of three miles and had a population of 300,000, Captain Frederick Marryat, visiting from England, noted that "many of the shops, or stores, as they are here called . . . have already been fitted up with large plate-glass fronts, similar to those of London." And shop signs began to show up strongly in the 1830's.

Young Charles Knox, who became an apprentice in the beaver hat business in 1835, soon established his business in a basement on Fulton Street known as "The Hole in the Wall." He acted as his own salesman, ironer and errand boy. He was one of the early experts in lavish and original advertising. Ball, Black & Frost, the oldest jewelry firm of its class in the country, opened in 1810 on Broadway, near Maiden Lane, and after many moves uptown eventually landed on Fifth Avenue, catching the swing of fashion. Jabez Gorham from Providence began in 1831 to manufacture the silver spoons that became so famous and he eventually joined forces with the older firm. McCutcheons, "The Linen House," opened in 1855 with its trademark, the Spinning Wheel, displayed in the window at 748 Broadway. Hanan & Sons founded its shoe business in 1849 with a custom boot shop on Dey Street. And William Sloane, a Scot, in 1843 opened a carpeting and floorcloth shop at 245 Broadway on borrowed money. He was destined to dominate the furniture trade and to carpet and furnish the more sumptuous homes and hotels of America. Five years after he opened his first shop old friends from Scotland, the Carnegies, stayed with him on their way west, bringing along their young son Andrew.

The Demorests were to have dealings with all these merchants as time went on. But in the meantime William Demorest viewed from a distance the fine new homes going up as the city moved steadily north in the narrow confines of Manhattan Island. Washington Square became the focus for some of the best. It had been fenced, and trees flourished in the enclosure. Men who would enrich art galleries, endow colleges, build up book collections and contribute lavishly to the culture and history of the nation settled close by. Among them were James Lenox, William C. Rhinelander, August Belmont, Henry C. deRham, Lorillard Spencer, Robert L. Cutting, George Griswold, George Opdyke and Moses H. Grinnell, of clipper ship fame. The homes around Washington Square had small front plots, gleaming door knockers, and back gardens where trellises, pergolas and borders of old-fashioned flowers dressed up an area that had once been a burying ground, and then a mustering point for soldiers. But the premier financiers were not in this group. Commodore Vanderbilt, who acknowledged a fortune of $11,000,000, clung to his home on Washington Place. John Jacob Astor died in 1848, leaving a fortune of $20,000,000 and an indelible stamp on the city.

The sweep uptown had been irresistible, first from Battery Park and Bowling Green to Broad and Wall Streets; then to St. John's Park, Lafayette Place, Bond and Bleecker Streets; and finally to Stuyvesant Square, Washington Square and Fifth Avenue, which was opened officially as a thoroughfare in 1824. Manhattan had a population of close to 100,000 when the Avenue acquired its name. It was not so long since woodcock and partridge had winged their way through the thickets and snipe had been shot where the Empire State Building would eventually stand. Trout had been caught in the stream that meandered close to Washington Square, and mink, otter and muskrat had haunted the brooks and marshes where Saks Fifth

Avenue, Bonwit Teller and Best's would flourish a century
later.

A stream flowing east fed the muddy little waterways where
the Plaza, the St. Regis and other luxury hotels were destined
to stand. Indian trails, cowpaths and country lanes were cut up
for the development of lower Fifth Avenue. The Brevoort
House was opened in the year of Mr. Demorest's first marriage,
to remain a city landmark until 1953. During his early years in
the city the social focus was shifting steadily from Stuyvesant
Square to lower Fifth Avenue. Gramercy Park had opened up
in 1831, Union Square in 1833, and Madison Square in 1847,
the year of his daughter Vienna's birth. Fashion soon clustered
around Madison Square, where oaks, elms and sycamores threw
shade on steaming days and flowers bloomed in gay borders.
Children with wide-brimmed hats and pantalettes rolled hoops
or skipped past the rows of hansoms and four-wheelers waiting
at the curb for customers.

On his walks Mr. Demorest was familiar with the sight of
Corporal Thompson's Madison Cottage, a post tavern well
known to travelers by "The Sign of the Buck Horn" it dis-
played, a landmark at Fifth Avenue and Twenty-third Street.
In 1853 it was torn down to make way for Franconi's Hippo-
drome, with its tent roof and brick walls. The Hippodrome
was abandoned within two years and the site was sold to Amos
R. Eno, who used it for the famous Fifth Avenue Hotel. The
Latting Tower, an observatory 350 feet high, aping the Eiffel
Tower but failing sadly on all counts, stood by the Croton
Reservoir. One of the most curious sights of the town, however,
was the pseudo-Gothic mansion known as "Waddell's Caster."
Its towers, gables and odd angles suggested a cruet jumble.
Fields of waving grain could be viewed from its windows and
Thackeray was one of its visitors.

By 1850 Broadway was changing from a street of homes to
one of shops, and the brownstone craze was bringing a certain
uniformity to row after row of buildings. Hotels, restaurants,
boardinghouses abounded and the Astor House at Broadway and

Barclay Street, with its elongated bar and its famous free lunch, was haunted by the better-off merchants and the politicians. The Metropolitan Hotel, a brownstone building a block long, and the St. Nicholas, a huge marble edifice at Broadway and Broome, served both visitor and citizen for reading rooms and parlors.

That same year Jenny Lind landed in the United States and became a national idol. Exploited at every turn by P. T. Barnum, her golden voice reaped rich rewards and the city went wild with enthusiasm. A crowd of 20,000 surged in the vicinity of her hotel and 300 volunteer firemen in red shirts, bearing flaming torches, serenaded her. Fourscore policemen could not handle the crowd that swarmed around Castle Garden on her opening night. Tickets went for $250 in some instances, and in addition to 6,000 citizens jammed into the auditorium, others floated about in small boats in the bay, hoping to catch the echo of the Swedish nightingale's voice. Jenny Lind opened the door to an endless influx of foreign artists and influenced the future course of music in America. Soon Henrietta Sontag, Adelina Patti and Marietta Alboni followed her.

But the stir over Jenny Lind was minor compared with the general excitement and influx of visitors for the opening of the Crystal Palace in the summer of 1853. With his strong taste for novelty and invention Mr. Demorest was inevitably drawn to the glass and iron building with arched naves, modeled after the Crystal Palace of London. It was billed as the Temple of National Industry and had 6,000 exhibits, illustrating the industrial and artistic progress of many countries. President Franklin Pierce declared it open and it had a heady start, but five years later it burned down in one of the most spectacular fires in the city's history, with visitors fleeing in all directions.

In the year the Crystal Palace opened there were 272 churches in New York, 8 markets, 13 parks and squares, 115 fire companies, 25 hotels, 5 theaters, 2 minstrel halls, 29 omnibus lines and 5 streetcar lines. The city was on the march. Fifth Avenue now ran north of Twenty-third Street, but was still unpaved and rural in aspect. A fine row of private houses had been built on Twenty-third Street, and the brownstone front was becoming a city symbol. When Spanish Row opened with a flourish in 1855 the first suggestion of a New York apartment house had come into being. It consisted of eleven brick dwellings, uniform in size, and with little suggestion of home. But then, as Mrs. Trollope had observed as far back as 1831, there was a strong tendency in the American woman "to board by the year, instead of going to housekeeping."

Mr. Demorest's own fortunes had not been going well in the early 1850's. Ever since he bought out his employer and embarked on a dry goods business of his own he had encountered obstacles. Times were hard and the big merchants were getting monopolistic in their practices. A crisis was reached when a note for $50,000 that he had endorsed for a friend was not made good. He went bankrupt and accepted employment in a Philadelphia merchandising house. He moved his family there in 1852 but still kept his links with New York, where he had trade contacts.

During the next few years he engaged in the manufacture of cloaks, did wholesale trading in clothing and had ties with the millinery business. His children flourished and he and Willamina took a vivid interest in the religious and political life of the city. The combined city and suburban population was more than 360,000 when he settled there. There was a strong abolitionist group, to which he belonged. He took special interest in the first Republican National Convention, which was held in Philadelphia in 1856, with John C. Frémont emerging as the nominee. In 1857, just before the crash, the Philadelphia Academy of Music opened with a grand ball. The new opera house was built of brownstone and red brick, with arched windows and baroque ornamentation. It had huge Corinthian columns and was much admired. The interior ran to gold, cream and red plush, and excellent operatic fare was offered in the years that followed. The great artists of the day who visited America invariably appeared there. But Mr. Demorest gave little thought to the opening of the Academy of Music, for in February, 1857, Willamina died. And by September of that year financial panic swept the nation. The Bank of Pennsylvania closed its doors and other banks soon followed suit. There were mass meetings in Independence Square and business houses shut down. Mills and factories laid off their workers. "Bread or fight" they murmured as a program of public works was introduced.

A depression followed the panic of 1857, with few businesses flourishing, although the construction of railroads went forward with strength. Mr. Demorest was in a low state of mind with his two young children to care for and business virtually at a standstill. He was in his late thirties, dynamically interested in politics and the world around him, and soon he was forming fresh plans. On April 15, 1858, he was married to Nell Curtis in Williamsburg, New York, by the Rev. Jesse S. Peck. Thomas Hart Benton died that week and Stephen A. Douglas made his famous speech on the Pacific Railroad. The Mississippi was in flood and the clipper ship *John Gilpin* of Boston had run into ice and foundered off Cape Horn. The Mormons were giving trouble in Utah. The Philadelphia *Press*, owned by John W. Forney, was belaboring New York as a commercial city provincial in tone and not in any sense of the word the leading city of the country, in the way that Paris and London were. But at the moment *Harper's Magazine* was serializing *The Virginians* by Thackeray and other solid fare was rolling off the presses.

On Nell's wedding day *Don Pasquale* was being offered at the new Academy of Music in Philadelphia. Lincoln, Wood & Nichols on South Second Street were having a big spring opening of hats with imported French flowers. And Mr. and Mrs. Demorest were planning fashion improvements of their own.

CHAPTER II

§

Birth of the Paper Pattern

THE DAY in the 1850's on which the Demorests first displayed two dozen trimmed paper patterns in the parlor of their house in Philadelphia, fronting on Franklin Square, was a landmark in fashion history. Women in tartans, with wasp waists, wide sleeves and flying bowknots, clustered around the narrow house and blocked the stairs and sidewalk. They were face to face with a provocative innovation at a time when the sewing machine was whirring its way into mass popularity.

It turned out to be a fashion show of real significance. The demand for patterns was immediate and overwhelming. Mr. Demorest decided to move his family away from the quiet square that William Penn had incorporated in his city plan. He gave up his position in Philadelphia and returned to New York, where he had first sought a fortune and had come a cropper. He returned with optimism and determination, opening up shop at 473 Broadway as the nation headed steadily down the road to civil war.

Nell had given up her millinery business when she married.

Watching her Negro maid in Philadelphia cut out a dress from crude brown wrapping-paper patterns, she had a flash of inspiration. Why not patterns in thin paper that could be duplicated endlessly and distributed at small cost? Why not assemble the assorted segments for demonstration purposes? Mr. Demorest hastened the development of this idea. To him it was largely a problem in mathematics. They labored over the idea of supplying plain and trimmed patterns for women and children. Perfection of fit, adaptability to varying figures, were the essentials, with enough flexibility in sizes to meet all needs. Nell and Kate had been working for some time on a system of dress-cutting that they felt outmatched in precision the results of seven years' apprenticeship under the prevailing system, which entailed endless pinning, cutting, trying and retrying, instead of what Mrs. Demorest called the "daguerreotype certainty" and scientific accuracy of their own charts. Two prize medals had been awarded at the Crystal Palace for their model dress charts for children.

The small exhibition in Philadelphia evolved quite logically from the dress-cutting system. The two became inseparable and Mr. Demorest, a natural promoter with a creative way of looking at things, quickly seized on the bonanza developed in his own home parlors. In the autumn of 1860 he brought out the first issue of *Mme. Demorest's Mirror of Fashions*, a handsome quarterly in royal blue with gold decorations on the cover. It cost 10 cents and had its own distinction alongside *Godey's Lady's Book*, so successfully run by Sarah Josepha Hale. It had the colored steel engravings that had long delighted Godey's public, with the enticing announcement that they were done directly from the original European models and were not reproductions of old French plates.

The name "Mme. Demorest" was adopted for trade purposes. It suggested Parisian fashions and was in the idiom of the day. The quarterly was embellished with decorations and was subtitled: *Mme. Demorest's Illustrated Quarterly Report and Mirror of Paris and New York Fashions for Ladies and Children's*

*Dress. In Style, the Parisian Beau Ideal of Beauty and Elegance.
In Accuracy, the Perfection of Artistic Excellence.*

The patterns were advertised from the start and a sample was attached as a premium, with instructions on how to order more. Women studied the plates and tried the sample patterns, and then they clamored for more of the magic tissues. Soon flat envelopes containing numbered patterns in packaged lots were penetrating mining settlements in Colorado, isolated farms in the Middle West, growing communities on the Pacific coast, and crossroads in the deep South, as well as plantation homes. Single patterns for mantillas, basques and bodices were 25 cents, and 50 cents "if elegantly trimmed." Cloaks were 37 cents plain and 75 cents trimmed. Blouses were 18 cents. Dresses "elegantly trimmed" were offered for $1, and infants' patterns were 12 cents each. Complete sets of fifteen articles sold for $5. At first the job could be done with 200 reams of paper a month but eventually the Demorests papered the nation with the patterns that made their name a household word.

Their business grew so rapidly that almost from the start they found it necessary to employ skilled designers with original ideas, in addition to importing the best dress models from London, Paris and Berlin. Here Kate Curtis was of immeasurable help to the firm, in adapting French fashions to American tastes. Mme. Demorest found the American woman much more conservative in her tastes than the chic elements abroad. Her husband and she always thought in terms of the country as a whole and not merely the metropolis.

Soon they were turning out the patterns in tinted paper—an added dash of glamour that stirred up home dressmaking instincts and became something of a parlor game. American husbands found themselves shuffling around looking for their pipes and newspapers on parlor tables littered with odd segments of rustling paper—violet bodices, gray sleeves, white ruchings—while their wives ran up their own and their children's clothes on one or another brand of the sewing machines that had flooded the market since Elias Howe inspired this whirl of creative effort. Mothers in particular valued the graceful little designs for children's clothes with the suggestion of style that went with the Demorest imprint. The patterns, numbered, graded and in a great variety of sizes, were a particular boon to the nation's seamstresses, who abounded in every community of any size. It added to their numbers and whipped up fresh waves of fashion consciousness at grass-roots level, and a better sense of cut and finish.

The Demorests undeniably brought a dash of excitement and high fashion to lonely women in remote parts of the country as the circulation of their magazine soared to 60,000, even while the Civil War raged. The distribution agencies across the country grew in number from eighty-four, reaching from San Francisco to Troy at the beginning of the war, to 300 by 1865, and ultimately to 1,500 in the United States, Canada, Cuba, the Sandwich Isles, and the capitals of Europe. Many of these were permitted to label themselves Mme. Demorest's Magasin des Modes, keeping alight the Parisian inflection and drawing in the modish customers. They received package lots of patterns to set up showroom displays, accompanied by ornamental cards. Invariably they ordered Mme. Demorest's Premium System of Dress-Cutting at $1, the complete guide to the consummation of the pattern process. Wherever possible, the agencies were given to widows or spinsters. Those already in business were urged to open agencies and profit by Mme. Demorest's up-to-the-minute fashion service.

The beautiful ladies on the colored plates, with their stiff brocades, their cloaks and basques, ruffles and tilted hats reproduced in glowing colors, were the pin-up girls of the period, displayed like Mme. Godey's models in boudoirs, as well as in millinery and dressmaking establishments. A seamstress who could produce a Demorest pattern was thought to be linking herself with the true world of fashion. The patterns served the feminine dynasty from grandmother to infant. They could be adapted to the family purse strings, however tightly drawn, and distributed in massive numbers to any given point.

Inevitably this had its effect on American styles, from Worth's most soignée customers to the isolated farm woman. The Demorests catered to the rich in their own private dressmaking and millinery emporium but through their pattern business they diffused fashions on wider social levels. The paradoxical formula worked like magic. High fashions at low cost. Worth, translated into Americanese by Mme. Demorest, with a catholic range, from the Empress Eugénie to Amelia Bloomer. Perhaps more convincingly than anyone else the Demorests helped to tie up smart fashions with everyday usage in the United States, and they were deeply involved in the battle that raged between imported and domestic wares. Only the affluent who traveled could shop in Paris, London or Berlin. Only the thoroughly well-to-do could buy direct from Worth or pick up imported models at A. T. Stewart's. But millionaires were coming strongly into view, even before the war. Philadelphia had twenty-five at the time the Demorests gave their first fashion showing.

There was nothing sybaritic about the Demorests themselves. Both had spent their early years in healthy, outdoor surroundings. Both had a heritage of simplicity and solid values, and in the spirit of the mid-nineteenth century were crusaders at heart. As they prospered they were liberal in spirit and attentive to the needs of the poor. Mme. Demorest's independence in setting up a business of her own, her growing interest in women's causes, her deep-seated approval (rarely voiced) of all the measures that spelled emancipation, were artfully concealed behind a stately and conservative façade. Her husband, on the other hand, was an articulate and forceful champion of the social crusades of the era, adding temperance reform to his antislavery campaign. He considered tea and coffee harmful stimulants and looked with disapproval on the besotted who gorged on ice cream. Both he and Mme. Demorest upheld the Negro cause in all their dealings and had a large sprinkling of Negro girls among the employees in their Broadway workrooms. They made a point of having them sit with the white girls, receive the same pay, attend the company parties, and share in every way the fate of their colleagues. When customers objected —as they sometimes did—they were told to take their business elsewhere. Contemporary newspapers commented on the Demorest policies in this respect. They observed it at the fashion showings, at a paper masquerade ball given for the employees and in various allusions to the Demorest Emporium.

In the beginning Mr. Demorest presided from a desk with many pigeonholes at 39 Beekman Street, directing his growing operations. In 1860 he was forced to move his business house from 375 Broadway to 473 Broadway in order to have more room. Soon women in victorias and broughams were driving up to the narrow building hung with the sign "Mme. Demorest's Emporium of Fashions." Two alluring windows at street level advertised paper patterns and corsets. Upstairs Kate, the small, rotund sister with a dry sense of humor, functioned in the background, spending endless hours over the paper pattern designs, insistent on precise fit and finish, working over her charts like a mathematician.

Mme. Demorest, like her husband, showed dash and imagination. She lent her own impressive presence to the salon and kept the workrooms humming with fresh designs. She watched the import market and gradually found her niche in the social life of the city. Twice a year her fashion openings were the talk of the ladies of New York. She was a reassuring sight as, fashionably turned out, she directed attention to the gowns, hats, corsets and paper patterns of the family emporium. But in the early days her activities were divided between the salon and her home. At the time of her marriage Vienna was eleven and Henry was eight, so that she had two stepchildren to look after. The Demorests lived at first at 45 Charlton Street, where on August 2, 1859, Nell bore a son who was christened William Curtis Demorest. Her second child, Evelyn Celeste Caradora Louise Demorest, was born on November 21, 1865, after they had moved to 27 East Fourteenth Street. For a period between they lived on Broadway, close to Grace Church. Mme. Demorest always treated the four children as if they were all her own.

But the fashion business did not suffer if Mme. Demorest did not get to work with total regularity in those early days. Kate toiled behind the scenes and Mr. Demorest was a powerhouse on all fronts. His energies were unbounded. He was vigorous, quick-witted, adept at seizing the moment to promote a new activity, and he knew how to push every aspect of his business. He was soon the business head of a spreading empire—the promoter, the inventor of innumerable gadgets, the distributor, and eventually the editorial chief of five publications. At one point their combined circulation reached a million. He became a merchant as well as an editor. Premiums ranging from a Mason and Hamlin organ to a boy's pocketknife were scattered across the country. A Purchasing Bureau was established, to fill orders at short notice. The range was wide—from a harmonium to a bridal or mourning outfit; from a Holy Bible to a set of furniture. Arrangements were made with the city's leading merchants for their lowest retail prices, and the Demorests dealt direct with importers and manufacturers of ribbons, flowers, feathers and all kinds of millinery goods. No "streaked straws" or outmoded styles went out to the customers. One day's orders included hats, dry goods, books, jewelry, hearse plumes, waterfall curls, boots and shoes, fine leather trunks, parasols, dressing cases, vest patterns, silk cloaks, dress trimmings, two fluting machines and military hat cords.

New York's population in 1860 was 814,000 and the value of its real estate exceeded $398 million. There were 303 manufacturers in the city turning out goods valued at more than $17 million while Philadelphia had 352 manufacturers responsible for $10 million worth of materials. Imports at this time were gaining on home industries. They were estimated at $112,350,-000 in 1860, and were definitely affecting both cotton and woolen industries. The political situation was tense and Mr. Demorest watched each move in Washington, consorting with the local abolitionists, and voicing his own theories as he moved around town and discussed the political outlook with such men as William H. Seward, Horace Greeley, Henry Ward Beecher, Dr. Charles B. Cheever and other notables.

War was already in the air at the time of Baron Renfrew's famous ball, held in the Academy of Music in October, 1860. The fair-haired young Prince was the toast of the town for the time being and every move he made invited newspaper comment. The beauties with whom he danced, the gowns they wore, the floor that collapsed, the brilliant lights and gowns and jewels all supplied lively observations. A number of Mme. Demorest's gowns were on view that night and the *Mirror of Fashions* commented:

All the élite of the city were present, and the scene was one of dazzling beauty and magnificence. All the ingenuity and resources of the most celebrated modistes were brought into play on this occasion, and the toilets may therefore be considered as fairly indicative of the standard for full dress during the winter. Velvets and moirés, relieved by the costliest laces, and jewels for ladies already past their youth, and tulle, tarlatane and crape flounced and puffed and gayly decorated with flowers, for budding beauties.

Thus Mme. Demorest wove together her fashion notes and the social news of the day. She made solid soundings as she moved around town and in this instance she felt that the ball had influenced the season's fashions and had made the low-necked gown imperative. As the nation headed into war, trailing vines adorned gowns of gossamer materials. Organdy and grenadine prevailed, or tulle and tarlatan garnished with grass, field flowers or sprays of lilac. The bertha made popular by Harriet Lane was worn by the smartest girls as they danced the quadrille and the polka. They went home in cloaks of moiré or velvet. The pelerine was back in style and dark furs were the rage, with sable "a recognized value, like diamonds, or cashmere." Mink ranked next, although skins had risen from 75 cents to $4 each. Fitch was popular in the South. Chinchilla was scarcely used except for children, because of its perishability. Ermine was most distinctive of all and like "costly jewels, diamonds if possible, was the ambition of all ladies," the *Mirror* observed.

"Lyons and royal velvets are the only materials for winter bonnets," Mme. Demorest decreed in 1860. Trimmings were feathers or lace. Colors were deep and brilliant, like magenta, gold, or fuchsia, contrasting strongly with somber backgrounds. Velvets and moirés, brocade silks, ottomans and velours, poplins, cashmeres, merinos and soft French empress cloth were the stuffs of which fashionable gowns were made. Bows were everywhere, as well as trailing vines and guipure laces in black and many colors. "Parasolettes" trimmed with black lace were supplanting sun umbrellas. Hair was worn in heavy masses, frizzed and combed up from the sides, with wide braids in coronet style. All sorts of supplementary decorations were applied, such as a roll of scarlet velvet ribbon twisted with gold, a bandeau garnished with transparent leaves of gutta percha or a wreath of white blossoms with a feather trailing down one side.

Fashion moved ahead regardless of the shape of events. Will Demorest was a toddler on the April day on which the first shot was fired and North and South moved into the deadly embrace of the Civil War. The excitement in New York, as across the country, was intense. Newspaper offices were besieged by people watching for bulletins. Parading regiments and rattling drums soon shot tremors of patriotic ardor and pangs of fear through the population. Relief activities were organized. The Sanitary Commission took form. Interest in fashions wavered but did not die as women scraped lint, worked on haversacks, bade their men farewell. Mrs. Lincoln arrived in town to shop at A. T. Stewart's and Arnold Constable's. In the autumn issue of 1861 the *Mirror of Fashions* commented:

The war, which has depressed nearly all our mercantile interests, has had its effect upon fashions. Money is not plentiful, even among the wealthy classes, and the fear of possible results has put a present stop to the finest and most costly importations. Fortunately for us, however, communication is too constant between great fashionable centres for even a war to make much difference in our knowledge of facts.

In other words, Mme. Demorest still spoke with the voice of authority. Scenes of peace and luxury, viewed through the pages of the *Mirror* which, like *Godey's Lady's Book*, ignored the horrors of war, brought intermittent hours of balm to harried wives and mothers in distant spots. *Harper's, Leslie's* and the daily press showed the battlefields, the soldiers, the hospital agonies, the assorted miseries and woes of war. The quarterly did not penetrate the South, where soon there were no materials of any sort from which to fashion clothes.

But new manufactories sprang up everywhere in the North, and notably in New England. Waterpower was harnessed. Money was invested on the tide of a wartime boom. Flour mills, sawmills, knitting and textile mills flourished. Wood pulp was a thriving industry as boxes, cartons, manila paper and even tissue for patterns was in demand. Heroes emerged overnight. Generals went down to defeat or found passing glory. While Abraham Lincoln wrestled with his wartime problems in Washington, New York was a hotbed of civic corruption and unrest. By 1861 Mayor Fernando Wood was out of office and discredited. George Opdyke, banker, merchant, and a Republican, had become mayor. But his hands were tied while Boss Tweed cracked the whip in the background. As the months went on, the Copperheads, demanding peace instead of war, emerged on the political front and among their chief critics was Mr. Demorest. He started an illustrated paper the *Phunniest of Phun*, in which by means of cartoons he kept driving home the slavery issue.

At the same time Mme. Demorest's two brothers were caught in the struggle between North and South. Zachariah Curtis, who had an orange plantation in the South when war broke out, was taken prisoner in New Orleans by Union troops but escaped by hiding in a barrel of refuse and winding up in the river. He managed to get through the enemy lines and to reach the Demorest home in New York. His sister gave him money and clothes, and he set off for the family home in Saratoga, where he remained for some time. He was an athletic youth, with wrists like steel, and later he joined a circus. Her other brother, Edwin L. Curtis, who had taught school in Virginia, joined the Fifth Virginia Regiment of Volunteers, part of Stonewall Jackson's brigade. When the war was over he took charge of a Normal School for Negro youths, and Mme. Demorest gave him funds to help this institution. Later the Demorests had warm ties with the South, and Demorest, Georgia, was named after William Jennings Demorest around 1890, in recognition of his work for temperance reform. At the same time excursions to Demorest were promoted from Atlanta by real estate developers.

As the war raged on, there was increasing emphasis in the *Mirror* on mourning attire, and a general recognition of the nation's sufferings. "People of independent ideas often refuse from conscientious motives to wear mourning at all," ran an editorial. "The war, unfortunately, has brought the subject of mourning very close home to nearly all hearts . . . and so shadowed our once happy country, that a black garb might not be considered out of place, if worn universally."

There was a strong demand for mourning veils and yard goods in black. Bombazine gradually gave way to French merinos, cashmere, alpacas, and rep cloths. Black marceline silk and grenadine were cool in summer. Bonnets were smothered in crape, and veils were long and heavy, unless they were made of lisse. Jet was the only ornament allowed and plain black kid gloves were worn, as well as Congress gaiters. Men as often as women used handkerchiefs with deep black borders and all wrote their notes on stationery heavily edged with the universal sign of mourning. By 1862 the mourning cloak with passementerie and jet trimming told its own story, and it was ubiquitous.

Crinolines had definitely won the day by the season of 1862-63, and rich taffetas and glacé silks kept them in full sail.

One of the most drastic of all fashion innovations, they blocked traffic, kept men at a distance, and went off at alarming tilts that gave sudden vistas of frills and legs. At times they deadlocked their wearers in the midst of luggage and packages. Conservatives thought them vulgar and the *Mirror* commented with some satisfaction when the battle was won: "Five years ago when hooped skirts were first introduced, every one predicted for them a speedy decline . . . but after encountering the shafts of ridicule and opposition in every conceivable form, they will not only remain a fixed fact, but have become a permanent institution, which no caprice of fashion will be likely wholly to destroy." Although Nell could turn out spectacular billowing effects, her most popular number was the small Quaker hoop skirt which was one of the wonders of the crinoline age and achieved immense popularity and distribution. It was neat and graceful, took up little room, and seemed to assist, rather than impede, locomotion. It took first prize at the Fair of the American Institute, and *Frank Leslie's Ladies' Gazette of Paris, London, and New York Fashions,* gave it a brisk tribute: "Madame Demorest deserves grateful remembrance for being the first to introduce a really excellent, cheap hoop-skirt; and so popular did they immediately become, that other manufacturers were compelled to reduce their prices, although none have ever pretended to vie with these in cost, quality of material used, and amount of labor expended upon them."

Hurrying demoiselles did not trip if they wore Mme. Demorest's hoops, which retailed at twenty springs for a dollar. She used the maximum number of standards, so closely placed together at the bottom of the skirt that the heel could not catch in them. But her most popular innovation was the Imperial dress-elevator, with weighted strings to raise or lower the skirt at will and keep it always clear of the sidewalk. It sold for 10, 15 and 25 cents and prevented the hitching up in one spot and drooping down in another that plagued the hoop brigade. "Are you wearing your Imperial today?" women would ask. This pleased Mme. Demorest, who had often observed women skipping the gutters and crossing under the horses' hooves in the dust at Saratoga, not to speak of the muddy mess when one went promenading on a winter day in New York. No generation ever had more trouble with their skirts than the girls of the crinoline age. Mme. Demorest, who had been cold to them at first, was completely converted. She described the crinoline as a fashion made in heaven, contributing to grace, health, beauty and convenience. Hooped skirts had saved women, she added, from the martyrdom of the heavy weight they formerly carried over their hips in the shape of underskirts, and from much physical suffering and disease.

The press on both sides of the Atlantic at this time was attacking extremely low-necked gowns and tilted hoops as being immodest. The Frenchwoman of fashion was wearing the short-waisted Pompadour bodice, a style that had invaded England and shocked the more conservative. The extreme décolletage had not found favor in America and Mme. Demorest saw to it that puffed lace chemisettes added the proper touch of decorum to her gowns. So, while the British press raged about low bodices, the American papers confined themselves to tilted hoops.

Just as *Leslie's* approved Mme. Demorest's crinolines, *Godey's* bowed to her French corsets, which were one of the most popular items of her establishment. "The most elegant and at the same time the most comfortable corsets are those made by Mme. Demorest," *Godey's* conceded in 1863. While physicians debated the dangers of tight lacing and the wearers of tight corsets from time to time fell flat on their faces in fainting spells, the *Mirror* cheerfully commented: "Who shall decide when doctors disagree, and therefore we have nothing to say for or against the wisdom and propriety of wearing corsets; we only know that many women do wear them, and that they are essential to that perfect elegance of form and distinction of style, which marks the thoroughly bred lady."

Women squeezed themselves into Mme. Demorest's French corsets, which emphasized comfort but insisted on "artistic grace and elegant proportions." The best in French coutille cost $7 and if embroidered they ran from $8 to $12. Her spiral-spring bosom pads were advertised for "those who require some artificial expansion to give rotundity to the form." Together, her French corsets and nineteenth-century brassière helped the fit of her clothes and saved many a girl from the doldrums. Her spring model skirt, her combination suspender and shoulder brace, her scissors-gauge for ruffling, binding and cording; her elevator platform, her universal holder and skirt-looper; her braid and embroidery stamps; her diamond needles of the finest English steel, and her hair-curling cream, made her a benefactor to a tortured generation.

By the time the crinoline furor had subsided Mme. Demorest was the unchallenged dictator of fashion. "What Madame Demorest says is supreme law in the fashion realm of this country," said a rival publication. "No boudoir is complete without this invaluable *Mirror of Fashions*, edited by one of our most celebrated arbiters of style," said the New York *Mercury*. But the *Mirror* sternly disapproved of the girls who went strolling on Broadway wearing black skirts covered with infinitesimal flounces and raised slightly to show off red silk stockings and high-heeled kid boots. Their gloves were flame-colored kid and the "ensemble is so startling as to have suggested the title of 'Flamingos' for the fast young ladies who adopt this extreme of the mode."

Winter walking boots at this time were usually of black kid with buttons or elastic. They were likely to be heavily decorated with braid or velvet plaiting. They had high heels, and thick cork soles helped to make them waterproof. In winter Balmoral Clumps with triple soles and double uppers were worn by the hardier walkers. The Soulier Fénelon was of delicately shaded kid, with velvet bows to match the gown, and large steel buckles. In the boudoir women wore velvet or buff kid mules lined with white silk and trimmed with ribbon. And the military influence was strong, for both women and children. The coachman cape and the Galway were seen everywhere. Balmoral skirts were popular, and so were talmas, cardinals and hoods. Military braid,

tassels, buttons and medallions showed the effect of parading regiments, and children ran around in Zouave jackets and Garibaldi
suits made of cassimere. Aprons were shaped like the United
States shield. Women wore Zouave vests with crinolines, the
Burnside riding habit, the Saratoga hat, the Russian paletot.

In spite of all the talk of austerity, luxury items flourished
during the war. Tiny bonnets with sloping crowns and diminu-
tive curtains sold for $40, $50 and $70. Even in 1864 it was
observed that one would not know a war was on, as women
wearing superbly embroidered carriage cloaks of amber velvet
whirled into Tiffany's to buy emerald necklaces and gold combs
for their hair. Frivolous bonnets of white or black sprigged lace
were a persistent fashion and women wore French lace capes as
evening wraps. Massed trimmings of roses, passion flowers and
water lilies were as common on the small new bonnets as
ostrich tips.

The long and dashing cloaks and mantles had begun to
give way to the English paletot or short sacque by the summer of
1863, as wartime dress became more utilitarian. Women went
about their relief work wearing the "Fifth Avenue Walking
Dress" of English alpaca in light-cuir color, braided in pyramidal fashion, with a hunting jacket cut deep in the back
and square in the front. Their sleeves were edged with velvet
quilling and their parasols were of black moiré antique. They
traveled to camp and reviews to see their soldiers in buff nankeen.
In the evenings they invested the dance floor with as much
glamour as they could summon up. They carried white lace fans
with mother-of-pearl stems, imported by Tiffany; and sometimes they wore wreaths of violets and camellias, with accompanying corsages, made in sets by Constantin of Paris. White
lilac appeared on bridal wreaths in place of orange blossoms.

At this time they parted their hair in the center and rolled it
down into the waterfall. The nets that held their coiffures intact
were of Solferino chenille, delicately knotted in a diamond pattern. The finer nets shimmered with crystal beads, suggesting a
shower of diamonds in the hair. A more solid effect was achieved

with gold or coral beads. Stewart's was selling what Mme. Demorest considered the costliest Alençon and point d'Angleterre
laces ever brought into New York. "Real lace, such as our mothers and grandmothers left under lock and key, is now worn in
profusion," the *Mirror* noted.

Hair bracelets were a fad and Ball, Black & Company was
selling massive bracelets, Etruscan style, like standing cuffs of
gold, buttoned with costly jewels. Mousquetaire gloves were
used for both day and evening wear and Stewart's had a strangle
hold on all of Alexandre's gloves, which enraged his fellow
merchants. The price was exorbitant and the *Mirror* speculated
as to why American manufacturers could not make good kid
gloves. Those they produced were coarse and ill-shaped. White
kid gloves for evening wear were embroidered with magenta,
lilac or a color matching the garniture that dripped from every
gown at this time and came strikingly close to nature. Garden
bugs hid realistically in misty folds of lace. Fig leaves, meadow
grass and simple wild flowers usurped the field—"the more
primitive and rustic in appearance the better." In summer, veils
of fine guipure lace protected the complexion from "the violence
of the spring winds."

"Shilling calico" was a thing of the past as the war continued
year after year. The best establishments, said the *Mirror*, refused to stock any but English and French prints, since the
common American calicoes cost as much as the English and
were inferior in quality. When the war ended the world was
stripped of cotton as it had never been since Eli Whitney per-
fected the cotton gin in 1793, with the Southern crop then
jumping from 2,000,000 in 1790 to 160,000,000 pounds in 1820.
Low prices set in around 1840 but rose pyrotechnically during
the war. Printed Irish linens, French prints and cambrics increased from 50 to 75 cents a yard. Indian foulards took hold,
being both smart and inexpensive. Poplins went up to $5 during
the war. Silks and satins ranged from $5 to $12 a yard.

Children at this time were miniature images of their parents.
Little girls wore poplin, plaid, cambric or calico dresses, with

wide skirts, full sleeves and plenty of tucking. They donned
changeable silk for parties, and grenadine in warm weather.
Their wide sashes were usually brightly colored and tied at the
back. For wraps they wore tight little paletots fastened with
bone buttons. Their high Polish boots were of bronze or light
kid. Their low slippers were white and their gowns all had
names—the Lucia, the Little Pilgrim, the Evalina, the Winnie,
the Henriette, the Lelia, the Fredericka dress and the Mary
apron. Small boys were sometimes attired in Highland dress, to
the rage and disgust of one of General Grant's sons, who thought
ill of the kilt. Their velvet bonnets were apt to sport a white
heron's plume or a tuft of cock's feathers fastened in front with
a crest. More often they wore sailor, Zouave or Garibaldi suits.
Or they ran around in black-and-white check suits, belted in
black morocco mounted with steel. And invariably they wore
black button boots or cloth boots tipped with black.

Mme. Demorest approved the fact that babies were at last
being freed from their swaddlings. Her infants' patterns were
a pet project, for by this time she was supplying them for any
item of dress from a baby's sacque to a man's dressing gown.
Soon it was apparent that she was affecting the dress not only
of women but also of men and small children. When the *Mirror
of Fashions* ran an engraving of the "typical" American family
during the war years, presumably engaged in "industrial, refined, and fashionable amusements," one of the daughters was
examining the newly arrived *Mirror*. Another was exercising on
Shaler's Parlor Skates, an early variety of roller skate. The baby
was enjoying his new perambulator while Mamma, in a gored
wrapper, was urging one of her daughters to play a splendid
piano from Horace Waters, "whose warerooms are located in
our immediate vicinity." A small boy wearing a Zouave cap and
jacket was firing away on one of Crandall's Patent Spring Horses,
and the oldest girl was busy with a Wheeler & Wilson Sewing
Machine. It was all a happy blend of trade and recreation.

By this time the *Mirror* was flourishing and it now took ten cartloads to convey one issue away from the plant. The cartmen would not burden their horses with more than 4,000 copies at a time. Mr. Demorest had long had his eye on Fourteenth Street for his business and also his home. The tide of fashion was now crowding around it and various merchants were opening up for business there. He was one of the first to see its possibilities and to invest heavily in property. He moved his home to 27 East Fourteenth Street at the end of the Civil War, but the Broadway offices continued in business and another of Mme. Demorest's Magasin des Modes functioned at 134 Pierrepont Street in Brooklyn. Besides the large staff they employed in the skirt manufacturing department the Demorests now had more than 200 women engaged in selling, cutting, fitting or designing patterns, and finding profitable employment in this "apparently small and trifling pursuit." It was part of the Demorest philosophy to prove that they could make jobs for women.

To the rear of his establishment was a large machine shop, where Mr. Demorest could work over his many inventions, and specifically on his own model of a sewing machine with sundry improvements, such as a tucking attachment that he found tied in well with his wife's dressmaking operations. The emporium did family stitching and superior tucking at one or two cents a yard, and tucking at this time was an occupation in itself.

It became the accepted thing for women shoppers to drive up to Mme. Demorest's Emporium as well as to Stewart's to see what was new from Paris, and then to sidle their hoops into John Taylor's café on Broadway. He was the city's premier caterer but it was considered daring for women to lunch unescorted in an establishment of this kind. However, Mr. Taylor made them feel at home and quite important. They were served simple dishes, admirably cooked and courteously served, instead of the pastry snatched from a baker which, according to the *Mirror*, "some ladies eat against their judgment from a dislike to enter a public restaurant." His ice cream was noted and many of his customers used his artistic molds when they gave their parties at home. The ingenuity of the confectioners was at its height during the Civil War as they whipped up turrets, citadels, forts, cannon and other martial fantasies. It all gave spice to the day—Taylor's confections, Mme. Demorest's models, Stewart's gorgeous silks and laces.

CHAPTER III

The Miniature Bride

WARTIME BRIDES drove up regularly to Mme. Demorest's Emporium to have their trousseaux made with the speed and style that she guaranteed them during the hectic days of the 1860's. But when tiny Mercy Lavinia Warren Bumpus, twenty-two years old, arrived one day in 1863, a crowd gathered outside to view the prospective Mrs. Tom Thumb. P. T. Barnum had given her freedom of choice in the style and price of her wedding outfit. Miss Warren was ecstatic.

It was a problem to fit a midget. She laughed as the fitters turned her this way and that, pinning, cutting and basting. Mme. Demorest took personal charge of this most uncommon customer, towering over the small figure who viewed herself from all angles in the pier mirrors. The *Mirror* later reported:

We have taken particular pains to ascertain by close scrutiny, that she is a very pretty woman. Her face is sweet and expressive, her complexion good, her eyes bright, and her dark hair abundant, and worn becomingly braided back from the side of her face. When she smiles she shows two very distinctly marked and charming dimples. Her figure, small as it is, is perfectly developed, and very fine.

Mme. Demorest considered the reception gown made at her emporium for Mrs. Tom Thumb to wear at the courts of Queen Victoria and the Empress Eugénie the prize item of the trousseau. It was fashioned from superb taffeta, shading from pale amber to a silvery white. The emblems of various nations ornamented each separate width of material, joined at the seams with marabout feathers and lace, which also bordered the skirt. The left side of the skirt was looped up nearly to the waist over a petticoat of white glacé silk, covered with puffings of fine tulle and seed pearl tracings. The bodice was arranged with tiny folds of white satin, edged with point appliqué, forming a little jacket. The sleeves were short and trimmed with lace. Miss Warren was particularly pleased with her bridal skirt, made with Mme. Demorest's unique system of springs, and with her tiny corset. It was like fitting a doll, but eventually the emporium delivered a miniature model in white satin.

Lavinia was proud of her miniature jewels. Ball, Black & Company designed her unique wedding ring; her green-enameled watch in the form of a leaf, studded with diamonds; her diamond pendants, earrings, brooch, bracelet and hairpins; and finally her coral set. Her wedding gifts had the same sort of amusing charm and the guests hovered over Tiffany's silver horse and chariot, set with rubies; Barnum's miniature music box, and a tiny rosewood sewing machine inlaid with silver and pearls. Crowds surrounded Grace Church as Tom Thumb and Miss Warren were married, with General Ambrose E. Burnside, Mrs. Cornelius Vanderbilt and other military and social figures looking on, as well as her friends from Barnum's. She carried a bouquet of roses and camellias and her small pink face was crinkled up in smiles throughout the ceremony. Her sister Minnie, billed as the "smallest woman in the world," was her bridesmaid, and General Tom Thumb was unquestionably the man of the hour. Their wedding reception was held at the

Metropolitan Hotel and afterward they left for Washington to visit President and Mrs. Lincoln.

The Tom Thumb romance had been widely publicized. Barnum had played it to the limit and had worked up competitive interest for Lavinia's hand. But aside from this the public viewed the pair of midgets with genuine interest and affection. Lavinia had joined Barnum's American Museum in 1862 by way of a Mississippi showboat. She had reached her full growth at the age of ten. She was alert and intelligent and was presented to the public as being fond of poetry, music and art. After her marriage to the General she traveled around the world and became both rich and famous. She was widowed in 1883 and later married an Italian midget, Count Primo Magri. She toured with a Lilliputian opera company and lived until 1919, as forgotten at the end of the First World War as she had been famous in the days of the Civil War.

Like Mr. Barnum, Mr. Demorest did not overlook the publicity value of the General and his bride. Each new subscriber received a carte de visite of Mr. and Mrs. Tom Thumb with Minnie and Barnum. Photographs of Mrs. Tom Thumb in her reception dress, and of Mr. and Mrs. Tom Thumb together in their wedding attire, were sold for 25 cents apiece. These little souvenirs turned up in attics for years after the midgets were little more than a memory. Tom Thumb's wedding was a brief but diverting interlude in a year of stress and strain. Each day's papers told of victory or defeat, of further sufferings, of the Sanitary Fairs and women's work in hospitals. But women still danced, dressed smartly, held rendezvous and kept their spirits up.

The year began with President Lincoln issuing the Emancipation Proclamation in its final form and reached its climax with Gettysburg in July. The tide of victory rose in the North as Vicksburg fell to Ulysses S. Grant and by November the Confederate Army in the West had been driven from Tennessee. Stonewall Jackson had died at Chancellorsville in May. The draft riots in the summer of 1863 threw New York into a state of panic. The Copperheads flourished at the time and Governor Horatio Seymour, speaking at the Academy of Music on July 4, gave them impetus when he attacked the draft. After he had left the city for Long Branch bedlam broke loose. The mob surged down Broadway, waving torches and a collection of weapons. They started fires, tore up car rails, pillaged stores, knocked down telegraph poles, and damaged a million dollars' worth of property. Whole city blocks burned as they brandished their torches, smashed windows and brought all traffic to a standstill. They hung Negroes to lampposts and set fire to the Colored Orphan Asylum at Forty-third Street and Fifth Avenue, but the children were led to safety. They menaced the Little Church Around the Corner, which was sheltering Negroes at the time. They besieged Mayor Opdyke's house on Fifth Avenue, and were starting to wreck the main floor of Horace Greeley's *Tribune* when quelled by troops. The city shut up tight while the plundering went on, and the Draft Riots went down in history as one of the black spots of the era.

By this time the writers, artists and cartoonists were giving the nation a visual image of what went on at the battlefields. The war correspondents were a new breed who would loom large on the horizons of the future. They were alternately courted and spurned by the generals and politicians of the day. *Harper's Weekly* and *Frank Leslie's Illustrated Newspaper* with text, picture and cartoon, kept the public informed, shocked, angry, saddened and hopeful. Mathew Brady moved from point to point taking his memorable pictures, a steppingstone to the war photographs of the future. Currier & Ives etched the scene. New England's authors carried the torch for the Union. The transcendentalists had long been vocal on the subject of slavery. Stephen Foster wrote the songs of the South and died an alcoholic in Bellevue early in 1864. Walt Whitman did volunteer work in the hospitals. Thoreau's *Excursions* was published posthumously, a tranquil note in an era of conflict. The authors most widely read at the moment were Dickens, Zola, Balzac and Victor Hugo, and, among the American writers, Washington

Irving, Nathaniel Hawthorne and James Fenimore Cooper. The nation was avidly absorbing current news, and newspapers and magazines abounded. When the war broke out 200 periodicals of one kind and another were being published across the land. *Harper's Magazine* had been in the field since 1850 and seven years later the weekly, which gained great strength from its coverage of the Civil War, was founded. The *Atlantic Monthly* and *Russell's Magazine* also entered the lists in 1857.

Studying this fertile field, Mr. Demorest decided to extend his range beyond fashions, and in January, 1864, he bought the *New York Illustrated News,* one of the first picture papers. He experimented with it for eight months and then decided to consolidate it with the *Mirror of Fashions,* which had come out for the last time as a quarterly in the summer of 1863. The combined result was the first issue, in September, 1864, of *Demorest's Illustrated Monthly Magazine and Mme. Demorest's Mirror of Fashions,* a publication that was to stay in the family's hands until the 1890's.

This brought the Demorests into the field of general publishing. Both were listed as editors of the new publication and it flourished from the start. The fashion tie-up already established led to a circulation of 100,000 by August, 1865. With all the profitable sidelines—the inventions, agencies, colored plates, patterns and purchasing operations directed by Mr. Demorest—he soon became a wealthy man. The magazine was a small quarto in size. It was priced at $3 a year. Each subscriber received an engraving 18 by 24 inches, either sentimental or historical in nature, to hang in the family parlor, as well as a dollar package of patterns. A home paper dress pattern was stapled into each issue. In the mood of the day premiums soon became one of its major attractions.

Mr. Demorest announced that the consolidation would not limit the fashion department but would result in more literary and pictorial features. He had decided on a monthly because the quarterly had created a demand for more frequent issues. The colored steel plates at once became a notable feature of the consolidated magazine, which combined serials, verse, fashions, science, education, the arts, editorial comment and serious articles aimed realistically at women. Social reforms, family life and homemaking had a heavy play. So did science and world events as time went on. The travel note was emphasized and a sense of the larger world pervaded the magazine. There was strong emphasis on music, a family taste, since Vienna was already showing promise as a singer. The chromolithographs, woodcuts and ornate embellishments were in the best publishing tradition of the day. It was always tidily made up typographically and had excellent engravings. Portraits of famous men and women that could be detached were thrown in later for good measure.

The moral tone of the magazine was lofty at a time when this was a highly developed trend in publishing circles. Many had religious affiliations. The Demorest stories were accepted with "distinct reference to purity of tone and the inculcation of high moral principles." At the same time a certain sophistication of tone was maintained, for the Demorests moved in the main stream of events. The first poem published in the new magazine was by Theodore Tilton, a friend of Mr. Demorest's at this time although they quarreled later. The first serial was written by Virginia F. Townsend. Alice Cary and George W. Bungay, both family friends, contributed verse with some regularity. From time to time the names of top-ranking American and British writers appeared in its pages.

The magazine laid the foundation for Mr. Demorest's solid career as an editor, zealous crusader and reformer. He was soon devoting time, energy and much of his profits to social movements and particularly to the temperance cause. He was as much the crusader as his wife was the fashion expert. Reformers, educators, clergymen, writers, editors, politicians visited him at his home and their names appeared in the columns of his magazine. In its early years he did not make it the voice of propaganda, however, except for a constant drive on behalf of women's causes. His editorials ranged the field in a bland, contemplative way, in the style of the essayist, and without the bite that invested much editorial comment at the time.

Mr. and Mrs. Demorest were perhaps the first of the husband and wife working teams and the trademark "Mme. Demorest" blanketed the work of both, so that the merchants downtown sometimes speculated as to where Mr. Demorest's functions ended and Madame's began. The combination was so subtly worked out that it became a legend in time that the name "Mme. Demorest" was more a trademark than a fact. She chose to remain a shadowy character, rarely writing under her own name. But while he was the working partner who ran all the ramifications of the business, his wife gave her own special distinction and common sense to the fashion end. From the start Mr. Demorest saw the advantage of their mutual trade label, but no one who knew them well doubted that his was the mastermind and that Mme. Demorest carefully observed the conventions of the day and held her peace while other eloquent women pushed hard for emancipation. She had her own means of getting across a cause. She avoided the hustings and let others do the talking, but hers was a propelling hand in the steady drive for the advancement of women.

Mr. Demorest usually chortled when anyone suggested that it was Mme. Demorest who ran the business. He knew better, but he also realized that the family label led to misconceptions on this score. He sometimes solemnly assured his sons that if ever a man was boss both in his home and in his business it was he. And Mme. Demorest, the diplomat, would have been the last to deny it. Aside from their business each had separate interests and strong views, but they never argued.

The body beautiful was zealously nurtured at Mme. Demorest's Emporium, and it was her husband who employed chemists to work out the beauty formulas that made his wife the Elizabeth Arden, the Helena Rubinstein, of her day. She became more than a mythical name to the public when her picture appeared in a medallion on the beauty preparations.

From the emporium flowed a steady stream of cosmetics: "Mme. Demorest's Lily Bloom for the Complexion, an unequaled and delightfully perfumed toilet preparation for imparting a white, soft, clear and beautiful texture without injury to the skin." It was put up in neat boxes at 50 cents and was sold by druggists and perfumers, or was sent out by mail.

"Mme. Demorest's Roseate Bloom for the Complexion," another variation, gave a "natural and youthful freshness without injury to the skin." To this magic lotion was added "Mme. Demorest's Everlasting Perfume Packets for bureau drawers, glove and handkerchief boxes, reticules and the pocket." They would last for years. They would shed an exquisite perfume. And they cost only 50 cents. The ladies who bought the patterns soon followed up on the beauty preparations and for several years bureau drawers here and there across the country smelled of Mme. Demorest's Frangipani (the Eternal Perfume), of Jockey Club (Everybody's Favorite), of Night Blooming Cereus (the latest sensation), of Heliotrope (so very natural), of violet (everybody loves it), of Rose Geranium (a general favorite), of Bouquet (very exquisite), of Rose (the Ladies Choice), of Jessamine (a delicious perfume), of Verbena (very sweet), of Millefleurs (the odors of a thousand flowers combined), of Musk (this perfume exceeds all others), and of Patchouly (a delightful perfume). In time the little perfume packets, the skin lotions, the curling cream, appeared less and less in the advertisements.

The Demorest premiums were alluring, from organs to the miniature "Gem" souvenir booklets loaded with jokes, and useful oddments. Subscribers received knives, paintboxes, harmonicas, compasses, lithographs, songs, all manner of inducements. Anyone rounding up three, five or ten subscribers received a photograph album bound in gilt. Two subscribers clubbing together were treated to Mme. Demorest's System of Dress Cutting, an Imperial Dress Elevator or a gold pen. Eight subscriptions were good for a Universal Clothes Wringer. A Wheeler & Wilson sewing machine went to the smart saleswoman who rounded up thirty-five subscribers. Thus the momentum grew.

Advertising was a dull and static art at this time. Emphatic black lettering caught the eye, as crowded, declamatory sentences hammered home a message. There was little white space and much fine print. *Demorest's*, like the other magazines of the day, advertised patent remedies, magic cards, opera glasses, cabinet furniture, and a multitude of items linked to the era. Columns were devoted in each issue to advertising the Demorest wares. But behind all the promotion was the steady beat of the editorial contents and impeccable fashion news. These were sober, sound and well-edited until Mr. Demorest's zeal for temperance reform overcame his editorial judgment. From "Diamonds of Thought" to architectural plans for the home his magazine spoke to the families of America and had its influence right through the Age of Innocence. His experience in merchandising served him well as his new magazine penetrated the outposts of the nation, along with showers of assorted paper patterns. He was both merchant and editor. It all served as a fillip to mass fashions and helped to bridge the wide gap between New York couture and the country store and village dressmaker.

Songs were one of the most popular sidelines of the house. It was an era when families gathered around the newfangled pianos and organs to sing hymns or the popular songs of the day. Mr. Demorest offered wartime sheet music that penetrated many parts of the country. And when peace came he offered a $100 prize for a national jubilee song celebrating the "moral victory" achieved by the war. A typical package of Demorest songs included:

> Yankee Doodle and Yankee Ann
> Little Joe the Contraband
> Kiss my Mother Dear for Me
> This hand never struck me, Mother
> The Song of All Songs
> The Dying Drummer

She was all the world to me
Dost thou ever think of me, Love
The new Emancipation Song
Golden Dreams and Fairy Castles
The Pure, the Bright, the Beautiful
Fairest Rose of Summer

Mr. Demorest took a bold stand on the quack medicine advertisements that showed up in many of the current publications. Two had crept in with false claims that he did not like, and liquor was involved in both instances. He smelled a rat when rum got into bitters, denounced it as a "swindling dodge" and observed: "We can afford to be independent of all quack medicines." But he approved Reeves Ambrosis to make hair grow, with an illustration showing hair to the heels like the Sutherland Sisters. He sponsored Rigaud's Extract of Ylang-Ylang, Colgate's honey soap and Ivins Patent Hair Crimpers. Bay Rum Soap was a staple with men at this time. Mme. Demorest's boxes of aniline colors in eight shades were promoted for tinting cartes de visite. Mason & Hamlin organs sold for from $50 to $170.

In fact, if the ads did not lie, the New York ladies of the period stepped out in J. & J. Slater's promenade boots with scalloped sides, buttons, tassels, and a one-inch heel. They wore Stewart's scarlet waterproof cloaks and adorned themselves with Tiffany diamonds. They bought their clocks and watches, their Sèvres and Dresden china, their notepaper and their diplomatic cases of rosewood, ebony or leather from the same firm. They used Peter Cooper's gelatine and played on Steinway pianos. Their parlors were lit with Ives's patent lamps. They had their phrenological charts made out by Fowler & Wells and they read phrenological and psychological journals as well as Victor Hugo. They sang "Sweet Nell" straight from the pages of Demorest's, and their laundry went through the Universal Clothes Wringers, 58,818 of which had been sold by 1863.

They stitched away on a variety of sewing machines—those made by Singer; Grover & Baker; Wheeler & Wilson; the Howe

Machine and the Weed Machine. From 1866 on they also had the Bartlett & Demorest machine, noted for its elastic stitch and sturdy wear. Among its fascinations was the fact that it sewed either way; that the looper reciprocated instead of revolving; that it had only one threading before reaching the needle; that it featured the chain or loop stitch; that even with screw driver, clamp, extra needles and full directions, it cost only $25. Mr. Demorest acknowledged that the chief difficulty was to market it against the other well-known brands, particularly that of Issac Singer, who spent a million dollars a year on promotion. The itinerant journeyman, cabinetmaker and actor from Troy who had borrowed $40 to make his first sewing machine pulled out while the war was on. When he died in Devon at the age of sixty-three his estate was estimated at $13 million.

During the war the sewing machine was fully exploited and by 1867 a thousand a day were produced at an average cost to the customer of $60. Adelaide Ristori took an American sewing machine back with her to Italy. One was shipped to the Queen of Madagascar and another was given to Mrs. Ulysses S. Grant at the Sanitary Fair in Philadelphia in 1864. "The mournful melody of the Song of the Shirt is lost in the cheerful music of the Sewing-Machine," commented *Demorest's*, which had helped the sewing machine industry considerably with its patterns. Soon sewing machine journals were added to the clatter, along with a rash of fashion magazines strongly committed to the flying stitch.

Mr. Demorest's high-wheeled bicycle would come later but his watch guard was a popular novelty designed to outwit the ubiquitous pickpockets of the Civil War era. It consisted of a short chain with a holder and swivel attached, and sold for 25 cents in steel or gold-plated metal, and for 50 cents in black enamel and gold. It inspired a quatrain in the magazine:

> Pocket your watch and watch your pocket,
> Is a proverb as old as the hill;

But Demorest's guard can lock it,
Defying the pickpocket's skill.

When he had a free hour he liked to tinker in the machine shop behind the emporium. He turned out one improvement after another for sewing machines and obtained a patent for a method of cooking and heating with gas. He was the inventor of many of the dress attachments that were sold on the premises. He always found time to think up another improvement, to draw charts, to call in the right workmen and get something on the market. He worked closely with the merchants and many of them profited by his operations. A mention in *Demorest's* often went a long way in popularizing a shop or material.

Although he took out patents on cosmetics, machines, hoop skirts, his bicycle, his sewing machine and many of the emporium gadgets, by some strange mischance he failed to protect himself on the most important of all—his patterns—leaving the way open for Ebenezer Butterick to reap a great fortune in this field and eventually to mow him down at his own game. Butterick, who has generally been credited with the origin of paper patterns, first launched them on the market in 1863, and promptly patented them. He was a farmer's son and a tailor, a man of simple tastes and inflexible will. He sold his patterns first in Sterling, Massachusetts, his home town, then moved his business to Fitchburg, where he sold men's fashion plates accompanied by cut patterns. Toward the close of the Civil War he arrived in New York with a bed of his own invention that folded against the wall. He rented a room at 442 Broadway and used it as storeroom, workshop, and home. In 1867 he took into partnership Jones Warren Wilder and Abner Pollard, and the business moved to 589 Broadway, where they issued the *Ladies Quarterly Report of Broadway Fashions*. At this time he started turning out paper patterns for women, where he had previously concentrated on men and children. His modest *Metropolitan* was established a year later to advertise his patterns, and in 1872 the flourishing E. Butterick & Company founded the *Delineator*.

It was a long time before the Demorests felt the competition. They held the field solidly through the 1870's but began to feel the pinch in the 1880's.

While vanity was getting its due in one part of the magazine, the sober pen of Jenny June (Mrs. Jane C. Croly) was urging women to live more sensibly—to cultivate their minds as well as their bodies, to educate their daughters, to make them read, to stop being slothful, to depend less on their servants and more on their own efforts, to discipline their children, to refrain from marrying young or for money, to stop aping foreign fancies. She was more of a stimulant than a soporific to Demorest readers and soon women across the country were quoting Jenny and relying on her advice.

She had joined the Demorests with the first issue of the *Mirror* and remained with them for twenty-seven years—from 1860 to 1887. In the early issues her name appeared with theirs as one of the editors. But in actual fact she was the staff writer and turned out millions of provocative and often refreshing words. The Demorests valued her, and when she was retiring she said that in all their years together she and Mme. Demorest had never had a moment of discord. Their interests interlocked as consistent advocates of the greater emancipation of women, but Jenny was the editorial spokesman. The Demorests crusaded for reforms even more ardently outside their magazines than they did on the journalistic level, but they had the medium to back their views and promote their aims.

The constant drive for women's causes was attributed largely to Mrs. Croly, although Mme. Demorest backed her on every count and, some suspected, originated quite a few of her projects. Neither needed much help from the other, however. Both were clever women. Although Jenny constantly spoke up for what she considered women's rights, she and Mme. Demorest were cold to the aggressive tactics of the suffragists. Nell shared her husband's interest in social reform and devoted much of her time to philanthropic work. She was never the dedicated journalist in the sense that Mrs. Croly was, but she knew how to push things along. Both women sugar-coated the pill when a feminist drive was on. Their husbands were strong-minded men. As wives and mothers they spoke with the voice of knowledge and authority. Mme. Demorest brought up four children; Mrs. Croly had five, one of whom died in infancy. They paid due attention to their homes, were admirable hostesses, and never came under fire as did Susan B. Anthony and the other rampaging feminists. They were always gracefully gowned—how could a Demorest product afford to be otherwise? They were well-read, well-informed and well-spoken.

The Demorests and Mrs. Croly made a rare triumvirate—the bearded Huguenot brimful of energy and ideas; the reserved grande dame that Mme. Demorest had become; and graceful, eloquent little Jenny June, with her mournful blue eyes, her heavy pile of auburn hair, and her determined chin. She was nearsighted, thoughtful, and desperately efficient around an office in an unobtrusive way. She was an essential part of the organization, for she filled countless columns with material that was much ahead of the times. Her advanced views on women's interests, her fluent style, her place in the social life of the city, made her valuable on many counts. Because of her wide journalistic experience she understood all the technical aspects of publishing, and she wrote with drive and originality. She could read proof, do makeup, review books and plays, and cover general news. Her talks to women in *Demorest's*, her essays on the life and habits of the era, her skillful handling of the Ladies Club (a popular section devoted to correspondents), gave her solid standing in the organization and spread her own fame still further.

She was already well known around town, having written for the *Tribune* and the *Sunday Times and Noah's Weekly Messenger*. When she joined the *Mirror* she was writing "Parlor and Sidewalk Gossip" for the *Sunday Times*. She ran her own syndicate and turned out what she called her "manifold letters" for papers in New Orleans, Richmond, Louisville and Baltimore. By the end of the war there was scarcely a newspaper or magazine of any consequence that had not used her work. The London magazines often quoted her as an authority on American ways. She came originally from England and was born in 1829 in Market Harborough, Leicestershire. Her father, Joseph Cunningham, was a nonconformist who held classes for workingmen in his Tudor cottage. When their house was stoned and they suffered from persecution they fled to America and settled first in Poughkeepsie, then near Wappingers Falls.

Jenny's education was sketchy, although in later life she received an honorary degree from Rutgers Women's College and was appointed to a chair of Journalism and Literature there. She was by all odds one of the more literate women of her day and got her start in journalism from Charles A. Dana, when he was managing editor of the New York *Tribune*. She arrived in New York in 1855 after living for some time with her brother, who was the Unitarian pastor of churches in Southbridge and Worcester, Massachusetts. In the year after she moved to New York she married David Goodman Croly, then a reporter for the *Herald*, making $14 a week. He, too, was a reformer with a stiff spine and unbending will. He flourished when the *World* was established, and in time became its managing editor. Jenny was fashion editor of the *World* and also of the *Times* and her association with the Demorests was a logical development in her burgeoning career.

Jenny addressed herself to men as often as she did to women, and at times she must have confused them about their status. Soon they were picking up *Demorest's* from the parlor table to see what she was saying on their behalf or how she was excoriating them. They were abject rogues one month, cheating on their helpless wives, and browbeaten slaves shockingly treated by their women in another. At times they felt they had a friend in Jenny. In the issue of October, 1864, she attacked the lazy American woman and spoke up strongly for the American man. She deplored the violent and domineering tempers women indulged in at home, and she wondered how men could stand them. She noted that travelers had failed to find in American

women anything but love of dress, beauty of person, and grace
of manner—all admirable in themselves but qualities that
should be used as a means, not as an end. American women
lived at pedestal level. In no other country had they been so
praised, flattered, cared for and even worshiped. They were
like "pet spaniels in the home." To what end? Nine out of ten
were unable to give birth to healthy children, or to nurse them.
And men, poor things, went astray all too often, Jenny reasoned, because so many of the wives preferred to live in hotels
or boardinghouses instead of having a "quiet, loving home of
their own." She particularly deplored the wives and daughters
who had no gratitude for the results of their men's hard work
and despised the means by which they made their livelihood.
"It is surprising that men will bear so much from women,"
Jenny concluded, pointing out that they had a right to expect
care, good supervision of their homes, and attention to their
comforts.

She found the lives of too many city women "the merest
round of nothing" since they could not cook, wash or sweep,
make or mend their own clothes. But they could discuss by the
hour *Traviata* or the latest bonnet. "Pretty pegs to hang clothes
on, but not much heart," said Mme. Demorest's chief assistant.
She regretted that so many girls who would have made good
milliners, dressmakers or servants chose instead to be "female
writers of piles of manuscript that lie, read or unread, in every
editor's and publisher's drawer." But with all the certainty of
her own happy state Jenny added: "Nearly all women can have
their own way if they do not demand it and make a fuss about it."

Jenny did most of her scolding in her frank "Talks to
Women." She was mellower in her answers to correspondents
through the Ladies Club. Here she functioned like an early
Beatrice Fairfax, Dorothy Dix, Dear Abby and Mary Haworth
rolled into one, dealing with the combined problems of love,
marriage, food, fashions, etiquette, health and manners, until
she became the oracle of her day in all such matters. In her talks
she advised her sisters what to do in all manner of circumstances

and grappled barehanded with some problems never before brought into the open in a woman's magazine. Sex, hygiene, the fallen girl, all were treated in the twentieth-century manner. There was none of the pussyfooting indulged in by *Godey's*. She advised sex knowledge for the young, exercise for the expectant mother (a radical departure), freedom of movement and an end to swaddling clothes for babies. "Go easy on the layettes and seek the open air," she advised expectant mothers, ignoring the whirling sewing machines so ardently cultivated by her employers. Babies at this time were fed bread crumbs, potatoes, sometimes even strawberries, arrowroot, barley gruel from the bottle with milk, alternated with chicken or mutton broth. *Demorest's* advertised a riding chair with a mock horse behind it for babies to use before they could walk.

Jenny discussed housing conditions and comforted old maids with the cheering assurance that innumerable wives would gladly change places with them if they could. The homely woman was not forgotten. She was advised to avoid striking colors, to buy good materials and to confine herself to small patterns if she used figured materials. There was hope for everyone in the comforting pages of *Demorest's*. Jenny demanded full equality in marriage and attacked the "arrogant pride which asserts that women can not, shall not be doctors." She urged girls to find occupations and hobbies outside of their homes and to learn to breathe the fresh air, to take cold baths, to exercise and go for brisk walks, and not to loll about waiting for some good—or more likely bad—man to rescue them from maidenhood. Training for jobs would soon cure their vapors. "The real want of girls is less matrimony than a vocation," she wrote, in advising them to resist their mothers' drive for marriage. But in another issue she showed her hand clearly on the subject of marriage:

The great and most important right of women is the right to work. All the rest will follow. They must not lose sight of the fact, however, that their natural field of labor is *at home*—that it is the one which exerts the most influence for good or ill. It is better to be the mother of Kings than to be a King—and what does a woman want with a vote who has six sons, each one of whom she can train to vote as she pleases?

Her own zeal for education and jobs for women was so strong that at times she seemed the foe of marriage, which was far from being the case. There was no consistency in Jenny. She could argue her case persuasively from a number of different stands and had the flexibility that her job required. But at times she seemed to be spreading insurrection as she harped persistently on what women should look for in marriage, urging them to insist on perfect equality in income and property rights. It was all sharp talk for the chief writer of a magazine purveying fashion and beauty news. But it made women pay attention. Mr. Demorest and Jenny were bolder in their approach to social problems than Nell. Both women consistently refused to approve the Bloomer costume as such and called it "not only too revolutionary, but extremely inelegant and unwomanly in appearance . . . odd enough to attract universal attention, and neither pretty nor graceful enough to atone for its eccentricity."

They felt it was better to conform to fashion than to outrage it. That left bloomerism out in the cold so far as the Demorest Emporium was concerned. Yet Jenny looked longingly in the direction of dress reform. She was constantly meeting its advocates in the salons of the day. Many of them were her friends and she entertained them in her home. But Mme. Demorest let nothing interfere with the drive of fashion, although she discouraged extremes. The Empress Eugénie gave sensible dress a lift when she took up linsey-woolsey, and this gave Jenny June satisfaction. Real Aberdeen linsey or wool linsey-woolsey was unquestionably the best material for winter gowns, she told her readers in February, 1866, and scolded the girls who were making spectacles of themselves when promenading:

It is shocking to walk Broadway and see the long lines of young girls painted and dressed in the very extreme of the most outrageous mode—small hats bedizened with gold, and furbelows of every description, but affording them no protection against cold or storms; long veils drawn into a string; fancy jackets and coats, displaying any quantity of expensive buttons; but without a suggestion of either warmth or comfort. . . . While this love of dress is fostered in young girls, we cannot expect much self-control or earnestness of purpose from them when they become women. The last and only resource is to make linsey-woolsey and its attendant virtues the fashion.

The war had brought many changes in women's attire, as in all else. The nation was drained at every pore when at last Lee surrendered to Grant on an April day in 1865. The end had come, with victory for the North, misery for the South, where women had ceased to hunger for fashions and thought only of human life and food. Jubilation was matched by suffering and Ulysses S. Grant did not gloat over his victory. The scars of war ran too deep for that. Within two weeks Abraham Lincoln was dead and all New York turned out for his funeral. The catafalque moved along Fifth Avenue from Fourteenth Street to Thirty-fourth Street after the lying in state at City Hall. The Demorests had known him and had attended his second inauguration. They believed in everything for which he stood. A full-page picture of the assassinated President ran in their magazine of June, 1865, with an accompanying view of the funeral procession and a song "The Nation in Tears," with music by Konrad Treuer.

CHAPTER IV

Transatlantic Links

CARRIAGES ROLLED UP TO Mme. Demorest's Magasin des Modes on a dim November day in 1866, a cholera year. Her fashion openings had become semiannual events, with echoes heard across the country. Even *Godey's Lady's Book* was forced to admit that "Mme. Demorest of New York has produced some very elegant novelties in the dress line." By this time there were 300 branches throughout the United States, Canada, Latin America and in Europe. Each one was a prosperous business in itself, run by enterprising women who drew on the fountainhead in New York. The paper patterns were turning up in England, France, Sweden and Germany.

The New York *Dispatch* commented on the "cheerful showrooms, newly carpeted and decked with fresh, gay-colored patterns, exercising quite a fascination upon throngs of dames and demoiselles, because of their peculiar charm." And the New York *Herald* noted the handsome gowns that were on view but was even more impressed by the immense variety of patterns. Mme. Demorest, tall, gracious and knowledgeable, moved about among her models, explaining the procedure to buyers and reporters alike. By this time her name was becoming known on the international fashion front. It crept into the conversation wherever dress was mentioned, and this was still the favorite talk among women everywhere. How did she get her news so fast from Paris? How did she convert it so rapidly into models well adapted to American tastes? A letter from "Parisienne," a correspondent writing from Paris in September, 1867, to Mme. Demorest, summed it up: "I fear that not even Paris can add much to your stock and store. . . . We scarcely become accustomed to the newest style in Paris before, lo! the American lady comes with the same style improved, unified, and beautified."

Actually, the Demorests had scouts lined up in Paris, London and Berlin, who rushed information across that was quickly translated into fabric and tissue paper. They imported models, too, and fast copying went on in their emporium. They had a solid theory behind their operations. It was expressed in their magazine in November, 1867. French fashions, they pointed out, were taken from two sources—those designed for the ceremonial of courts and those aimed at the demimondaine. Their own technique was to draw the best from each, avoiding both extremes and turning out gowns that they knew the American woman would like and find wearable. Of the demimondaine cult *Demorest's* wrote: "To reproduce them as models with their coarseness or exaggerations, necessarily some time after the date of their first issue, is useless for all the practical purposes of American women and only serves to vitiate and deprave the public taste." Mme. Demorest had a deep and abiding faith in the "ladylike" tastes of her clients. It was an age when to be ladylike was all-important, and particularly since the wild tribe seeking emancipation was breaking out in different quarters.

The Demorest forces had launched a *Juvenile Bulletin of Fashions,* something never tried before, to outfit the young from babyhood up. But the big Demorest sensation at the end of the war was the mammoth fashion plate the house offered with more than seventy gowns, exhibiting all the latest styles. This was independent of the magazine and sold for $1.50. It was a yard long and three quarters of a yard tall, with an imposing array of spring and summer fashions done in color. The Demorests called it "the largest plate of fashions ever printed," which undoubtedly it was, and it hung in innumerable homes and stores.

One of Madame's admirers, George W. Bungay, writing in the New York *Independent* in September, 1866, paid tribute to her: "A lady of fashion who has the courage to strike out as she did, on a new and untrodden path, making fashionable France on more than one occasion look to her for style of dress . . . can not fail of appreciation and support. No woman in this country has done more than Madame Demorest to secure the best interests of her sex. She has proved, in her vast business transactions, the capacity of woman to care for herself; and she has been instrumental in placing many others on the path of prosperous trade which leads to independence."

This was pleasing to Mr. and Mrs. Demorest because behind all that they did was a fixed desire to enlarge the field of employment for women, a cause that constantly came to the fore in the family magazine. By July, 1867, the enormous growth of their business forced them to move again—this time to 838 Broadway, a spacious building with bay windows, occupying the most eligible site north of Stewart's marble block. They were close to Grace Church and below Wallack's new theater, and actresses going into the playhouse would pause to see what was new in Mme. Demorest's windows. Their downtown house at 473 Broadway remained in operation. Entire families visiting the city would drop in to be outfitted at the new quarters and the magazine advertised the fact that "ladies stopping at hotels can have all orders executed at a few hours' notice, and will find the fit, style and finish of the work unsurpassed outside of Paris."

This was a successful year all round for Mr. and Mrs. Demorest. It began with a triumphant display at the Paris Exposition of a showcase bearing the Demorest imprint, and was the first chance the Parisians had had to see the made-up paper models, as well as her beautifully fashioned corsets, her dress loopers in various designs, her stocking supporters, combination suspender and shoulder braces, dress charts and cosmetics. The exhibits the officials wanted most from the United States for this occasion, *Demorest's* reported, were such practical items as stoves and kitchen ranges, washing machines, sewing machines, brooms, shoes, clocks, rubber goods and, above all else, "an American restaurant, where pumpkin pies, corn bread, roast turkey, buckwheat cakes and other American specialties can be obtained with the true Yankee flavor." The paper patterns fitted well into the category of useful novelties.

Now that the war was over, Americans traveled freely again and Paris and Rome caught this lively tourist trade. The American colony in Paris was busy with fetes, concerts and reviews in connection with the Exposition. Magnificent entertainments were given at the Tuileries, and General John A. Dix, the United States Minister to France, appeared with his wife and daughter at the great balls and parties. The soft accents of Mississippi and Alabama were heard no more around the Tuileries, except for the diplomats and permanent residents who had long been there. The South lay quiet and stricken under the dawning reconstruction measures. But the "shoddies," or war profiteers, were observed at many of the functions. A great review of the French Army, with several sovereigns present and every civilized nation represented, was part of the summer's entertainment.

But the sensation of the Exposition was an impulsive act by Dr. Mary Walker, the doughty physician who had functioned right through the Civil War in men's attire. She tore down a picture of Robert E. Lee exhibited in the American Department. There was always news from abroad as well as from home to enliven the lives of the ladies who hung Mme. Demorest's colored plates in their bedrooms. From the East and Middle West sculptors, artists and writers now drifted to Paris, Rome and Florence to study, to pursue their various arts, to live the bohemian life. Willian Dean Howells, who had been in Venice as consul all through the war, was back and had joined the staff of the *Atlantic Monthly*. He helped materially to stimulate the literary pilgrimages to Italy.

A serious rival to *Demorest's* moved into the field in 1867 with the birth of *Harper's Bazar* as a "Repository of Fashion, Pleasure and Instruction." It was edited by Mary L. Booth, well known to both Mme. Demorest and Jenny June. It cost $4 a year and ran up its circulation to 80,000 within ten years' time. It, too, featured patterns, woodcuts of styles, serial fiction by leading writers, verse and miscellaneous attractions. It had cartoons by Thomas Nast, the artist who flayed Boss Tweed in *Harper's Weekly*. *Hearth and Home*, founded in 1868 for "farm, garden and fireside," also loomed formidably on the horizon at this time, with Harriet Beecher Stowe in the editorial chair. Gail Hamilton edited *Wood's Household Magazine*, and in 1873 the *Home Companion*, which eventually became the *Woman's Home Companion*, started as a small monthly juvenile magazine in Cleveland, Ohio. Many of these publications went in heavily for mail-order advertising. Only a few maintained the literary tone sustained by *Harper's* and *Demorest's*.

But in one way or another they had considerable effect on the generation growing up. Young girls became more than ever conscious of style. Everyday speech was affected. Fashion clichés took hold. *Demorest's* started a column on etiquette and sprayed out advice on many subjects. In January, 1867, the thought of the day was obviously beyond contradiction:

Avoid subjects in society such as politics or religion, upon which persons are most likely to differ. . . . It is as ill-bred to use foreign terms in your conversation as it is to whisper to one person when there are others present. Be careful how you encourage a reputation for saying smart, sharp, or sarcastic things; it will make you both uncharitable and unpopular.

Now and again a humorous note was injected into the fashion news. Commenting on the hair styles of 1868, *Demorest's* turned to verse over the "balloon," or bouffant, effect:

For light-headed ladies this fashion will prove
Good ballast in case of hysterics or love.
While the hat, termed Policeo, is dignified quite
And will keep the brain-pulses all perfectly right.
For thoughtful young ladies, whose heads are inclined
To be heavy by having a surplus of mind,
This aerial fashion will suit to a T
And render their ideas quite buoyant and free.

At this time golden hair was transcendent in Paris and many women were sprinkling gold powder over theirs or were having it cut off in order to wear golden wigs. At one New York wedding the bride and all her bridesmaids had their hair dyed red. Everything shone. Small veils were bordered with beads, and nets glittered with crystal and malachite. Immense pins and shining daggers were thrust through the waterfall, helping to hold the little fanchon-shaped bonnets in place. Women were glamorous objects, all gleaming with dew and spangles. There were frizzes, short curls and rats but the Empress Eugénie was frowning on the waterfall and Grecian curls. Gowns and gloves and hats had romantic names. Pearl-gray gloves, popular at this time, were known as "moon on the lake."

In selecting a flounce of Honiton lace for the adornment of her wedding dress Queen Victoria had made this native lace a fashion. An effort was being made to revive the rich brocaded silks that had become almost obsolete and Mme. Demorest helped this movement along. The distress of the Lyons silk weavers had been felt. She always kept an eye on the Empress to see which way the wind blew or her hoop tilted, but the crinoline was definitely shrinking in size, and the straighter, gored skirts were coming into view. Only the vulgar still sailed around in battleship hoops.

Correspondents abroad kept the emporium informed of every mood in fashion. At the last ball given at the Tuileries in the winter of 1865-66 the Empress wore a gown that Leoline, the Demorest correspondent, considered much too young for her. It was made with clouds of tulle as light as gossamer, with green water grasses for decoration and a fringe of diamonds on the corsage. The gems that lit up this costume were "as large as hickory nuts." Apart from the jewels, the costume might have been worn by a girl of sixteen, wrote Leoline. "The Empress never commits a fault of taste," she added, "but she has changed very much within a year, and though still beautiful and extremely graceful, with fair sloping neck and shoulders, which constitute one of her great charms, could no longer pass for a young woman. She looks all of thirty, when she is at her best; pretty well, after all, for one who will be forty upon her next birthday."

But *Demorest's* never subjugated the American scene to the pomp of Europe, although it drew from all the fashion centers abroad. Mrs. Emilie J. Merriman, who corresponded regularly from Italy, reported from Turin in March, 1866, that bonnets were scarcely worn there at all, which was hurtful to the millinery business. The traditional fashion was a black veil thrown over the hair and festooned at the neck. Italy seemed to this correspondent to be more independent of Paris fashions than New York. She thought it strange that few women should wear bonnets in Milan, the city that had given its name to "millinery." Mrs. Merriman felt that crowned heads were becoming noticeably intimate with the public. She wrote from Baden-Baden in September, 1865: "We have been permitted to bathe so near Her Majesty the Queen of Prussia, that her royal splash was echoed by my republican splurge—and afterward, when issuing from our respective rooms and tubs, she graciously bows, a recognition of mutual tastes, which is condescendingly reciprocated."

Mr. Demorest might disapprove of smoking, liquor, tea, coffee or other stimulants, but his magazine was bright with the popular songs of the hour, with the history of great stars, with dancing lessons—the galop or valse in two-time, three-time, or the Redowa Valse, with precise instructions. There were demonstrations of riding lessons, of good skating techniques, of deportment at watering places. The range was wide, from the view of gowns worn at balls given in St. Petersburg to the trees, the birds, the rambles of Saratoga. Active in civic affairs, much around the town in a business way, Mr. Demorest by this time was firmly established on the contemporary literary front. Editors and writers were in and out of his comfortable home on Fourteenth Street, from James Parton and Robert Bonner to Alice Cary and Horace Greeley. Nathaniel P. Willis, an old associate, died in 1867, leaving a sorrowing widow in Fanny Fern, who wrote extensively for Robert Bonner's *Ledger*. Jenny June and David Croly had their own salon, where Jenny kept her ear to the ground on women's causes as she handed around unspiked punch on silver trays to New York's literati. Increasingly the reforming note crept into the magazine, in spite of its worldly air and fascinating color plates.

New York was a rowdy town in 1867 and Mr. Demorest, the reformer, observed with disapproval the grogshops and dance houses along the Bowery, the concert saloons, billiard parlors and shooting galleries. The war had not improved the morals of the population and he saw much to deplore in the fleshly tastes of his fellow citizens. There were more than 9,000 saloons and 700 houses of ill-fame and Dr. T. De Witt Talmage was hammering away at civic corruption and the wild night life of the town. Crime stalked the dark alleys where two feuding gangs, the Dead Rabbits and the Bowery Boys, slugged it out with clubs, knives or crowbars. Cow Bay and Murderer's Alley were notorious. In the Five Points close to City Hall 382 families lived in a single block and thousands existed like rats in cellars. Pawnbrokers flourished and the strange street cries of the period rang down dark alleys—the ragpickers, cinder collectors, street sweepers, hot corn vendors and lamplighters. It was not like the simpler days when Mr. Demorest's grandfather, Cornelius, watched cartmen, stevedores, laborers and porters doing the city's work, often by lantern light.

Streetwalkers paraded past the emporium, even in the daytime. Their route of march was from Canal Street to Madison Square. They hung around the smart hotels, even the Fifth Avenue Hotel, which Paran Stevens had opened in 1859 and which had harbored the most noted men of the day during the war years, from Abraham Lincoln and Ulysses S. Grant to Baron Renfrew and Edwin Booth, who liked to stroll in from the Fifth Avenue Theatre nearby. Mark Twain, Cyrus W. Field and Peter Cooper all were habitués, and Alice and Phoebe Cary, the sister poets from Cincinnati, darted through its lobbies like frightened rabbits.

The streetwalkers avoided the sweep of fashion through Twenty-third Street from the Ladies Mile, the popular shopping area frequented by the most fashionable wives. It ran from Eighth Street up Broadway to Twenty-third. They had no fear of the policeman with helmet and white gloves who directed the horse-drawn traffic at Madison Square with his rattan stick. They strolled in a leisurely way past the rows of victorias, landaus, broughams, phaetons and hansoms drawn up against the curb by night and day. They haunted Madison, Union and Washington Squares. They rode in the omnibuses, hung around hotel doors, traveled up and down the river and visited resorts. They mingled with the crowds coming out of theaters and ogled from park benches.

The ballrooms, concert saloons and parlor houses represented varying grades of carnal entertainment, with Greene Street the most degraded, and the Louvre, close to Madison Square, along with John Morrisey's notorious gambling house, the most luxurious. Here the demimondaines, in a glitter of chandeliers, sashayed around amid rosewood furniture. marble columns and paneled walls to mix with the town's sports, just as the judges, politicians and merchants focused on Harry Hill's Houston Street establishment. But the most difficult purveyor of sin for the reformers to understand was John Allen, who had made the transition from being a divinity student to running a dance hall on Water Street. His girls wore the traditional scarlet dresses and red-topped boots with jingling bells, but had Bibles in their rooms. Finally the evangelists caught up with him in 1868.

The waiter girls and barmaids of the era were a lively lot.

Many of them had been camp followers during the war. The more high-toned "lady boarders" functioned from their private parlors. They did not walk the streets, but played the piano, attended church and observed the accepted social usages. They were none the less deadly to Jenny June's distracted wives. She and Mme. Demorest were interested in all these social manifestations, for at this time they were trying to help the wayward girls, those juvenile delinquents of the 1860's and 1870's who were often cast into the gutter. Some were extremely young. A number were engaged in the hoop trade and were fresh from the country. Frequently they showed up in hospitals, and all reformers at this time were interested in the operations of Mme. Restell, the notorious abortionist and midwife who lived in luxury on Fifth Avenue, attended church, drove around town in an elaborate equipage, and finally cut her throat when Anthony Comstock rejected a bribe she offered him.

While the seamy side of life was getting a thorough airing in the daily press and the clergy were hammering away from the pulpits, the social life of the town became ever more sophisticated. The war had widened horizons. The arts were flourishing. Fashion was at its peak, with Empress Eugénie leading the field and Worth the master creator. He had helped to kill the crinoline and banish the poke bonnet, which he felt had been deadly to feminine charm. He favored jet and bright colors. He felt that women did not dress to please their men but to impress one another and to build up their own self-esteem. He draped the Empress Eugénie in the most costly laces and piled on ornamentation as it had never been known before or since. His forte was not simplicity but complexity. He was hard to copy, as Mme. Demorest soon realized. And his prices were astronomical by any standards.

Fashion was seen at its most extreme at the watering resorts, and the Demorests did justice to this aspect of the social scene. They returned regularly to Saratoga each summer and Jenny June kept up a lively flow of communication for the magazine. A great many things had happened to Saratoga since the war broke out. The great ladies of the South were seen no more on Broadway. The war profiteers, the gamblers, the politicians, the grafters had taken over, although fashion still flowed to the spas. *Godey's Lady's Book* decided that the resorts were getting fast, and in 1865 thoroughly condemned the use of mascara by the fashionables at both Saratoga and Newport, terming these two spots "the Sodom and Gomorrah of our Union." But *Demorest's* always spoke up in defense of Saratoga. In a sense it was the family stronghold and at this time the Demorests were improving and developing the Curtis homestead. A firecracker tossed into the water in 1864 had started the great fire that had wiped out fourteen buildings along Broadway and Congress Street. A year later the United States Hotel was in ruins from fire. The Sans-Souci at Ballston Spa had by this time become a Ladies' Seminary, although it would again be a hotel in 1875. It had sheltered Henry Clay, John Calhoun, Martin Van Buren, R. Barnwell Rhett, Franklin Pierce, Jerome Bonaparte, Washington Irving and many another celebrity.

The Clarendon, built by Mrs. Mary Mason Jones, was still the bastion of the conservatives and here Peter Lorillard, a neighbor and friend of Mr. Demorest, died in 1866. Cornelius Vanderbilt still displayed his trotting horses and played whist at night. Jay Cooke, the banker whose fame had become legendary during the war, brought his hearty, pious presence to this worldly paradise. John Morrisey, the friend of Boss Tweed, came first in 1861, a handsome figure, six feet tall, with a black beard and dominating air. He was soon followed by a trail of politicians and gamblers. By this time Lake House, opened in 1853 by C. B. Moon, was a popular rendezvous, with its spacious piazza, its groves, ponds and winding walks.

Jenny June studied postwar Saratoga with considerable interest and wrote for the magazine that scholar and artisan, gentleman and boor, author and ignoramus all met there under the same roof and did their devoirs before the same shrine, as the man of the world and the woman of fashion. Yet Saratoga was the best, in her estimation, although Newport was more exclusive and did more for a woman's complexion if she hung out of her window and breathed in the morning dew. In a tour of the watering places Jenny appraised each one in turn. Long Branch was doing well, with General Grant summering there, and West Point had gained in popularity since the war. But she soon decided that Saratoga had the "most marvellous displays of wealth and fashion," plus a genuine claim to front rank in its mineral waters, which seemed to her unrivaled, an opinion shared by both Mr. and Mrs. Demorest. She enlarged on the splendid equipages, the grand cuisine, the leisure, the indulgence, the spirit of dolce far niente.

But an editorial in August, 1865, probably written by the master himself, took a sterner view of the scene, pointing out that the income spent on dresses and on the balls of the season, including a spectacular one given for General Grant, took enough revenue to support a frugal family all the year round. Although it dismayed him that five hundred gamblers should make Saratoga their summer quarters, he observed that "very mentionable visitors" were sojourning in the Saratoga hotels just after the war—men whose characters he admired.

In the autumn of 1867 the Demorests crossed the country from New York to Chicago for the inauguration of the new line of Silver Palace Sleeping Cars by the Central Transportation Company. They set off from Communipaw Ferry at the foot of Liberty Street on July 22 and took five days to cover 1,900 miles. Eleven cars held the party of celebrities and writers who shared in this epochal junket. The cars were of solid black walnut with silver mountings and decorations. They had marble washbasins, ice-water fountains, velvet carpets and well-upholstered seats. The curtains were of rose silk and the doors of ingrained glass.

They stopped first at Easton, where bouquets of flowers were presented to the women. They lunched luxuriously on game and hothouse peaches. They had supper in Altoona, then retired to curtained beds in staterooms. They dined next day at

Fort Wayne and stayed at the Sherman House, where a ball was given in their honor. There had been no warning of this festivity, so that even Mme. Demorest was caught without a ball gown, much to her chagrin. But she and her husband enjoyed to the full the magnificent panorama crossing the Alleghenies on their way back. Their final comment in their magazine on this excursion was in the spirit of 1867: "A through trip to Chicago in thirty-six hours without a single change of cars and surrounded by the most luxurious accommodations, need no longer be a matter of dread even to the most nervously fastidious lady."

CHAPTER V

Paper Dolls

A PAPER DRESS MASQUERADE, unique in the social annals of New York up to that time, was given by Mme. Demorest on Christmas Eve, 1867, in her emporium at 838 Broadway. Her two hundred guests rustled like falling leaves in October as they danced. The prevailing fashions for three hundred years were faithfully reproduced, to the last ruff and plume. The *Evening Mail* of December 26, 1867, noted that it was a "Vanity Fair of lace, gold, silver, crystal powder, wonderful headdresses, impossible skirts and forgotten combinations in dress."

The fashionable women of all ages met and shook hands; 1740 danced with 1614, and 1802 smiled at 1580. Mrs. 1860 chatted with Miss 1515, and 1700 trod upon the toes of 1260. All the butterflies, birds of paradise, flowers of Eden, macaws of Brazil, and artificial flowers of a whole street of French milliners' shops seemed to have been heaped up into one vast pile, which suddenly, at the strains of music, formed into quadrilles, and whirled, like a thousand flying dervishes . . . covering the carpets and furniture with a perfect shower of débris.

Although odds and ends flew off, the dancers did not lose their draperies, for the paper was tensile and firmly gummed to a thin muslin base. Mme. Demorest moved majestically among them—Queen Elizabeth in rich black brocade, with an underskirt of royal blue. Her hoops were enormous. Gold edged her pointed bodice and her ruff rose high against her dark, piled-up hair. Jenny June was Margaret of Provence in a 1260 cerise velvet basque edged with ermine, and a trailing blue skirt. Her own reddish hair was powdered with gold. Kate Curtis, archgoddess of the patterns, was Morning, her white silk gown spangled with gold stars and a gold crown on her hair. Her sister Matilda was Night, with the same effect in black and silver. Court dresses abounded and trade got a bow from the walking dresses and shopping gowns of 1800. The historical note was strong. The ruffs, the plumes, the laces, flowers and ribbons all were reproduced with accuracy. Even the dominoes of the masked guests were of period vintage. Mr. Croly of the *World* sauntered around with W. H. Burleigh, the poet, since both of their wives were participants. There is no record of the fact that Mr. Demorest looked in on the masquerade but his daughter Vienna sang and it was all admirable promotion for the house, as well as being stimulating for the girls.

"A noticeable feature in the affair was the perfect good will with which the fair ones of the company mingled with their associates of color," commented the New York *Times* next day. "Altogether the party was a deserved success." And the *Tribune* observed that when Mme. Demorest issued invitations to her employees she made no distinction in race or color. "American, Irish and German girls participated in the pleasures of the evening, and many intelligent-looking and ladylike Negro girls as well." By this time it was a well-recognized fact that Negro girls were always welcome in Mme. Demorest's workrooms, not a common state of affairs at the time. Many of her employees were from the country and bore such curious names as Trifeny, Plunny, Plumy, Elgardy, Florilla and Samantha.

The paper masquerade was just an echo of the great flourish of balls and masquerades that gilded the prosperous years following the Civil War. They were held all over town, in assembly rooms, in the Academy of Music, in Delmonico's, in hotels and private homes. And the artists shocked the town with their own Bal d'Opéra which the *World* viewed as a "tumultuous orgy." The most magnificent of all the balls was Mrs. Pierre Lorillard Ronalds' costume ball as the war neared an end. The gowns, the flowers, the revelry, and her own appearance as "Music," with a lyre lighted up in her hair by miniature gas jets, and her scarlet boots jingling with bells, were discussed for weeks. Mrs. Ronalds, who sang and acted, handled horses in a masterly way and was a favorite of Leonard Jerome's, cut solid ice with the more swift-paced sophisticates.

Worth's original creations appeared increasingly on American hostesses. Mme. Demorest could vouch for the fact that a young bride rounded up as many as 300 items for her wardrobe, costing all of $20,000, provided her family could pay the piper. More than forty gowns were needed to sustain her through a New York season alone, and they ranged in price from $80 to $2,500 when Worth was the creator. Added to this were her fans, her lingerie, her laces, her jeweled combs, her sables, her shoes, her gold whist markers, chatelaines and card cases. Even her fine lace handkerchiefs at balls were held by tiny springs to solid gold fans in miniature. And by this time the tinted French kid gloves that women wore in the evening had become so expensive that their wearers, most reluctantly, were having them cleaned instead of throwing them away. Pearl gray, primrose and canary had taken the place of white gloves after the war and Stewart's struck a romantic note with gloves in sultan red, marigold, deep purple, claret brown, mulberry and garnet, ornamented with small gold studs and finished off with gold-mounted tassels. It was costly and took a great deal of time to prepare for marriage in the 1860's and 1870's if one belonged to the inner social circle.

But Mme. Demorest knew how to map out a less expensive

454222222222222222

trousseau for her brides across the country. One of her typical outfits for the girl of comfortable means seems abundant today:

Bridal gown of white satin trimmed with old point lace
Reception dress of pale-pink grosgrain trimmed with puffings of tulle and blond lace
Evening dress of mauve silk, trimmed with knotted fringe and ruches. Pearl ornaments
Dinner dress of blue silk, trimmed with black and white lace. Coral ornaments
Black silk dress, with Valenciennes lace
Walking suit of green velvet, trimmed with sable
Traveling suit of gray Irish poplin, trimmed with velvet and fringe
Watteau morning dress of scarlet wool
White opera cloak of frosted plush
Real cashmere shawl
Black lace shawl
Two real lace handkerchiefs; six trimmed with lace; two dozen cambric
Two dozen hose, cotton lisle
Two dozen pairs kid gloves
Six pairs slippers
Two pairs walking boots
Two dozen of all articles of underclothing, richly trimmed
Riding habit of dark-blue cloth, hat and whip
Striped traveling shawl, done up in strap
Bonnets to match every costume.

The European touch—or what Jenny June referred to as "foreign fancies"—impinged increasingly on the home scene as travel became more general. French chefs in many instances supplanted Negro cooks. European china, silver and table manners cut across the American tradition. Rosewood furniture supplemented the austere colonial inheritance. Satin curtains and upholstery from materials woven in gold and imported from France dressed up the homes of the newly affluent. There was much talk of war profiteers and pretension as the more cautious and conservative looked on with disapproval. Champagne suppers and ornate effects reflected the great prosperity of the

Flash Age. Carriages with liveried drivers and footmen left lady callers with their card cases at the doorways of the new mansions. Social rivalry was gaining ground and hostesses tried to outdo one another on decorations, food and the distinction of their guest lists. Jerome, always original, challenged the skill of Lorenzo Delmonico by inveigling August Belmont and William R. Travers into competing with him for the perfect dinner, planned by the three sportsmen and executed by the great restaurateur. Delmonico rose to the occasion and presented them with a flourish as the Silver, Gold and Diamond dinners. The result was a tie. Men had time, money and the taste for such gourmet entertainment in the leisured 1870's.

New York was changing drastically at this time. The shift of property became an everyday matter after the war and the steady drive uptown was insistent. The population approached a million when the first elevated railroad was tried experimentally in 1868. But this made little impression on the carriage trade. Fifty new models were turned out each day in New York, including the Clarence for large families, the landau, the landaulet, coupe, pony phaeton, tandem, dogcart and four-in-hand drag. Gay packets swept along the Hudson, their decks crowded with excursionists. But the rural touch persisted and Isaiah Keyser dealt in ice, cattle and garden supplies where the Vanderbilts would eventually build mansions at Fifty-first and Fifty-second Streets.

Visitors from abroad were not enamoured of the New York they saw in the postwar days. They considered it architecturally ugly, its streets dirty and untended, its narrow houses monotonous and uninviting. It kept changing from month to month but always in a chaotic way. The fashionables rarely went north of Murray Hill, for beyond that they encountered something of a wasteland of unpaved streets, on which brownstone houses rose steadily in solid rows. But lower Fifth Avenue preserved its air of tranquillity. Its mansions had grace and solidity, and sometimes the owners, wearing cutaway coats and white cravats, stood at the railings of their gardens greeting passers-by. The

gleaming door knockers and white-capped maids washing flag-
stones were a familiar sight to passengers in the stages that went
whisking past.

In the 1870's the coaches went in for decorative effects, startling to quiet strollers. They flaunted pictures of Swiss landscapes, Indian fights, steamboats tossed in stormy seas, and
dashing trotters. Chains roped off the church streets on Sundays, ensuring total peace for worshipers. Madison Square was
in full flower and much of the shopping excitement centered
close at hand as women paraded along their own territory—
the Ladies Mile.

The Demorests had a new neighbor when Tiffany's moved to
Union Square in 1870, bringing the Atlas-supported clock made
originally for their place at 550 Broadway. And a year earlier
Brooks Brothers had settled beside the Singer Company on the
Square and adopted the sewing machine for making suits. But
all garments still were finished by hand.

That strange object, the high-wheeled velocipede, which had
been lurking in the background since early in the century, had
finally caught the public fancy. On a fine day they could be
seen curvetting in solid masses in the neighborhood of Central
Park. But *Demorest's* was withholding judgment. "It is an open
question yet whether they can be used by ladies; but we think
not—at least in their present form," ran an editorial. "The very
appearance of a lady upon such a machine would be so obviously incongruous and out of place as to prevent them, except-
ing as a joke or mere piece of bravado, from ever applying them
to their own use."

However, Mr. Demorest inevitably was attracted by their
speed and convenience, and the fact that women who could not
afford carriages or horses might find them practical. He thought
that an improvement in style would supply the answer and he
began to tinker in his workshop with a high-wheeled velocipede
with ball bearings. "Light, pretty and tasteful, the ladies'
velocipedes might become an institution, especially for use in
parks and large private grounds," he commented on second

thought. "We are quite sure riding them would supercede croquet as a fashionable summer amusement." But the girls who whacked the croquet mallets went doggedly on in their gored piqué dresses with Breton jackets or in striped cambric suits with white muslin hats trimmed with black silk ruches. Croquet had brought them out into the open. Young friends dropped in to run up points and drink lemonade in the sunny outdoors. The family as a whole could play. Le Cercle had brief popularity. It required more skill than croquet. Wood wickets took the place of iron hoops. The mallet was spherical and the balls vibrated when struck, but this variation of croquet did not take hold. Nor did any of it interfere with the craze for the velocipede. The art of riding it was being taught at thirty establishments in New York and every town and village across the country was taking up the sport. The nation was on wheels.

Skating was the perennial winter delight of the graceful girls who skimmed across the ponds in mulberry costumes of plush trimmed with black marten fur, carrying tiny muffs. Their caps were of plush, beaver or velvet, Glengarry shape for the most part, and trimmed with fur or birds' feathers. They did the Dutch roll with a flourish of colored petticoats above the black kid boots that laced high over their ankles. Tartans were sweeping the market at the moment, the influence of Queen Victoria extending to the Glengarry and Balmoral caps. Friends and rooters watched from sleighs drawn up close to the rinks. The New York Skating Club in the wastes of Fifty-ninth Street was a sight on icy days with its shifting panorama of men and women cutting swiftly across the ice, cheeks glowing, scarves floating behind them, blades gleaming in swift turns. There were many private ponds and Beekman's flourished in a swampy area close to the East River. Alexander McMillan's was at Forty-sixth Street, still a remote spot for the fashionables. Young girls sometimes cut into their skating time to concentrate on German. French was so universally known in this set that German was "now the fashionable linguistic acquirement," *Demorest's* pointed out, with the added note that seventeen was much too young for girls to come out. Yet they were doing it, and wearing short dresses into the bargain. Jenny June didn't approve.

At this time Mme. Demorest was pushing riding hats and the magazine was running equestrian lessons, with charts and directions. The Atlanta model was a black velvet riding hat with a long black ostrich feather that created a dashing effect. The Duchess was of white felt with a crimson bullion cord around the crown and crimson marabout feathers floating over the side. Correspondents wrote in for the hats by name, just as they ordered their gowns by number. The typical riding habit was of dark-green cloth trimmed with velvet, embroidered with jet. A neat tucked chemisette was fastened with studs. A long plume, like a long train, was now a mark of the highest distinction, Mme. Demorest ruled.

The driving focus had shifted from the Battery to Central Park, which was still an unfinished dream. For years it had been the fashion to drive to the Battery or to promenade on foot at the island's tip, where the neat walks, the bright flower beds, the band, the observatory on Castle Garden, the cool breezes off the bay, were an irresistible attraction to the citizens who dwelled below Fourteenth Street. A small group habitually drove along the Bloomingdale Road to their summer estates overlooking the East River, to return laden with flowers and garden produce. Their shaded lawns and gardens ran to the water's edge. The country seats of the Goelets, the Gracies, the Rhinelanders, the John Jacob Astors, the Schermerhorns, the Lenoxes, the Beekmans and others were in this region. And Mme. Jumel, whom Nell Curtis had been seeing from childhood at Saratoga, would clatter into town from her mansion with her four-in-hand. The rough surface of the streets created a bone-rattling effect and it was not until the 1870's that upper Fifth Avenue was graded.

But by this time trotting had become the rage, and society, the stars of the theater and the more raffish elements were finding suspense and excitement in this new diversion. All roads led to Harlem Lane and the fans cheered from the porches of wayside inns as the trotters broke into the open terrain. Men of such disparate tastes as Ulysses S. Grant, Robert Bonner, Lester Wallack and Henry Ward Beecher were enthusiasts. Bonner, like Demorest, frowned on betting and fought the gambling elements that went with the trotting horse. But he could not resist the sport itself and every afternoon after leaving the massive *Ledger* building he went to his stables on Twenty-seventh Street, changed into driving togs and set forth for his daily trot through the park. Lester Wallack, who had put up a handsome playhouse at Broadway and Thirteenth Street, where orchestra seats sold for $1 and gallery seats for 25 cents, was drawn irresistibly to the tracks. It was the speed racing of the era, with its own quota of collisions, mad spurts and favorite horses.

Ulysses Grant, the horse lover, succumbed to the trotters even while he occupied the White House, and he liked to watch Commodore Vanderbilt's entries at Saratoga, along with a great many other men whose chins were variously adorned with Dundrearys, Imperials, Vandykes, Galways, sluggers, goatees or walrus whiskers. Because of the gambling elements that had invaded this sport, horse racing was in some disrepute with the social set until Leonard Jerome founded the American Jockey Club. But swearing, drinking and gambling, commented Mr. Demorest, were fashionable vices which could not exist if women did not tolerate them. At this time the crusading note began to sound more strongly in his magazine. In April, 1869, he launched a vigorous attack on gambling, speculation and lotteries:

Religion and charity are the mantles which lately have been made to cover this blackest of sins. . . . Let no one of our readers be tempted under any circumstances to buy a ticket in a lottery or gambling enterprise. Denounce it to your children and family in terms of the utmost severity. . . . The church raffle, and the ticket to the gift-concert, with not the remotest chance of obtaining the house and lot, are steps which lead directly down to that lowest perdition—a gambling hell.

He was equally censorious of the spiritualistic rappings that Margaret and Kate Fox of Rochester had touched off and that seemed to interest even such friends of his as William Cullen Bryant and Horace Greeley. The Fox sisters had started a cult that ran its course and aroused lively debate. People were playing planchette, studying astrology, and tinkering with psychic phenomena. Mr. Demorest's own advertising columns plugged some of the mystic wares. But he solemnly warned his readers that it behooved Christian men and women to be careful how they encouraged "such a species of blasphemy by introducing Planchette into their families, or allowing so grave a spiritual joke to be disseminated among their children." However, tables continued to fly into space, spirit voices were hearkened to in the home, and Kate Field, among other intellectuals, lent herself to these dubious manifestations.

When Mme. Demorest had her spring showing in 1868, exhibiting at both 473 and 838 Broadway, it was evident that the pouf of the pannier was killing off the Civil War sashes, and jet was having a revival, pushed on by Worth. Visitors from the country joined with the city regulars in viewing the Grande Duchesse pelisse, the costume à la Marie Antoinette, the Pompadour, the Mantilla Royale, and the Dauphin suit for boys. Every costume for adults or children had a name. The Maud dress. The Latour suit. The Lamballa cloak. Thus they assumed identification in the shopper's mind and were useful in the pattern trade. Children were still quite rococo in their attire. They were apt to be tucked up in tiny sealskin or ermine jackets. Black velveteen suits trimmed with large pearl buttons and black sashes were for party wear. White silk and satin quilted hoods often adorned the very young and white felt hats the older children.

Boys suffered greatly from tartan sashes and shoulder knots, long cassimere trousers, and hats with curled brims jammed

on their too-long silken hair. Or, if running about in Newport,
they might wear tweed knickerbockers and tucked striped
shirts, finished with collars and cuffs, if they had reached the
age of eight. At three they wore gored piqué dresses with cape
attachments and chip hats trimmed with blue velvet and white
ostrich feathers. Little girls could be joyful in the rambles of
the park in French cambric with flutings and ruffles. Their
skirts reached to the calves of their legs and were wide like
crinolines. They wore high boots and sailor hats of glazed straw
like their mothers', with flying ribbons.

Women at this time were taking up the suit for street wear although they still clung to cloaks and mantillas for dressier occasions. A new Alma or Scotch cape was fashionable that spring
to throw over Spanish linen and China cloth for seaside wear.
The polonaise in linen had become an institution and the bustle
was in sight. Bridesmaids favored white organdy and tarlatan.
Bridal wreaths in America had a new tilt after Mme. Demorest
noticed that Adelina Patti wore hers at an uncommonly low
angle when she married the Marquis Henri de Caux in the
autumn of 1868. She also did everything she could to make
life simpler for the lady sojourner of the period. It had taken
enormous trunks to hold the crinoline gowns and the puffings,
flutings and flouncings that persisted after their decline. Much
as she disliked the bloomer dress she suggested a modified form
of it for riding or boating excursions.

Two traveling gowns, one dark and serviceable and the other
light and dressy, should be carried in a carpetbag to be worn
while stopping at a hotel for a day or two en route to one's
destination. Waterproof cloth, buff nankeen, alpaca, or English
shepherd's check were suggested, with the "skirts properly drawn
up over appropriate under-skirts." Thus did the *Mirror of
Fashions* give the woman traveler precise instructions on dress
and conduct, never forgetting that the average woman was being
addressed rather than the sojourner de luxe. The same simple
rule was applied to those traveling abroad. They were advised
to take one dress for shipboard that could be thrown away on

landing. Two suits, one of black silk and the other of Japanese poplin, would serve with a waterproof or long sacque and cape. A black straw toque with blue gauze veil and a box of paper collars and cuffs were essential. Several changes of underwear were suggested but the rest of the wardrobe could be bought cheaply in London—gloves and shoes in particular. Travelers were also urged to set forth with a box of Messina oranges, some lemons, sugar, tea and equipment to brew it, since "raw lemons or a cup of good hot tea are great panaceas for seasickness."

There was much for them to do in Europe and traveling correspondents sent back glowing letters to *Demorest's* about the functions at the Tuileries, the art galleries, the spas, the wonders of the Swiss mountains, the joys of dining with British authors and Italian artists. The engravings from month to month were exhilarating, whether Hudson River scenes, Riviera vistas or Alpine peaks. In September, 1870, the Demorests added Prang's Chromos, a series of popular illustrations, to their magazine. Chromos, or colored lithographs, were a favorite form of household adornment, and housewives cleaned them with a soft feather brush or wiped them with chamois and a dampened linen rag. Among those that hung in countless homes were "Flowers of Hope," "The Maiden's Prayer," "After the Storm," "The Captive Child," "At Close of Day" and "The Three Tom Boys." But the chromo "Home Sweet Home," with its horse trough, dairy house, well, orchard, shed and woodpile, was the prime favorite. The subscriber could find a little of everything in *Demorest's*, from plans for a country house and a poem by Edgar Allan Poe to Alice Cary's favorite pudding recipe or advice on whether or not to leave one's husband. The May issue of 1870 ran *The Raven* with elaborate decorations.

By degrees the women of the South were beginning to think in terms of fashion again. One of Jenny June's correspondents wrote in 1868: "In my life, I do not think I ever saw anything so beautiful as the box of things you sent us in the spring of '65 . . . occasionally someone would come from the North, and

bring a Demorest. What rejoicing! What borrowing and alter-
ing!" A few months later a second correspondent added her
testimony: "Another prominent feature of reconstruction is in
our wardrobes. . . . I have just completed a very stylish-looking
Fanchon, from a New York bonnet of 1860. A lady has found
she could make a very genteel dress from an old silk, laid aside
in palmier days. Waterfalls have been turned into chignons,
fine dresses have been gored, panniers added, and new trimmings
and a general reconstruction of our wardrobes."

She wondered what now became of the fine fabrics that once
were brought to the Southern homes, and if Stewart and other
merchants did not miss the heavy orders they used to fill for
the South. "But though we are under a cloud, and bend before
the blast, and must give up so many of the luxuries and even
comforts of life, we dare to hope that, under a new system, we
shall again rise in the sunshine of prosperity." She paused to
recall the dried sweet potatoes, barley, okra, cornmeal, bran
and ground peas they had used for coffee; the sassafras and
pear leaves to make tea; the poke berries for rouge; the slippers
made from dog and hog skin; the goose-feather plumes that
kept their vanity alight.

A new order prevailed as Thaddeus Stevens and Charles
Sumner pushed reconstruction measures that opened the way
for the carpetbagger invasion from the North. Both men and
women suffered under the harsh spirit that had taken the place
of Abraham Lincoln's benignity. Fierce battles raged in Congress over reconstruction issues as the social pace quickened.
General Grant's blunt report after a tour of the South was so
sympathetic in tone to the people of the Confederacy whom he
had helped to humble that the unyielding New Englanders
attacked him at once. Bitter feelings delayed conciliation.
Mourning was a stern reality in innumerable homes. It was a
slow and painful awakening from an era of excitement, danger,
dissension. The world had changed. The American home had
changed. The publications of the day reflected the change. The
social, business and political worlds would not be the same again.

Gloom spread through the land when the gold operations of Jim Fisk and Jay Gould created panic on Wall Street and precipitated "Black Friday" in September, 1869. The Grants had been in the White House only six months and already the President was heading into scandal and abuse. He was playing croquet in a hamlet in western Pennsylvania when he learned of the gold crisis. He moved to checkmate the swindlers but did not escape without assaults on his own integrity. Fisk, the financier with waxed mustache and showy manners who had reached Wall Street by way of Jordan, Marsh & Company and liked to ride up Fifth Avenue with French chanteuses he had brought over to the Grand Opera House, barricaded himself in his office to escape attack after his fantastic bidding. The day was one of Wall Street's landmarks. The market was in an uproar. The sale of gold had exceeded $500 million. Gambling had reached a point where the grooms, bootblacks, newsboys, porters and coal heavers, among others, were dabbling in stocks and occasionally making fortunes, or, more often, being pushed to despair. Speculators abounded in the dry goods field, too.

The gold crisis was President Grant's first big ordeal and others would follow, as he coped with corruption in his own administration, tariff problems, inflation, the Alabama claims, civil service reform and racial tension in the South. Greeley, a miserable man at this time, ill and humiliatingly defeated in his bid for the Presidency, thought that the public treated Grant "harshly, captiously, unjustly," as the popular General, in his shift from the battlefield to the White House, found storms roaring around his ears. Bigelow thought that he had not grown in public estimation and had "never said or done anything to individualize him, or give him the kind of personality which inspires a national or popular enthusiasm."

By this time women were using the new and fascinating telegraph to send to Jenny June some of the queries for which they needed speedy answers. She tackled every topic with an air of unassailable authority, reflecting the Demorest point of view as well as her own. Her advice sometimes had bite and was salutary. It was also eminently practical. Like many others, she thought that standards had slipped since the war.

"A little common sense, exercised in the choice of a husband, is just as needful as in the selection of a dress or cloak," she commented sagely. "We are glad to see in intelligent and fashionable circles a decided intention to discountenance, as vulgar and improper, privileges which, like the old Dutch custom of 'bundling,' have become so universal, that no one felt like being the first to denounce or break in upon them."

Girls were advised to remember that to be happy and honored wives they should be esteemed as well as loved. Parents should not permit them to sit up alone in the parlor until all hours of the night. "Sitting in a darkened room until two or three o'clock in the morning with any man, is so obviously and shamelessly indelicate, that it is only a wonder the instinct of parents . . . has not forbidden it long ago," Jenny wrote. Young women were warned that a man who wiped his feet on the doormat before entering a room would make a good, domestic husband. If he put his handkerchief on his knees while taking his tea he would make a prudent one. If he picked up the last griddle cake he would unquestionably make a selfish husband. But that a mother should warn her daughter not to say anything smart to a man since "gentlemen are so afraid of clever girls" was sheer tosh, in Jenny's opinion. It was her experience that the smartest men also liked brainy girls. She had some home knowledge of this situation. But any man who visited a girl for six months and never mentioned marriage to her was either not a "marrying man" or he was a cad.

Anxious subscribers were told to rub sulphur followed by lemon juice on recalcitrant freckles; to use the magic comb to color their gray hair; to apply "golden" ointment to their faces and wash it off with horse-radish steeped in buttermilk; to make their spring medicine with yellow dock, gentian root, ginger, rhubarb and wormwood steeped for a day with sugar. They learned how best to polish their diamonds, get the most out of their gardens, and tend their parlor plants; to answer a wedding invitation, set their tables and discipline their children. But while all these familiar matters were treated with due respect the steady drive for women's rights and better education went on. Girls were urged to study business as an art, to perfect themselves in specialties, to form societies, to make a bid for financial independence, to attend Cooper Institute and learn telegraphy, or to work up businesses of their own. "Keep your tools instead of your fingers at the grindstone," Jenny advised. "And do not be driven to that most poor and despicable of all means of obtaining a livelihood—marrying for a home."

At this time there were 150,241 teachers in the common schools of the country, and 100,000 were women. In Massachusetts there were six times as many women as men teachers. In Vermont the proportion was five to one; in Iowa it was three to one and in New York eleven to one. Jenny harped unceasingly on educational opportunities and went to Poughkeepsie to see how things were getting along at Vassar, which had been founded in 1861 and loomed up as an interesting experiment. *Appleton's Journal* on October 8, 1870, had said that "the competition of women with each other in swimming or rowing matches is intensely repugnant to every conception we have of the sex." Jenny didn't think so. In fact, after taking careful soundings she decided that Vassar could go much further in all respects. Without any hesitancy she predicted coeducation:

The next step will be the education of the sexes together, possibly the throwing open the colleges already in existence to young ladies, as well as their brothers and male cousins. There is no reason why it should not be done at once. . . . Instead of dissipating their energies, as many suppose, it would stimulate them to further effort.

This was bold talk for the era. But Jenny did not waste any bouquets on the college as it was. It was not the perfect school for women, the college of the future. Indeed she found it only slightly in advance of the men's colleges, but she decided that it had great possibilities and eventually would help to change the tone of modern society and create public opinion among women "altogether superior to the conventional code."

Both Mr. and Mrs. Demorest were intensely interested in educational matters and closely followed every advance across the country and abroad. A Japanese village on display in Madison Square Garden suggested to Mr. Demorest that one day education would be provided by photographs, pictures, stereopticons and visual exhibitions. Their magazine proposed a great free college for women in New York, where they could take courses in millinery, plain sewing, telegraphy, bookkeeping, German, music, drawing and English.

House hunting at this time was nearly as popular a diversion for women as prowling through the small shops along the Ladies Mile. Although the city was growing fast, it was hard to find suitable homes, and children were unwelcome in many cases. Houses rented at from $200 to $1,000 a year but "babies are looked upon as obstacles to social ease and comfort," Jenny reported indignantly. She theorized that men were driven to the street, the barroom, the billiard saloon and the theater "to find consolation in the best way they could" because of the difficulty of finding decent, roomy houses. The girls arriving at Castle Garden made good servants and their wages ran from $10 to $15 a month with board. Workers in dressmaking establishments, mail writers and women bookkeepers in publishing houses earned from $5 to $30 a week. There was much rudeness on the streetcars and women could scarcely find seats in the cabins allotted to them on the ferryboats because men who did not like the "smoke and reek of the Gentlemen's Cabin flocked in to the Ladies Cabin." But the Easter Parade had arrived with a gentle whisper of the future in the spring of 1869. It was noticed for the first time when one of the papers commented: "The day being pleasant, the streets and parks were filled with pedestrians gladly enjoying the first airs of Spring. The ladies were out in full force, looking doubly charming under the influence of those genial skies." They whirled around the churches as they would for the next century.

While New York's social life grew in grace, there was a

mounting note of dishonesty and debauchery as the 1870's followed the war-ridden 1860's. Charges of corruption which had brushed the White House were ten times heavier at the civic level where the depredation of Boss Tweed, in command of Tammany Hall, were being sharply pinpointed by Thomas Nast in a series of blistering cartoons in *Harper's* that helped to unhorse him finally and land him in jail. Nevertheless, railroads were being built. The postal system was revised. There was a vigorous drive for progress, whipped on by the restless giants of journalism, Horace Greeley and James Gordon Bennett, whose days were nearly over. The new decade opened with a great funeral procession along Fifth Avenue for Admiral Farragut and a murder that stirred the city to its depths. Benjamin Nathan, a wealthy banker and broker, had been bludgeoned to death while seated in his nightshirt at his desk. No crime in the city's history had caused such excitement. For days crowds surrounded his home on Twenty-third Street and stage drivers walked their horses past to satisfy the morbid curiosity of their passengers. But the murder of Mr. Nathan went down in history as one of the great unsolved.

CHAPTER VI

A Club Is Born

IN THE YEAR 1868 Jenny June, with the backing of Mme. Demorest and several other pioneers, conclusively channeled the future course of American womanhood. They organized the Sorosis Club, official starting point of the club movement for women which eventually affected their status around the world. Mme. Demorest was one of its early officers and was potent in the club councils. She did not live to see the organization of the General Federation of Women's Clubs that had grown out of it by the close of the century, but Mrs. Croly did.

Unwittingly Charles Dickens triggered off this revolution on his second visit to the United States. Having etched the American people in acid after his earlier trip in 1842, this time he had decided to mollify and conciliate. But he was suffering from gout and felt ill-tempered when he hobbled down the stairs at Delmonico's on Horace Greeley's arm on an April night in 1868. New York's most shining wits and intellectuals had turned out to greet him at the banquet given in his honor by the New York Press Club. A total of 187 guests dined appropriately on crème d'asperges à la Dumas, Côtelettes à la Fenimore Cooper and les petites Zimballes à la Dickens. It was a literary night to remember and the town's most intellectual women did—for they were excluded from the feast and the resultant indignation gave America its start as the incubator of the woman's club.

When news of the reception became public, men with remote literary connections added their pleas to those with authentic claims and were accepted as guests while talented women actively engaged in newspaper and magazine work were ignored. David Croly, then managing editor of the *World*, was on the executive committee and his wife applied for a $15 ticket through him. The members considered this a joke and snubbed the proposal, although they were accustomed to seeing little Jenny whisking around in their offices wearing Mme. Demorest's elegant fashions and carrying bundles of her "manifolds," or hurrying in from a theater to write a review of a play. They also had every reason to know that the copy of Fanny Fern, James Parton's wife, was more sacred to Robert Bonner of the *Ledger* than that of Henry Ward Beecher or Alice Cary. Not one word could be changed. She was a born circulation getter and received $100 for a single column. Fanny did not live to see Sorosis flourish, since she died four years after it was founded, but at the time she and Jenny June had good cause to consider themselves quite entitled to sail in at the front door of Delmonico's and to take their places at the literary feast. They were two of the nation's most quoted and prolific women writers. But it was not so much the feminist urge then sweeping the country that stirred them as genuine pride in their craft.

Horace Greeley, James Parton, David Croly and Parke Godwin, son-in-law of William Cullen Bryant, took their proposal seriously. Greeley, always the champion of women's causes, said he would not attend unless they were included. Under pressure from the formidable Greeley the committee at the eleventh hour wrote to Mrs. Croly in a challenging way. If enough ladies could be found willing to pay the price to make

a good showing and thus "prevent each other from feeling
lonely," they would be permitted to buy tickets. The note arrived three days before the Dickens reception. Jenny considered
it a "churlish and conditional assent," tantamount to a refusal.
She crisply retorted that since the ladies had not been treated
like gentlemen, they would prefer not to attend. By this time
the suppliants had plans of their own. The revolt had begun
at the annual St. Valentine party given by Charles Edwin Wilbour, a *Tribune* man, and his wife. Among the guests were
Jenny June, Mme. Demorest, Alice and Phoebe Cary and
Fanny Fern, all women of substantial reputation. "It serves
us right," said Mrs. F. J. Ottarson, wife of another *Tribune*
man. "We women will never get anything until we get together.
The thing for us to do is to start a club of our own."

Mrs. Croly saw the merit of this and inspired the others. It
took courage at that time to launch such an idea. But indignation over the Dickens episode spurred them on. The matter was
further debated from the plush easy chairs of the Cary home
at 53 East Twentieth Street. And when Jenny June ran down
the fascinating, auburn-haired Kate Field, of the *Tribune*, exercising her nimble body at the "Light Gymnastic School" of
Mrs. Z. R. Plumb, and tackled her over the dumbbells, Kate,
the writer, the poet, the mystic, the actress, singer and wit,
gave ear. A woman's club? Of course, that was the answer. Fifth
Avenue at the time was lined with luxurious quarters dedicated
to the comfort of man. The Union League Club, decorated by
Tiffany and John La Farge, had flourished at Fifth Avenue and
Thirty-ninth Street ever since its establishment in 1863 "to op-
pose disloyalty to the Union, to promote good government and
to elevate American citizenship." The Manhattan Club, home
of "Swallow-tail Democracy" and the haunt of Sam Ward,
Joe Jefferson, Dion Boucicault and Commodore Vanderbilt,
stood at Fifteenth Street and was famed for its cuisine. The
New York Club, founded for literary and professional men,
faced the home of Levi P. Morton, and the Athenaeum was
one block up the Avenue. The ivy-covered Calumet was at

Twenty-ninth Street and the St. Nicholas Club was at 386
Fifth Avenue. The ancestor of them all, the Union Club,
founded on Bond Street in 1836, had settled in a brownstone
house at Fifth Avenue and Twenty-first Street, facing the Lotos
Club. All exuded well-being, good cuisine, a comfortable refuge
from life's annoyances.

Kate Field promptly enlisted the interest of Mrs. Henry
M. Field, of Boston, and Jenny approached Mrs. Vincenzo
Botta, whose Saturday night salons were as famous in their
way as the Cary Sunday evenings. Emerson was a regular visitor
when he came to town. For a score of years Mrs. Botta, who
had once been secretary to Henry Clay, entertained the wits,
actors and artists at her brownstone house on Thirty-seventh
Street, just west of Fifth Avenue. She lectured. She wrote
verse. Her husband, an Italian professor, made Adelaide Ristori's
conversation clear to Edwin Booth. Henry Ward Beecher,
Julia Ward Howe, Richard Watson Gilder and, of course,
Horace Greeley were as likely to be found at Mrs. Botta's as at
the Carys'. The poetic sisters and Anna Lynch Botta, already
soundly established priestesses of literary salons, could see
nothing but promise in a woman's club. The next move
was a meeting at Mrs. Croly's home on West Fourteenth
Street to set up an organization. They must find a name for
their club and outline its aims. Mrs. Botta brightly suggested
that it should be called the "Blue Stocking." The majority
voted this down. This club, said Jenny, should be homogeneous
—hospitable to women of different minds, degrees, and habits
of work and thought. It should be representative of the whole
woman, and not of any particular class. Actually, small groups
in different parts of the country could claim priority on the
club idea, although they never gathered strength.

Kate Field held out stubbornly for calling it the Woman's
League, which she felt would give it political prestige and ally
it in a sense with the powerful Union League Club. Alice Cary
suggested the Sphinx but surrendered readily when Jenny

222222

22222222222

pointed out that they did not wish any suggestion of mystery to surround their club. Phoebe, as well-cushioned and cheerful as her sister was ethereal and withdrawn, suggested the Columbia Club, but this was rejected as being hackneyed. Finally Jenny and Mrs. Wilbour ran through several dictionaries and settled on Sorosis. Jenny liked its "full, appropriate signification and sweet sound." Mrs. Wilbour thought that it needed explanation but she consulted her husband and he gave her masculine reassurance that it was good. Thus the first woman's club got its name. It was taken from the Greek, a botanical term meaning growth, the product of many things. In the simplest terms the founders hoped for the "advancement of women through unity and co-operation."

Mme. Demorest, who listened rather than talked at meetings but who always lent most effective and practical aid, took home the rough preliminary notes on the constitution and asked her sister, Anna Mary, to copy them. Anna had been living with the Demorests since she was fourteen. Her handwriting was classically good and Nell cautioned her to hold her peace about what she was doing. Sorosis was just being hatched and any men around were not to know too much about it until the image was complete.

The object of this association is to promote agreeable and useful relations among women of literary and artistic tastes.

It is entirely independent of sectionalism, or partisanship.

It recognizes women of thought, culture, and humanity everywhere, particularly where these qualities have found expression in outward life and work.

It aims to establish a kind of free masonry among women of similar pursuits, to render them helpful to each other, and bridge over the barrier which custom and social etiquette place in the way of friendly intercourse.

It affords an opportunity for the discussion among women, of new facts and principles, the results of which promise to exert an important influence on the future of women, and the welfare of society.

Within a month after the Valentine party Sorosis had been incorporated. Alice Cary was elected president by acclamation and Mrs. Wilbour became secretary and treasurer. The other women in at the founding were Jenny June, Kate Field, Phoebe Cary, Mme. Demorest, Mrs. Agnes Noble, wife of a Brooklyn lawyer; Mrs. Celia M. Burleigh, an ordained minister; Mrs. Ella M. Clymer, a beauty who had attended Robert Dale Owen's Utopian community in New Harmony, Indiana; Sara L. Hopper, active in feminist drives; Josephine Pollard, a brilliant young writer, and Mrs. Lucy Gibbons, making a round dozen pioneers.

It was agreed that members should be proposed and admitted by ballot. The initiation fee would be $2 and they would meet monthly for business, luncheon and social conversation. But they had trouble finding a suitable meeting place. No one wanted these impetuous females and their club. One possibility after another faded until they reached the gallant Delmonico, more used to catering to millionaires, gourmets and stage stars than to earnest-minded women. The restaurant was still quartered in the old Moses H. Grinnell mansion on Fifth Avenue at Fourteenth Street. The master restaurateur cheerfully gave them a large room on the second floor and there they met for years. They could scarcely have done better, since this was the haunt of the sophisticates.

Soon the jeweled women and whiskered men who lunched off Delmonico's Lucullan fare would watch for the Sorosis ladies on their way upstairs. Some were modish; others let their skirts drag and their waterfalls escape their nets, but bloomerism was conspicuously absent. Occasionally the lines crossed, since all manner of celebrities visited both the Demorest and Croly homes. Eventually it was considered a distinction rather than a blight to belong to Sorosis, although some of the projected schemes seemed wild to the sedate hostesses who sat in their gloomy mansions along Fifth Avenue and pondered over their doings. Here were women discussing science, education, art, drama, current events and philanthropy as if they were running the world. The chief annoyance was their passion for holding down jobs. Mme. Demorest, no mean tradeswoman herself, thought it outrageous that some considered it a disgrace for her good friend, Miss Susan A. King, to be rolling up a fortune in real estate. But it took some time for the club to reach a state of respectability.

The members made no secret of the fact that one of the purposes of the club was to get away from home. It was considered daring at this time for women to lunch out by themselves, but since some of the members came from Brooklyn and other suburban points, and had family responsibilities, the middle of the day was chosen as the most suitable time for meeting. It was pointed out in *Demorest's*, which became the chronicler of Sorosis doings, that none need shy away from the simple tea and chocolate, lemonade, salads, sandwiches, cakes and ice cream that inaugurated a million women's club luncheons yet to come. After all, this was far removed from the "eating and drinking, the carousing, card-playing and the like of the men's club." This reassuring editorial sounded as if it might have been written by Mr. Demorest himself.

Their first official meeting was at Delmonico's on April 20, 1868, and fireworks spurted at once. Some of the husbands had been growling and grumbling about these subterranean doings that had kept their homemakers whirling around the town— and particularly Professor Botta, who had the European conception of woman's place in the world. Mrs. Botta was the first to resign. Kate Field also became difficult because of her determination that the club should be named the Woman's League. She pulled Mrs. Field with her and they swung the vote, but at the next meeting the name Sorosis was restored by an overwhelming majority and Kate Field, always independent and individualistic, walked out with some of her backers. Mrs. Field excused herself by saying that she was too much out of town to be an effective member.

Alice Cary delivered her inaugural address but was so upset by Kate Field's insurrection at the first meeting that she resigned as president the following week. However, in her hail

and farewell speech she coined a phrase that spread like wild-
fire and brought gibes as well as applause. "We have tipped
the teapot," said Alice diffidently. "We have proposed the
inculcation of deeper and broader ideas among women." Beyond that, Sorosis promised to open up new avenues of employment for women, to discourage idle gossip, to make light
of the follies and tyrannies of fashion, and to encourage women
to speak their minds without fear or hindrance. The Sorosis
sisters had decided to find a place above the salt. "Women
have nothing of their own," said Alice in conclusion, "and an
organization that aims to become an order, that recognizes
women of representative thought and culture, will, in time,
become a power and confer distinction upon its members."

They were quickly bathed in ridicule. Cartoons, gibes and
jokes hemmed in the Sorosis members as the Dickens banquet
went off with great splendor. All unconscious of the storm that
raged among the wives of some of his most distinguished hosts,
Dickens spoke of the astounding changes for the better that
he saw on every side. He promised he would "manfully,
promptly and plainly . . . bear testimony to the unsurpassed
politeness, delicacy, sweet temper, hospitality and consideration" of the American people. He was not in any way responsible
for the slight from which the ladies of the press felt they suffered on this occasion. But when the true situation dawned on
him he, too, got into the act and declined an invitation to
lunch with them. It happened that he was turning down all
manner of invitations, spurning courtesy calls and avoiding
social contacts, so as to concentrate on his work and his own
interests. This, John Bigelow thought, was far from being a
gentleman, and he had a poor opinion of Dickens' stumbling
delivery in the readings that netted him $6,500 a week in New
York.

With the Sorosis Club an established fact, the lampooning
at home and abroad became withering. The editor of one of
the leading New York dailies prophesied its early death, insisting that no woman's society outside of a sewing circle could

hang together for any length of time. *The Queen,* published in London, said there was a good deal of head-shaking and holding up of hands in wonder at the proceedings of Sorosis. The idea seemed simply ludicrous. In short:

What would be the feelings of the British public if some fine morning it were announced in the *Times* that a number of ladies— say Mme. Bodichon, Miss Emily Davies, Miss Garrett, the authors of *Adam Bede* and *John Halifax* and other well-known writers . . . had invited the members of a literary club to dinner, and had made speeches and proposed toasts. No one would believe it—the whole account would be treated as a hoax.

However, fundamentally *The Queen* wished them well, if only to prove that women could act harmoniously if they chose to do so. As a final touch the British magazine ran as a particularly amusing and incredible item Jenny June's reply to the handsome and accomplished Robert B. Roosevelt who had sought membership, perhaps as a joke or possibly to test the members' sincerity. Jenny June informed him that he was being turned down not because he had been found lacking in character, position or personal merit but simply because he was a man. "Personally, you have been found very agreeable by several members of Sorosis," she wrote to him. "Sorosis is too young for the society of gentlemen, and must be allowed to grow. By and by, when it has reached a proper age, say 21, it may ally itself with the Press Club . . . but for years to come its reply to all male suitors must be, 'Principles, not men.' "

But the husbands of the ringleaders were powerful men in the literary world and in the end they did not like the ridicule. Between the badgering they got at home and the strong image their wives were creating in the public mind they weakened and the Press Club invited them to a breakfast—"but not to speak, or do anything but sit still and eat, and be talked and sung to." Jenny June led this parade of controlled robots, and then Sorosis slapped back with a tea at which the girls did all the talking and also paid the bills. This function was quite an ex-

perience for some of New York's most glib toastmasters. The
guests, who numbered 125, arrived at half past five, just as
Delmonico's was sparking up for the evening. Each woman
slipped each man a boutonniere and shepherded him to his
particular corner, with the full understanding that he was to sit
there and be quiet. Since the gentlemen of the press were not
noted for their silence, this proved to be a hilarious interlude
for them.

When all had arrived, the company moved into the large
dining room and again each member led her quarry to his appointed seat, with the understanding that he was not to open
his mouth except to drink tea and enjoy the refreshments. No
wine was served but each table had its own urn and the toasts
were drunk in tea. The women responded, while their guests sat
speechless. However, the food was Delmonico's best and it kept
them contented until the speeches began. Jenny June addressed
them with a touch of sarcasm, implying that Sorosis was paying them back in kind for their own speechless breakfast. She gave
them permission to laugh, since the principal desire was to
entertain them, and the men promptly roared. The first toast
proposed was to the "Man of the Period" and Fanny Fern
answered this one with her usual eloquence but without solving
the question as to whether the clergyman, the editor, the businessman or the politician deserved the title. Mme. Demorest
responded to the toast "Man the Monopolizer." Rising to her
majestic height and looking around her with the severity that
her features suggested but her eyes denied, she gave the assembled men a closely reasoned talk in which she reminded
them that a daughter might inherit her father's capacities, his
qualities and his fortune, but she must not put any of them
to good use. She could not share his education or strike out for
herself. And no matter how well she performed her role as wife
and mother she still was subject to husbandly caprice and her
services were recognized only as a duty she owed. She charged
that man had monopolized the right to declaim, lecture, preach
and do any public speaking, while women were cut off from

the worldly contacts that might give them self-possession and experience. Mme. Demorest wound up with an observation picked up in her own fashion emporium:

Why wonder that she learns to smile at suggestions of extravagance in dress, and adds another yard to her train, or buys a more expensive set of lace for the next party, and sprinkles gold-dust over her glossy hair? She is none the poorer for the outlay, for ordinarily a wife owns only her own wardrobe.

The toasts went on and on—some of them with bite, others quite innocuous: The Professional Woman. The Newspaper Man from a Domestic Point of View. Heroic Women. The Committee Women. The Gentlemen. The Literary Woman. The Man of the Future. Blondes and Brunettes. Men and their Buttons. Woman and Art. Isabella of Castile. The Girl of the Period. Exhilarated by their own eloquence they all sang "Robin Gray" and recited from Longfellow. The men smiled and bowed wordlessly, then picked up their hats and walking sticks and headed for home—some in the same carriages as their Sorosis wives—to the same houses, the same children, the same dull old routine. It was all good fun but with serious purpose behind it. Mr. Demorest was not among those present. He gave Nell and Jenny their heads while he attended to business but he always saw to it that his was the master's voice. The struggle was more acute in the Croly home, where David was a nervous, ambitious man, often less amiable than Mr. Demorest. In fact, Jenny June had worries of her own.

The third function shared by both sexes was a dinner at which men and women paid their own way, Dutch style. They divided both the honors and the responsibilities and the evening was a success. Things were back in perspective again. The big relief for the men was the fact that the bloomer influence was totally missing. The harridans looked soft and lovely in Mme. Demorest's cunningly fitted brocades. They were smartly coiffed, jeweled, and adorned with the Sorosis badge on their left shoulders, a rosette of white lace, with a gold pin in the shape of an "S," bearing the Greek letters in enamel. Mme. Demorest sailed in to the dinner, a model of what the well-dressed woman should wear. On the whole they were out to show that brains and style could go together. Jenny June, with her fashion job, was smart enough to make a point of this. They were more than a little triumphant in a quiet way, and, as one paper put it next day:

We believe we violate no secret when we say that the gentlemen were most agreeably surprised to find their rival club composed of charming women, representing the best aristocracy of the metropolis —the aristocracy of sterling good sense, earnest thought, aspiration, and progressive intellect, with no perceptible taint of the traditional strong-mindedness.

Jenny June argued that the mutual entertainments given by the Press Club and Sorosis were a refining influence for the men accustomed to whooping it up with liquor and cigars. Sometimes the wives had to cope with this contingency on the home front. By joining them they had shown the cold sober men how much more agreeable things could be with women present. Along with many of her sex Jenny was thoroughly tired of hearing men ask why women did not stay at home and attend to the children's socks and their husband's buttons. Since Mme. Demorest, Jenny June and some of the others were doing a good job with the socks and buttons and were even fattening up the family exchequer, they seemed to have some justice on their side at this point. "Whatever they do, except stay at home and mind the baby, their motives are sure to be maligned and misrepresented, their acts tortured, caricatured and falsified," said Jenny June, who was quick in debate and eloquent on the platform.

Overnight the membership of the club grew to fifty, and on June 1, 1868, three months after its incorporation, Mme. Demorest sent the members an immense circular basket of roses, with the name "Sorosis" in white carnations and violets in the center, to symbolize the fact that they had battled for their name, had planted it and now the club would grow. It did. In March, 1869, Mrs. Croly was elected president by acclamation and in May she swung the club into ambitious action with a plan for a Woman's Parliament. Her dream was an institution as permanent as Congress itself, serving as a center for a "great united womanhood" with branches all over the country, electing their own representatives and sending delegates to annual gatherings in New York. Jenny reached for the clouds. She hoped her plan would crystallize the intelligence and influence of women into a moral power and give them "that voice in public affairs which is theirs by virtue of their humanity." She argued that a Woman's Parliament would offer them the privilege of the vote, without the humiliation of asking for it from those who had no right to withhold it.

This was a challenge, even for the women already out on the hustings, but it never developed in the way that Mrs. Croly had hoped. The National Woman Suffrage Association, headed by Elizabeth Cady Stanton and Susan B. Anthony, had just been formed and Lucy Stone was battling for suffrage through amendments to state constitutions. Miss Anthony was running *Revolution,* a paper demanding many reforms, from personal purity to educated suffrage. Victoria Woodhull, a dashing siren in a field of Quaker gray, had been cutting a wide swath on the political front since opening her brokerage office on Wall Street. Soon she would be aiming at the Presidency.

Jenny's original measure was defeated by a small margin but she, Mme. Demorest and several others held firm to the outlines of the plan. Mrs. Horace Mann, Miss Elizabeth Peabody, Catharine Sedgwick and Mrs. Charles Pierce arrived from Boston to organize the Women's Council of New York City as part of the Woman's Parliament. They took the stand that charities were palliatives rather than cures for social ills and that having learned to work in the small areas of their own churches and communities women should now turn to the greater things of the world itself and bring their experience and their energies to the task of social regeneration. Papers were

read on co-operative housekeeping, education, distribution of
the family income, prison reform and the legal status of women
in regard to property. School workshops were considered and
sanitary and hygienic reforms suggested.

Although much of the Sorosis agitation was talk, some of it
crystallized into action and a special committee was appointed
to investigate foundling asylums. The city had no sound institution of the sort and the subject had been ignored. Mme.
Demorest, Jenny June, Mrs. Horace Greeley, Dr. Anna Dins-
more, Mrs. Mary C. Owen and Mrs. Celia Burleigh made up a
vigorous committee. They collected facts, compared notes with
institutions abroad, and their findings were published in the
New York *World* during June, 1869. The revelations of infant
mortality and abuses in such institutions as existed were sensa-
tional. As a result of this exposure a good Protestant foundling
home was organized, and soon afterward a Catholic one. From
this point on Mme. Demorest devoted time, money and effort
to surveying local institutions involving women and children.
She took special interest in the Young Women's Home established by the Ladies Christian Union at 176 East Fourteenth Street, close to the Demorest stronghold. At the time
there was "not a roof to shelter a virtuous girl unable to pay
the prices demanded for board."

At the close of 1869 the membership of Sorosis had risen to
100 and standing committees on literature, art, music and the
drama were at work. New clubs were already forming, notably
the successful Woman's Club in Brooklyn. Mrs. Demorest and
Jenny were thankful that the club had set an example in dress
and had enforced early hours; that it had stimulated literary
and artistic tastes, rather than noisy demonstrations. The founders felt that, although they might still be slandered and misrepresented, the club itself was already past ridicule. Some
found in Sorosis a steppingstone to public careers; others a
resting place from labor and anxiety—the pleasant shadow of a
green tree in a barren land. Nine years later Jenny recalled that
Sorosis had never admitted a professional agitator to its ranks.
It remained a ladylike club.

She refused re-election as president on the second anniversary and Mrs. Wilbour took over to serve until 1875, when Jenny was back in office. She was president until 1886 and was honorary president at the time of her death in 1901. Mme. Demorest was a charter member, vice-president and treasurer at different times. Mrs. Phebe A. Hanaford, minister, lecturer and writer from Nantucket, served as president in 1874 while Mrs. Wilbour was abroad.

In speaking at the second anniversary Jenny urged stronger motivation for Sorosis. The men's clubs were the focus of political organization. Only the Century functioned in its early days on a purely personal basis. The republican government, she pointed out, made no provision for the employment and incorporation of women in state or national affairs. It was the only form of government which did not recognize in any way the existence of women except as creatures to be punished. Marriage, she conceded, was the refuge of some, but it had also been the grave of many clever women—especially of those who had married clever men. She thought Sorosis should recognize the work of women—not just that of authors, artists or professional women whose work was equal to men's, but in the less heralded fields. She favored a system that would recognize effort as well as results. To Jenny Dr. Elizabeth Blackwell, the first woman doctor in the country, was more truly a heroine than Joan of Arc. Sorosis had arrived at a point where its very existence meant power, she said. It was known at home and abroad and should function with style. Jenny took a long and accurate look into the future:

We shall live—live to see the woman's club the conservator of public morals, the uprooter of social evils, the defender of women against women as well as against men, the preserver of the sanctities of domestic life, the synonym of the brave, true, and noble in women. This is the mission of the Woman's Club, this is the mission of Sorosis. I pledge your future, ladies, only from your past.

Mme. Demorest was the main speaker at a preliminary meeting to the Woman's Parliament held in October, 1870, at

Packard's English Training School Rooms. Her topic was "Business Education for Girls," a subject on which she was expert. She argued that compensated labor was the only sound means of independence and of growth, physically, mentally and morally. She urged parents to steer their daughters toward remunerative business and pointed out the widening range of avocations. Women professors occupied college chairs. They had triumphed over prejudice in the medical profession, meeting vituperation with dignified bearing. Telegraphy, bookkeeping and typesetting were pursued with success. But the barriers of convention had been raised so high, and were so strongly cemented by time, that the only hope of overthrowing them lay in the union of numbers linked together by common opinion and effort, said Mme. Demorest. The voice of too few would be lost in the clamor of denunciation. But the "united watchword of *thousands* would strike at the foundation of the false system and annihilate it." The fashion arbiter finished on a characteristically practical note:

Therefore, to daughters, I say, fit yourselves for some congenial business or profession that will reward your labor—as men learn trades—so that the results may demonstrate the hand and genius of a master workman in its accomplishment, and the great world which has need of proficiency, of every germ of talent, of every resolute worker, must, by force of the mysterious magnetism of your power, recognize your claims to equality upon this plane with man.

Dress reform and attacks on slavish attention to fashion came up so persistently in the early days of the club that this drive must have been something of an embarrassment to Mme. Demorest and Mrs. Croly. Mrs. Wilbour instituted a series of lectures on the subject and also arranged talks on health and hygiene to be given by medical women in various halls and church vestries. This was a controversial matter at the time. Years earlier Dr. Blackwell had done the same thing on sex hygiene and had aroused horrified protests. Finally a Woman's Congress was called in 1873 which combined some of the features of Jenny June's proposed Parliament and a gathering suggested by Mrs. Paulina Wright Davis. Mrs. Wilbour sent 1,600 circulars to prominent women at home and abroad, and many signed it, including teachers, preachers, professors, physicians, artists, editors and philanthropists. This led to the creation of the Association for the Advancement of Women.

The delegates assembled in the Union League Theatre in New York on October 16, 1873, with Mrs. Mary A. Livermore acting as president. She was then editing *The Agitator* and *The Woman's Journal*, which later merged. Mrs. Stanton gave one of her whirlwind talks on coeducation. Maria Mitchell, the tall Quaker astronomer from Nantucket, spoke on the higher education of women. Other speakers dealt with such matters as the industrial arts, the enfranchisement of women, endowments for women's colleges, the lot of women in the medical profession, and in law. Julia Ward Howe went right to the heart of the matter in a sweeping speech "How Can Women Best Associate?" Messages of encouragement arrived from Frances Power Cobbe, Jean Ingelow, the Crown Princess of Germany and other European women of advanced views.

Sorosis continued to flourish. And the shadow of Jenny June, quiet, earnest, systematic in her work and eloquent on the platform, stretched into the distant future—an innovator who had left her mark on the feminine world. Few areas of public life would be left untouched by the women's clubs of the future. Their strength would grow.

CHAPTER VII

A Glimpse of the Empress

IN THE AUTUMN OF 1869 Mme. Demorest descended on Paris
with all the zest and alertness of her practical nature. She
invaded the salons of the designers and dressmakers. She studied
"beautiful designs for autumn and evening wear, and some very
singular costumes for the spas." She was welcomed by shopkeepers as a distinguished fashion expert and good customer
from the United States. At least thirty houses catered to the
luxury fashion trade in Paris at that time. She went to the races
where the "demimonde is supposed to set the fashions for the
world" and took mental photographs of the gowns she saw.

In the end she came to the conclusion that every woman in
sight was gorgeously attired except the Empress and Mme.
Demorest. Eugénie on this occasion wore a "dust-colored stuff
suit, black tulle bonnet with white pompom, and is not as
blonde as I expected to find her," she reported back to her readers. She did not mention what she herself wore but her costumes
were always conservative, in high style, and of excellent cut
and finish. She decided that those who thought things cheaper

in Paris than in New York were mistaken, except for camel's-hair shawls and laces. Everything else was quite as much as at home, taking into consideration the discount on currency. Moreover, New York received and wore the fashions as soon as they appeared in Paris, she pointed out with a weather eye to the alert news coverage of the family magazine.

In October she was sending home her first impressions of the City of Light. She was struck by the quiet. The cement boulevards reduced the thundering noise of vehicles. The city was immaculately clean. The Opera House was in course of construction and the men worked on Sundays as well as weekdays. They attended early mass, then took out their hammers to build. She and Vienna went to the American Chapel and heard a Brooklyn clergyman preach. When introduced by a friend, "Mme. Demorest—you may have heard of her," he smartly replied, "Yes, I know. She makes one kind of habit, and I another."

"Good, was it not?" Mme. Demorest wrote. "Well, he knows besides how to preach, for I listened to a most excellent sermon. ... The church is small but exceedingly attractive, and you may imagine, seemed homelike when we were ushered to a pew with four or five sittings labeled, and scarcely a name in sight that was not familiar."

That same afternoon as they approached Notre Dame they caught sight of an object falling from one of the towers. Mme. Demorest watched with interest, deciding that it was something thrown by those above to see how long it would take to land. She was shocked to find that a man had flung himself from the tower. "The contrast of this horrible incident with the beauty and gayety of the most attractive city in the world was fearful; I could not rid myself of it," she wrote to Jenny June.

She and Vienna were charmed by the floweriness of Paris. She wrote of the scarlet geraniums, fuchsias, ivy and vines that gave the city an air of "universal window gardening." She liked the flower borders in solid colors and reflected that the Parisians made all out of doors attractive. But she found Paris in August as destitute of fashion as New York. However, she stayed for the fashion openings and the couturiers had plenty to show her. Black satin, or combinations of black and white, were being worn by the Empress and, therefore, by everyone else. She thought Americans would consider the French use of colors "excessively outré" and she heartily disapproved a white and yellow silk, checked with scarlet and trimmed with scarlet fringe. That, definitely, was for the courtesan and the races. But she thought well of the new apricot shot silk that looked its best with white lace. And equally good for evening wear were the Watteau checks and stripes, "wonderfully ancient in appearance" and needing nothing for trimming but lace and black velvet bows, which were used in profusion on everything.

"The length of her train no longer marks the lady," Mme. Demorest ruled after studying the Paris scene. This was a hot issue on the home front, since all the dress reformers were attacking the trains that women dragged through the gutters. Street dresses now just touched the ground and evening trains had shrunk to a yard and a half. But walking was not a popular pastime in the French capital, Mme. Demorest observed, simply because a lady could not walk alone without being insulted.

I am told, however, that there is a little change for the better; formerly a lady could not go out to buy a spool of thread without taking a carriage; now they are beginning to walk quite independently, and ladies of high rank sometimes set the example of leaving their carriages, and taking a stroll down the boulevards. The influence of American women in Parisian society has, it is said, had something to do with this.

Thus Mme. Demorest reported from the spot as if it were the 1960's. She sent specific notes on costumes seen at the opera. She saw that the crinoline was dying but not yet dead in 1869. She commented on the violet toques, the hats like an archbishop's miter, the black strings of handmade lace on black velvet bonnets, the round hats trimmed with gauze to match the gown and ending with a veil a yard and a half long looped around the neck to form a hangman's knot. She noted the high-crowned hats that led the field, with long streamers down the back and plumes drooping over the chignon. Altogether she summed up the Parisian scene shrewdly for the American trade after talking to the leading couturiers and milliners. With the utmost speed her findings were screened, gowns and hats were copied, the paper patterns were cut, and the magazine carried the designs in a smart transfer of fashion news across the Atlantic.

The Princess von Metternich's wardrobe caught her attention, as well it might—119 silk gowns, 164 morning gowns, trimmed with thousands of buttons; 61 walking dresses and cloaks, 51 shawls, 152 petticoats, 275 undergarments, 365 pairs of stockings, 156 pairs of gloves, 49 pairs of boots and shoes, 71 sashes and belts, 24 parasols and 1 umbrella. On the more serious side she was struck by Eugénie's role in public life when viewed at first hand, and commented:

The Empress of the French is impressing her stamp not only on the fashions, but upon the politics of France. She assists . . . at every Council of Ministers, and her advice, even in opposition to the Emperor's, is frequently acted upon. For American women, however, it is a curious reflection that while they are denied the suffrage here, one of the sex is paramount at the Tuileries.

Her return home from what she described as the "most beautiful, the wickedest, the most polite and the most impolite, the most agreeable and most disagreeable city in the world" was stage-managed most effectively. The Demorest house was decorated with flags, wreaths and bird cages filled with canaries. Baskets of flowers were handed to her as she landed, and more flowers and fruit awaited her at her home. Her employees were assembled to welcome her and in a short speech she assured them that their devotion would stimulate her to greater concern for their interests and more effort for the cause of women in general. By this time both Demorests were considered notably good employers. Isabella Grant Meredith had written "Song of

Welcome" dedicated to Mme. Demorest and her husband had composed a poem for her which ran in the family magazine of November, 1869:

A WELCOME TO MY WIFE
Our brave, our dutiful and true.
Are words of welcome now addressed to you.
We greet you with exulting pride,
And joy to know you once more by our side.

Your long, long absence has but tried
Our chain of love; each link now ratified
Speaks welcome to a home so true.
A joyous welcome we now give to you.

The result of her foray on Paris was apparent in her autumn showing and she could justly claim that her models represented the latest from France. She exhibited the originals and paper copies of the designs she had selected personally while in Paris —street suits in Marquis of Lorne tartan, bonnets, gowns and opera wraps "representing the most tasteful novelties to be found abroad." She had returned loaded with inspiration and New York's most modish women gazed at the originals with keen interest, viewing among other items the Metternich mantle and the Russian bashlyk in white velvet, trimmed with scarlet satin and white fringe. She brought home the news that in Paris the big rage was crêpe de Chine, with magenta satin, shot silk and stiff Watteau silks on view at all the smartest haunts. The changeable vert d'eau, or shot silk, that she displayed in her own salon cost $25 a yard, and the price for a finished gown ranged up to $375. At this time Mme. Demorest started having her paper bonnets trimmed with artificial flowers instead of paper replicas. The frames on which they were mounted could be used later for the real bonnets. This was a popular innovation with her pattern customers. Thus the rich and the poor were served.

Fresh from her triumphs in Paris Mme. Demorest found herself in mild controversy with *Harper's Bazar*, a magazine that was digging deep into the consciousness of the more elegant American women. They had been sparring for some time about the priority of their fashions but matters reached a crisis in the winter of 1869-70. *Harper's* was getting its duplicate electrotype plates from *Der Bazar* of Berlin, a German fashion publication that sent out a pattern sheet with every number. The editors supplemented the German plates with their own material on New York styles.

Demorest's expressed surprise that American women should be asked to accept Parisian fashions that came by way of Berlin. Moreover, it was pointed out, German styles were not right without adaptation for the spirituelle American woman. They needed refinements. Mme. Demorest invariably modified French models to suit more conservative American taste, and fostered propriety, decorum, and the appropriate as well as the merely fashionable. But *Harper's* held its ground, and even accused *Demorest's* of borrowing some of its fire. This was indignantly denied with a further blast of countercharges: "We never knowingly copied a line on fashions from any journal published in this country. We have their representatives calling upon us almost daily for facts and information, which we cheerfully furnish . . . and it may be that, with our usual good nature, we have furnished to the local correspondent of the journal in question valuable facts, which we have used afterwards ourselves."

The editors admitted that *Der Bazar* of Berlin was received along with all the other prominent fashion journals from Europe and they had sometimes availed themselves of its hints. Nor did they pretend always to preserve entire originality of expression in minor instances involving mechanism. With this admission on the record a conclusive statement, which seemed to leave *Godey's Lady's Book* high and dry, was added:

We claim, and are justified in claiming, to be almost the creators of American Fashions. When we commenced issuing our own designs and forming our branches nearly twenty years ago, such a thing as American fashions had hardly been heard of. Ten years ago, when we started the Quarterly *Mirror of Fashions*, which in three years reached a circulation of sixty thousand, fashion articles and fashion journals were mainly confined to translations and republications of French and German modes. The popular demand induced us to turn our Quarterly into a Monthly, and generalize its departments in such a way as to make it a more complete Family Magazine; we succeeded so well that the leading authorities among the Press united in pronouncing it the Model Parlor Magazine of America.

This same editorial emphasized the fact that original designs were sent out four times a year to three hundred branches, representing most of the important urban centers in the Union. The dress-cutting system was in the hands of innumerable seamstresses. The emporium had consistently furnished the basic facts for dressmaking projects and was consulted regularly on "the detail and personnel of fashion." To crown it all, they were able to present Parisian fashions in New York in advance of French publications. Their circulation went up steadily and they had flattering offers from London for republication there. *Palmam qui meruit ferat*, finished this challenging editorial.

Harper's Bazar, meanwhile, pursued its chic course down the years, weathering its ups and downs and bearing the torch always for high fashion. But the Demorests never failed to challenge rival claims and to insist that their magazine sometimes beat the field by a span of six months. The issue was a hot one in the fashion world in 1870 with the house of Demorest making a bold bid to shift the fashion center from Paris to New York. The newspapers of the period pushed this cause. The Franco-Prussian War and the Siege of Paris had knocked the French capital hors de combat for the time being. Mme. Demorest attacked Worth, the master craftsman, citing his clumsy pannier as a "mere bag with drawing strings," far different from the looped and graceful overskirt that followed it and that owed its distinction entirely to American modistes.

While the Bois de Boulogne was a cattle park and sheepfold, and cartloads of grain, vegetables, and fodder were streaming toward the city, the New York *Herald* was urging American women to awaken to a sense of responsibility and to consider it an honor to wear American styles. The public was tired of the eternal revival of old styles and the dead past, and looked with hope to the New World for an infusion of fresh ideas in dress, as well as in railroads and other practical developments, said Mr. Bennett's journal. The drift toward emancipation from foreign dictation in matters of dress and taste was never so strong, the *Herald* added, pointing straight at Mme. Demorest as the leader of this movement. She had given convincing proof that a drive was under way at her autumn showing in 1870. She even produced proof that some of the leading London fashion magazines copied her styles and had made arrangements to get her fashion plates and descriptive cards.

She had not gone abroad that year because of the war. Her designs were wholly original and she took this occasion to underline the fact that she had never slavishly copied European models, or submitted to absolute dictatorship, but had "actually originated or modified, according to the best American ideas, every design submitted to the public for the last twenty years." Therefore, she wished to make the claim, without egotism, that the Demorests were the founders and representatives of popular American modes. During 1871 they were speaking out more strongly than ever. The downfall of Paris presaged a "great and most important change in dress, habits, and even the very aspects of our social life." It did not mean the inauguration of an age of simplicity or dowdyism; rather it would ensure the absence of "frippery and stage display" so characteristic of the Parisienne. "Hereafter, America will undoubtedly take its place as a leading power in the world of fashion," the magazine announced authoritatively.

The issue went right up to the White House. Mrs. Grant was not noted for her chic, nor did she pretend to be a fashion leader. When the newspaperwomen challenged her to name a style dictator who would swing American fashions away from the Eugénie influence, she simply said, "In matters pertaining to good sense and fine tact, I reply upon Mrs. Fish."

The wife of Hamilton Fish, Secretary of State, picked up the challenge adroitly but with tongue in cheek. She cheerfully voiced the opinion that every woman should seek her own convenience and comfort "whilst thinking of other things than dress." She felt perfectly comfortable herself in the new short street dresses, and she approved American fashions for American women rather than those dictated by people "who differ with us in the spirit of our institutions."

The issue was discussed across the country, and throughout 1871 correspondents of the Ladies Club were campaigning hard for American fashions. From New England to California they were demanding that Eugénie's scepter pass to American designers. The New York *Star* urged the "belles of New York to have a friendly tilt with the Grandes Dames who set the fashions in Paris, Berlin and London." What could be more sensible, this paper demanded, than Mme. Demorest's business suit, with its comparatively short skirt, flat trimmings and large pockets? "We can only say that not only has *Americanism* in dress become a success on which New York may congratulate itself, but a very pleasing innovation. We have American taste in art, racing, tobacco, architecture, furniture, gardening, cuisine, etc. Why not have American taste in dress?"

By the end of 1871 all trades in France were ruined and in particular the trades that had helped to make the fortunes of Worth and Laure, lamented the *Moniteur de la Mode*. But faith died hard. "Give us back an empress, or a queen, destroy the Republic, and in six months France would recover from its horrible nightmare, and Paris would again be telling female Europe how to dress."

In time this came to pass and Kate Chase Sprague, the nation's most modish woman in the 1870's, bought her gowns from Worth again. *Demorest's* reported the wedding of her sister, Nettie Chase, to W. S. Hoyt in Washington in the spring of 1871. This was one of the most fashionable events of the year, with Chief Justice Salmon Portland Chase looking on. The bride's gown was composed of many thicknesses of white illusion, and flounces bound with white satin. Her overskirt was caught up with orange blossoms and her jewels were pearls and diamonds. But she was outshone that day, as always, by the radiant, red-haired Kate in a costume of Nile green faille, with a court train of rose-pink faille, trimmed with green ruchings. A point lace overdress and point lace shawl gave Kate the final dash of glamour that all expected of her. "Mrs. Sprague, according to her habit, wore her hair plain, showing the shape of her well-formed head," *Demorest's* noted. Kate was ever the individualist—the beauty who knew her points and accented them. The ushers wore English morning dress, frock coats and light pantaloons. Their gloves were pale lavender, and blue satin rosettes anchored their buttonhole blossoms. The dandyish touch was not yet extinct.

That year the Demorests announced that the family magazine would be published simultaneously in London and New York, and that branch houses abroad would be added to the galaxy that had spanned the American continent for twenty years. Soon after the war they opened an office at 5 Rue Scribe in Paris and their patterns began to circulate all over Europe and around the world. Most of the smart American women who could afford to do so had returned to Worth, but in the meantime American fashions had had their innings and there was consciousness of a native drive for style. It stimulated the industry as a whole. And the pattern business flourished. Cutting machines had just been introduced and a revolution was under way in the wholesale clothing industry. A long knife took the place of the old-fashioned shears. It operated like a saw and went through eighteen thicknesses of cloth to one by shears.

This made a marked difference in the cut of clothing and within two years there was a heavy demand for ready-made garments. Jordan, Marsh & Company in Boston and B. Altman & Company in New York were two large stores operating at this time without signs. It was a matter of pride with them. Altman's had opened in 1864 with a small shop at 39 Third Avenue and had then moved to Nineteenth Street and Sixth Avenue. Jordan,

Marsh had 650 employees, passenger elevators, large salesrooms for every department and a "fine silk room, always brilliantly illuminated, where ladies can judge of the effect of gaslight upon a silken fabric at any hour of the day." With some of the Demorest speed the store claimed that it could sell, cut, trim, sew and furnish a dress complete in half a day.

Since the Demorest fortune was built largely on paper, the magazine reported jubilantly that paper of great strength and flexibility was being prepared by a new process and that it could be made into petticoats, chintz, curtains, table covers and even simulate leather. The prediction was made that eventually people would walk around "paper clad" with an entire new suit every day. But more immediate was the battle of the stays, which was under way with a vengeance. Tight lacing was discussed even in the pulpits. It had taken the place of long trains as a controversial issue. Too many beautifully costumed women were sinking to the floor in faints for the situation to be ignored. The *Arena,* which advocated dress reform, insisted that women had actually died of pleating. Mrs. Elizabeth Cady Stanton attributed her good health to the fact that her father had never permitted her to tightlace and had discouraged sewing and other sedentary occupations. When Susan B. Anthony fainted on one occasion, not from tight stays but from overwork, Mrs. Stanton wrote to her: "How funny for you to faint! Did you do it gracefully? And did you happen to fall into the arms of a son of Adam?"

Always ready to present different sides of an argument, *Demorest's,* while advertising the house's famous corsets, which substituted firm quilted cords for whalebone, at the same time lent its columns to a debate on the ills and advantages of tight-lacing. Dr. David Rice led the attack by categorically detailing the physical infirmities induced by tightlacing. His wife retorted with a strong argument in its favor: "I say that women are injuring themselves and their offspring by *not* making use of them. . . . We believe the tidy and trim way of dressing is by far the most healthful . . . we do not advocate wasp-waists, neither do we admire flattened chests but we believe a right use of a good corset will do more for health, than will the non-usage of it, in a lady's dress." And to press home the point still further, the use of Mme. Demorest's new health corset to round out the figure was strongly advocated, with the dismaying comment: "American women lack fine physical development, whatever the cause. . . . They are often narrow-shouldered, generally flat-chested, and as they grow older, from weakness, or want of exercise, are apt to stoop . . . in a way that gives them the appearance of marked and premature old age."

Meanwhile Jenny June, who sometimes deplored such vanities in her correspondence column, was forced to stand by while a campaign was launched for the "improved breast protector with hinges" that had supplanted the earlier spiral-spring bosom pad. But she carefully pointed out in one of her talks on "The Physical Life of Women" that the adoption of these by girls "in order to form an artificial bust, is an outrage upon truth and nature which no sensible mother ought to permit." However, both mothers and daughters seemed to be ready to cope with any discomfort, not the least of which was the false hair that added its weight to their tightly laced figures. Masses of false curls, switches and loops made a complex hairdressing cycle. Two million dollars were being spent annually on false hair. Flax and manila, or old rope, frayed, dyed and fashioned into plaits, chignons and curls, were piled on heavily burdened heads. Most of the false hair came from Germany and France, and some from the Southern states. A single switch cost $25, and pouf bonnets ornamented with heather, mignonette or tea roses, sat precariously on Alpine peaks of hemp.

With his infallible sense of promotion Mr. Demorest had the knack of seizing on the mood of the hour to push one of his wife's fashions. When Christine Nilsson, the Swedish soprano, toured America in 1871, causing a sensation second only to that of Jenny Lind, she was dressed by Mme. Demorest. On her arrival she had ordered an all-American wardrobe, a desire that fitted in well with the campaign of the hour. For her debut at Steinway Hall in September, 1870, Mme. Demorest set her girls to work on a ravishing gown of white grosgrain with Duchess lace flounces and blue grosgrain train, bordered with lace and lined with white satin. The antique sleeves had deep lace ruffles. The bodice was cut in Raphael style and it was considered one of the emporium's more arresting models. A diamond butterfly in the artist's hair was valued at $2,000. Fair-haired, slender, smiling, almost austere, Miss Nilsson was Marguerite and Ophelia to wild applause and bravos. Men and women rose, waved their handkerchiefs, and flowers almost hid the stage—a ship, a harp, a firescreen of flowers, a hurricane of strange devices.

Mme. Demorest had been dressing the celebrities of stage and concert hall for some years, but she had a particular interest in Miss Nilsson, who had taken Vienna under her wing and was helping to promote her musical career. Vienna had made progress since showing signs of being a child prodigy. She studied with Signor Bassini and Mme. Clara M. Brinkerhoff and did some composing. Her "Birdie" was taken up by Miss Nilsson as her signature song and she made it a popular number. Vienna's polka, mazurka and galop, which appeared in the family magazine, were played by Dodworth, Baker, Grafulla, Operti and other bandmasters of the day. She had grown into a handsome, dark-haired girl of twenty-four by the time she made her debut at Chickering Hall on February 25, 1871, wearing a shimmering green satin gown, trimmed with Alençon lace and May rosebuds. The décolletage was modest and the designer was her stepmother. Both parents drove to the concert hall with her, with fond expectation. A great musical career had been predicted for Vienna. "Seldom has a début of a cantatrice been made with such satisfactory results," commented the New York *Herald* after her soirée in Chickering Hall. "The universal verdict last night . . . was favorable; and we might say that there was a feeling of astonishment, as well as of admiration at the remarkable power, sweetness, range and purity of tone which her voice exhibited. . . . A year or two in Europe will develop Miss Demorest into an artist of whom America may be proud."

Vienna toured New England, Washington, Rochester and Chicago that year and her name became known to the public. Her brother Henry studied elocution and both performed willingly for their parents at impromptu musical evenings. Anna Mary, Mme. Demorest's sister, was one of the group. The young people had many friends. They went riding, driving, skating, sleighing, and kept the Demorest house a place of great animation. There were big family gatherings at Christmas and Thanksgiving, and the farm at Saratoga was a focus for all the young people. Mr. and Mrs. Demorest were tolerant guardians, in spite of their austere outlook on life, and both helped Anna Mary out of a scrape. She went out walking with a beau one evening, entering the park from the east side. At that time Union Square was completely encircled by an iron fence with flat-topped stone columns at the exits. The gates were locked at sundown and the young pair found suddenly that they could not get out. This was an unthinkable predicament for a well-brought-up girl in the Age of Innocence. Anna was close to tears when she heard Aunt Nell's voice. She and Uncle William were walking past. She called to them and Mme. Demorest stayed close at hand while Mr. Demorest went to the house and sent his butler to the rescue with a ladder. It was let down inside the fence and Anna Mary and her beau climbed to safety.

Mr. and Mrs. Demorest, who worked together all year, sometimes took their vacations separately and while she went abroad in 1869 he made a quick trip north by stagecoach and boat. He stopped off at Saratoga, where he always liked to take the waters, then proceeded by stage through the mountain gorges and around Lake George on a rough plank road. In the October issue of 1869 he described under his own byline the magnificent scenery as he passed through the historic grounds of Ticonderoga by coach and sailed across Lake Champlain to Plattsburg and Ogdensburg. He traveled through the Thousand Islands and had his first view of Niagara Falls. After doing the chute in a square wooden box suspended by pulleys, with a railway at an inclined plane of 35 degrees, he was glad to come to rest eventually on

the Canadian side. He proceeded to Rochester and paid a senti-
mental visit to Brighton, his childhood home.

His visit brought back one of the most tragic experiences of
his life—the fire in which his father and sister were burned in
1837. Before leaving Rochester he visited Vick's famous nursery
and flower farm five miles out of the city. It reminded him of
Grasse, with its great hothouses and gardens of carefully cultivated flowers, and was quite unequaled on the American continent at that time. Vick's chromos with their dizzying array
of flowers were having their effect on the horticulture of the
country. Where ten years earlier well-thought-out gardens had
been rare, now they abounded, and hard-fisted farmers who had
scoffed at their wives' efforts to raise a few flowers were willing
to prepare the flower beds and order seed and plants.

James Vick had contributed considerably to this effect. His
exhibitions of flowers at state and county fairs had spread the
fame of the flowers that sprang from his twenty-five acres of
gardens. His verbena, pansies, asters, zinnias, lilies and gladioli
were known from Maine to California, and acres of scarlet phlox
were followed by acres of pink phlox on the property. He had
150 employees filling seed packages, and amateur gardening had
become a national fad. Every year he issued lithographs in
colors with thirty varieties of his most popular flowers. English-
born, he began importing seeds and bulbs from abroad in 1850,
while he was still a printer for the *Genesee Farmer*. Soon he
was raising flowers in a small garden. His story appealed to the
news-conscious Mr. Demorest, who promptly gave it wide publicity. Flowers for the family were insinuating fare for a parlor
magazine like his own, and there were many ways in which he
could help along a cause. Frequently he did, thus putting his
stamp on the social life of the era. As small gardens multiplied
in number, the great estates were landscaped along traditional
lines with trimmed box hedges, tailored flower beds, and shrubs
imported from various parts of the world. Gardeners and horti-
cultural experts came from England, France and Italy to reproduce some of the effects of the old world. The accumulated

riches from whatever source were beginning to show up in private art galleries, landscaped estates with statuary, great mansions and country homes.

On his way home Mr. Demorest stopped off again in Saratoga. By this time he and his family had become regular summer visitors there and had improved the old family property. If Saratoga needed any advertising, which it scarcely did, *Demorest's* supplied a constant refrain. The fact was that Long Branch was offering stiff competition, with President Grant and his Julia settled there. Jenny June, making a tour of all the resorts in 1872, decided that the aggregation of artistic and fashionable social life at Long Branch was greater than at any other summer resort. Many new cottages had been built there in the preceding five years. Women drove about in low basket carriages wearing white muslin, soft silks, pineapple cloth or linens that resisted the salt air. The sports used tandems and four-in-hands. Lester Wallack owned the "Hut," Edwin Booth the "Snuggery," George W. Childs of Philadelphia had a cottage next to General Grant's, and things were lively at Long Branch morning, noon and night.

Bathing suits were a study in themselves. The girls stepped gingerly into the water wearing square-yoked blouses in blue twilled flannel or serge, trimmed with black alpaca braid. They added trousers gathered in at the ankle or flapping loose. Russian leather belts and white sailcloth shoes completed the outfit. They tied their Nantucket hats of coarse white chip coquettishly under their chins and tried not to wet their luxuriant masses of hair. Some sported ash-gray suits trimmed with scarlet. The very natty set forth in marine blue with white. The entire outfit cost about $10 in New York and could be hired for the day at Long Branch for 50 cents. Gray moreen was more popular at Newport, with bright plaid bands anchoring the trousers at the ankle. India-rubber shoes were attached to these bands and the bathers at this resort liked glazed sailor hats with oil-silk caps tucked inside the crown. Black serge with bands of scarlet merino was the uniform at Cape May, and the bather's

white canvas shoes had rosettes of scarlet merino. Whatever
the costumes, black stockings prevailed.

Jenny June decided that it was more complicated to go bathing than to don a ball gown, although the children splashed
about happily in bathing suits of scarlet merino with black
starred braid. Taking everything into account, however, she concluded: "Fashionable summer resorts seem to me the most
democratic places in the world, so far as dress is concerned. You
can dress and you can let it alone." There were extremes in both
directions and one seemed to be reached with the green ball
dresses treated with arsenic to whip up their verdancy. Newport
was exclusive and the New England abolitionists could be found
prowling along its rocky shores. But Mr. Demorest thought that
none of the resorts compared with Saratoga, and from time to
time he drew attention to the pleasures of sailing up and down
the Hudson with the People's Line. "Europe has nothing to
compare with these floating palaces, with their elegant and perfectly fitted state rooms, their spacious saloons and splendid
appointments," he wrote.

The summer of 1871 found a full revival of the gaiety and
style that had distinguished Saratoga before the war, when
fashionable women arrived with fifteen trunks for a stay of a
few weeks, and changed their costumes five times a day. Actually,
more people of wealth visited Saratoga after the war than before
it. Jenny June decided that, although there was less of an air
of high fashion and exclusiveness, the visitors had more money
to spend, and did. Fashionable women went in more for personal maids. "It is, as they say, almost impossible to dress oneself
in the present style, arrange one's hair, and give the last touch
to the drapery of the skirts," she observed.

The mint juleps, the famous brass spittoons of the Grand
Union—the hotel built by A. T. Stewart that outdid the hostel-
ries of the German spas—the French cuisine, the fast horses,
were not in the Demorest tradition, but Mme. Demorest herself contributed richly to the fashion picture at Saratoga. In the
summer of 1871 her gowns were showing up at all the resorts,

since the customers had not gone to Paris that year. Among the costumes she sent to Newport were a pale English pink faille, a walking costume of white satin bound with lilac velvet, a gown of ecru piqué entirely trimmed with ecru lace, and a walking dress of silver-gray foulard with an apron front and drooping basque with pleated frill and gray silk fringe. At the moment it was a runaway show for Mme. Demorest. The New York *Democrat* noted that her taste and ingenuity drew inspiration from her surroundings year by year. The *Telegram* said that next to Stewart's she was the "most prolific of beautiful articles, both in the millinery and dressmaking line" and was doing more every day to blend domestic and foreign fashions to the best advantage of the American woman.

Congress Hall, after being burned down, had been rebuilt, and the Grand Union had been enlarged to house 1,800 guests. Its huge allegorical painting of a cornucopia, representing the United States spilling riches to the rest of the world, was one of the wonders of the spa at that time. It was the most popular hotel, spacious and shady, with piazzas that invited conversation, leisure and observation. Velocipedes were now spinning in and out of the grounds of Congress Hall, as well as the carriages used by the older set, who seemed to prefer this hotel. The United States and the Columbian, which also had burned down, were in operation again. The Columbian had an air of sanctity and was haunted by invalids and reformers, although Saratoga was not the place for reformers to flourish. The Clarendon had always caught the conservatives. Peter Lorillard invariably stayed there. It also drew such sportsmen and public figures as William R. Travers, August Belmont, Jay Gould, General Ambrose E. Burnside, W. W. Corcoran, Henry J. Raymond until his mysterious death in 1869, Robert Bonner, Chauncey M. Depew, Commodore Vanderbilt, and other historic personages.

The day's routine at Saratoga was well established. The mineral waters were the morning's diversion. The most famous of the springs were Congress, High Rock, the Columbian, the

Washington, the Star and the Excelsior. High Rock was the farthest away from the hotels but it was noted for the purity and strength of its waters. Visitors liked to go to High Rock, Congress or Hawthorne Spring, and sometimes all three, drinking one or more glasses at each before breakfast, and finishing the morning's dissipation with a walk in Congress Park before returning home for a Gargantuan breakfast. At twelve they were drinking the waters again. Then the guests assembled on the wide piazzas, chattered, or listened to the band until dinner was served at two. When they could pull themselves away from table the carriages started the grand promenade to Moon's Lake-House, three miles away. Cool breezes swept its wide piazza, and the view over the lake, the fine oak trees, the winding paths through the woods, the artificial fish-ponds, all added piquancy to this expedition. Moon's had become famous for Saratoga chips, its own particular discovery. Potatoes were peeled and sliced to transparency, then the chips were put in pounded ice until needed. When the time came to use them they were dried and poured into boiling lard, to be taken out with a skimmer and shaken in a sieve.

Mr. Demorest deplored the guzzling that went on at Saratoga but insisted that it was not by any means the resort only of the fast and fashionable, as some people thought, but was more remarkable for its sylvan charms, its mineral waters, its fashion tradition. "We do not know of any watering-place that attracts so large a number of clergymen, and of quiet, refined, intelligent people, of all shades of opinion," he wrote at a moment when the Flash Age was at its peak. The war profiteers, the speculators, the carpetbaggers, the gamblers, the bonanza kings from the West, the men who were giving enormous impetus to the future of the United States as they built railroads across the continent, the quiet millionaires and the showy ones, the sports and the scholars, the politicians and the clergy mingled on the piazzas. It was almost as motley a grouping, and in some respects had the same elements, as the gatherings that Mme. Demorest could recall from her early days in Saratoga.

The chief difference was that where the accents of the South had once been pervasive, the visitors now talked in many tongues, and some with raw inflections, boisterous tones and profane terms. Gambling operations were in full swing. Boss Tweed and his followers strutted around, covered with diamonds, chewing tobacco and hatching plots as they wandered in and out of the saloons and gambling parlors. John Morrisey's Château du Chance operated close to a simple church. The races were of constant interest to most of the visitors and some fine horses came to the fore in the 1870's and early 1880's. Bramble won the Congress Stakes and the Saratoga Cup in 1879 and other horses much discussed were Volante, Alta, Modesty, Parole, Sultana, Iroquois, Hindoo and Foxhall.

Henry James found the people at Saratoga a "shoddy community of boasters" when the permanent population of 10,000 swelled to its summer dimensions and gambling houses multiplied. James Gordon Bennett called it the "cradle of fashion and intrigue, rendezvous of lackeys and jockeys." But it also became a boating center in the 1870's when rowing was the enthusiasm of the hour. The boat clubs of New York, Boston, Philadelphia and other cities sent professional oarsmen to Saratoga to compete for purses. On regatta morning the road to the lake was six deep in hay wagons and carts, as well as barouches and landaulets. It cost $30 to hire a barouche for the day, and even the cheapest carriage rented at from $8 to $15. New England farmers camped along the shore of the lake with their families. Students from the men's colleges shouted and sang as they traveled. The dust was choking for everyone, and water wagons were used to sprinkle now and again.

The Demorests pursued a quiet life at Orchard Lawn Grove. They lived on the original farm land that had been bought in 1794 by the two brothers, Henry and Zachariah Curtis, who eventually divided it. Henry Curtis, Mme. Demorest's father, was born there and Nell relived her own youth watching the children playing in the same woods. She and her husband had turned over a stretch of land a mile in circumference for public

use. The park was kept as a native wilderness and one day would
be part of Saratoga Raceway. Deer roamed at large and the
animal life of the woods was a source of constant delight to the
children who came from miles around to play in Demorest
Park. Regular outings were arranged for the sick and the needy.
Swings, seesaws, rustic benches, gypsy kettles, lent a touch of
enchantment to the woods. The show piece was Uncle Tom's
cabin in a tree with a rough-hewn armchair for the mythical
Negro. In autumn ripe chestnuts rained down on the children
in a grove close to the Curtis house, which stood on a knoll
sloping down to well-tended lawns and an orchard. A clear
spring ran near by. A carriage house and an old cider mill were
close to the family dwelling.

The Demorests passed much of their time on hot summer
afternoons sitting on the vine-shaded verandas in hammocks
and porch chairs. Even at Saratoga they kept a close eye on their
manifold interests. Mr. Demorest would get up early, prowl in
the woods, drink the waters, tinker a little at his machines, go
driving, study his mail, read the day's publications, and watch
the children at play. Nell liked to sleep late in the country and
drive in to Saratoga in the afternoon to visit friends. Kate worked
busily upstairs on new patterns. They entertained in the country as they did in town and many friends visited them at Orchard
Lawn Grove, including the writers and artists of the day. Since
the Crolys did play reviewing, the leading stars frequently visited
both the Demorest and Croly homes. Mr. Demorest did not include the theater in his list of worldly taboos but music was the
chief family interest, as Vienna was launched on a career of her
own. Musicians were particularly welcome. Theodore Thomas,
the knight errant of music who had despaired of popularizing
classical music, now gave concerts that drew great crowds.
Strauss waltzes were the most popular feature of his summer
programs, with Wagner, Meyerbeer and Beethoven introduced
at every opportunity.

Demorest's added musical and dramatic notes to its features
in 1871. More than a dozen theaters had flourished in New

York during the Civil War, playing all the year round. Stock was well established. The stars were pronounced personalities, who prized their status. They arrived from Europe with considerable fanfare, they toured the country and the public flocked to see them, for better or for worse. Burlesque had its own following, with broad satire rather than fleshy appeal, and so did that native institution, the minstrel show. Shakespeare had a heavy run on Broadway before, during and after the war. Edwin Booth's *Hamlet* broke all Broadway records for Shakespearean drama in the darkest days of the war and Charles Kean did an American tour during the same period. Laura Keene's name was inscribed in American history as the actress starring in *Our American Cousin* the night Lincoln was assassinated. The echoes of *Uncle Tom's Cabin* died hard and Harriet Beecher Stowe moved in the aura that she had created for herself. In the early 1870's Charlotte Cushman was electrifying New Yorkers crowding into the Booth Theater to see her Lady Macbeth and Meg Merrilies. Charles Mathews was playing at Wallack's and Joseph Jefferson, who had given the Church of the Transfiguration its popular name the Little Church Around the Corner in 1871, was receiving $500 a performance for his Rip Van Winkle. *The Black Crook* was flourishing at Niblo's Garden, and *Lalla Rookh* was drawing enthusiastic audiences to the Grand Opera House. The Lydia Thompson Troupe was at Wood's Museum. The arts were having a heavy play and all manifestations of increased interest in culture and education were encouraged in the Demorest family magazine, while fashions and the life of the home and family remained its basic strength.

CHAPTER VIII

Tea from China

O N A MELLOW October day in 1872 the *Madam Demorest*, a clipper ship, set sail from New York for the Orient on a curious mission. It was billed as the first ship ever purchased, owned, and sent out by women for commercial purposes. Bankers, merchants and the press sailed down the bay to see it off and the figurehead at the prow was the carved image of Mme. Demorest. One flag flashed the name of Mme. Demorest from the masthead and another advertised its purpose—the Woman's Tea Company.

Miss Susan A. King, who had made a fortune in real estate, was on board as mistress of the expedition, with half a million dollars in exchange to back her up. She was bound for Japan and China, to buy up tea that would be brought to the United States to be handled and sold by women in all parts of the country. Tea was to be a career, a livelihood for the growing army of impoverished women who had no men to support them. The company consisted of Miss King and Mme. Demorest. It was capitalized for half a million dollars and the plan was to distribute the tea through the Demorest network of agencies. Women, and women only, would handle it.

The two philanthropists had spent much time pondering over the best commodity for women to sell before settling on tea. They were looking for something "lady-like, light, profitable, not above the majority of intellects, and in all its appurtenances suitable for refined tastes," said Mme. Demorest. They sought something in great demand, to ensure widespread employment. Tea seemed to fill the bill. New Yorkers watched the venture with interest and for weeks the merchants and old-established tea importers had been strolling down Wall Street to study the clipper ship as it lay at rest in its slip. The press had a field day over this daring plunge into the world of the seasoned China tea traders. "The American tea trade is threatened with a monopoly by a firm of ladies," commented the New York *Sun.* "Woman has resolved she will no longer be only a tea-drinker; she aspires to be a tea-trader."

But the men who had had dealings with Miss King and Mme. Demorest did not view the project lightly. For years Susan had been one of the most successful and daring real estate operators in the city. As new streets stretched northward she bought and sold property, keeping ready cash on hand, always making fresh investments, quickly abandoning the unproductive. Her final coup before she concentrated on philanthropy was the $250,000 sale of the land on which Union Theological Seminary would rise. At the same time she gave the trustees a gift of $20,000. Both her beneficiaries and her competitors were among the group of distinguished citizens who went down the bay in a small launch to see her off on the clipper ship.

Flags fluttered. The holiday spirit prevailed and Miss King regarded with some satisfaction the city she had helped to build as it lay behind them in an autumn haze. She was the first to clamber up the rope ladder, a rugged spinster of strength, originality and purpose, wearing heavy leather shoes and her customary dark, durable and inexpensive attire. A close-fitting bonnet framed her broad face and wide black ribbons were tied determinedly under her chin. She already knew the bark from stem to stern. It was a 448-ton vessel, 130 feet long, 30 feet wide and 19 feet deep. Captain Gorham was in charge and young Henry Demorest was going as supercargo.

James T. King, Susan's brother, proposed the health of Mme. Demorest, who promptly replied with a brief speech that summed up her own and Miss King's attitude to business for women. In her own right Nell was essentially a businesswoman, who believed in everyone working, and she had given much thought to practical ways of helping girls get started.

All women should cultivate and respect in themselves an ability to make money, as they respect in their fathers, husbands and brothers the same ability. A woman thoroughly educated in mathematics, with some mature business qualifications, and minus the pride as to a woman's being in business, may choose her own position in the world . . . Miss King, to whose credit this enterprise is mainly due, is proud to assure you that she began her business life early and alone, believing it just as creditable for her to make her place in the world, to make money, be rich, as for her brothers . . . and she did not feel called upon to apologize to the world for her doing this, because she was a woman.

There were more speeches. Vienna sang. Henry recited. They lunched and discussed the future of New York. The party left Miss King to her great adventure. The sails billowed and the clipper vanished slowly from the harbor. Mme. Demorest returned to her fashions and philanthropy. Miss King headed for adventure, but the true safari to the Orient was already behind her. Before buying the ship she had traveled alone through China and Japan, studying the field, making contacts, ordering tea. Like the good businesswoman she was she wanted first to see for herself the methods of planting, harvesting, curing and preparing tea for the market. She had set off in 1870 and for eighteen months had traveled about like a visitor from Mars, stirring up interest wherever she went. She had survived a typhoon, acute fevers from food, climate and exposure, and fantastic adventures. The Chinese had come to appreciate Miss King. Her fame had spread and her novel trip had some of the excitement for readers of *Demorest's* that Nellie Bly's dash around the world would have for the public several years later.

Susan was born in 1818 in Gorham, Maine, daughter of a farmer and government agent who supplied army stores. As a child she accompanied him on his journeys to buy cattle and other supplies and thus learned how to bargain. Her education was flimsy, and when she reached New York in the 1840's she first gave guitar lessons, then helped to establish a girl's school in Philadelphia and another in New York. Susan liked to master-mind an operation, then drop it. The city was young and growing and soon she began to deal in land. Before long the businessmen were aware of sturdy Susan King, tramping the swamps and fields, spotting promising property, offering them deals that turned to gold for everyone concerned. She was shrewd, fair and hardheaded in her dealings and in time was de-scribed as a millionaire.

As she grew rich her interest veered to philanthropy. She had met Mr. Demorest in the course of her business, since he, too, was interested in real estate and had bought a great deal of property around Union Square. Soon she and Mme. Demorest were working together on philanthropic interests and she helped to found and maintain the House of Mercy for Fallen Women on condition that it should remain nonsectarian. Thus they came to be good friends and business associates. But Susan was tiring of the "quackery of benevolent institutions" when she took up the tea project as a business venture that would also give other women some economic advantage. She refused to help those who showed no inclination to help themselves, and she vowed that she would never give a penny to any woman who worked to help support "some idle or dissolute man." Unlike most of her sex, she found it easy to make money and believed it to be simply a question of management. She was cold to the suffrage movement and did not give a fig for the ballot, or for the ladies lustily beating the drums for the bloomer costume, free love and the vote. Her approach was as direct as a sledge-hammer blow. It was strictly nineteenth century, for Susan had the spirit of the fortune builders of her era.

The dollar is a language people understand all over the world. It chin-chinned and chow-chowed me all through Japan, China, Chinese Tartary, Borneo, Java, Celebes, the Malacca Islands, among the cannibals and the heathen Chinese. It has carried me all around the world. What do I care for the ballot? But now mark my words, if ever women do get the right of suffrage it will be through their showing the ability to win the dollar, and win it just as men do.

When the formation of the tea company was first announced in 1870 it seemed a radical departure for women but Mme. Demorest's reputation in the fashion world and Miss King's as a businesswoman inspired confidence and respect. The New York *Sun* called Mme. Demorest the "Sorosian and Queen Fashionist" and wrote of Miss King's practical good sense and success in large financial operations—a double guarantee that their importing business would flourish and perhaps do more than "any undertaking of the period to enlarge the sphere of woman's influence and increase her means of remunerative employment." But would they permit men to load the vessels that would transport the tea, or even to command them? Or would some "argosies of magic sail . . . come dropping down with costly bales into the port of Gotham"?

The New York *Globe* pointed out that the different brands of tea would be submitted to the Sorosis Club for testing. In a sense the whole plan grew out of the club aims to further women in business. The New York *Democrat* conceded that Mme. Demorest was a "lady whose name is a household word in every family throughout the country, and a synonym for untiring energy and genuine enterprise." The Springfield *Republican* felt that if only one needy woman in every town and village found support from this source, a worthy work would have been performed.

Heedless of both compliments and gibes the two women had

gone gravely ahead with their plans and Susan had set off on her earlier trip to the Orient in July, 1870, before the clipper ship was chartered. Her friends, knowing her purposeful character, feared that she would never come back alive. She crossed the continent, sending back graphic accounts of her adventures to *Demorest's*. While passing through Weber's Canyon, Devil's Gate, Echo Canyon, Humboldt's and "a great many other places too wonderful to describe" she gave careful thought to the pleasures of travel for women. "I do not see why women can't do business and travel as well as men," she wrote. "The idea of men living on all the luxuries, traveling and seeing the beauties of this beautiful world, and women remaining at home!" Susan expressed the hope that the tea club would give business to thousands of women who would make it pay to travel over the same road. She watched the herds of cattle and wild horses dashing across the plains. Prairie, desert, mountains, all swept along in grand panorama as she sat stiffly at attention in the rollicking coach and contemplated the life of woman.

San Francisco burst on her like a new world. By this time the glitter of gold had been transmuted into luxury living. Store windows had flashy displays of Oriental wares. The town was a blend of wealth and shabbiness, luxury and honky-tonk. She swept past the peddlers with baskets of flowers and headed for the haunts of the merchants. Susan put up at the Cosmopolitan Hotel and persuaded its New Hampshire owner to give Mme. Demorest's tea vendors the same privileges as he did men, and at the same price. She stumped in and out of the offices of the businessmen who dealt in the China trade and told them of her plans. Her arrival in Japan caused a stir. Here she encountered George F. Train, author and promoter who had been involved in the clipper ship trade with California. They joined forces briefly but neither one felt akin to the other and they soon drifted apart. Susan was the soul of independence. Dispatches reached New York from Yokohama that Miss King meant business and that with her "rapid, business-like movements she soon became the observed of all observers." She moved like a whirlwind, tested tea, talked to merchants, bought curios, explored the city and took stock of native life.

The president of the Oriental Bank escorted her to a reception given in her honor by Sir Harry Parkes, the British Minister. She gave Lady Parkes a copy of *Demorest's* and asked her to join the Tea Company. She called on C. E. De Long, the United States Minister, and with eight coolies and a sedan chair she then started off to view the Daibutsu, or Great Buddha, of Kamakura. After five days of jolting around in her sedan, and visiting tea plantations she concluded that the Japanese did not export their best tea. Little was grown and it was used chiefly by the nobility and the affluent. She bought samples, ordered quantities from the plantation owners, and made arrangements to get all the tea her company wanted. Before leaving Japan she wrote to Mme. Demorest that she could talk tea now to anyone she met, for she, Susan, had coralled the new spring crop and they would get their tea straight from the farmers in its pure state. "No good teas ever get to New York," Miss King wrote. "It is said here, 'They are not willing to pay the price there, and they don't know a good cup of tea from a poor one,' but we'll see, when I get there with our good tea. I tell you, it is *nice*."

Susan sailed from Yokohama for Hong Kong in the bark *Adelia Carlton* and for a time was believed to be lost at sea. They had run into an unusually severe typhoon and had gone far off course. But by late October she was eating Tientsin grapes at Chefoo and was close to the Great Wall and also the spot where the "Chinamen had killed off the French missionaries," she wrote to Mme. Demorest. Miss King had promised that she would look into the work of the missionaries while she was in the Orient. Both Demorests gave solid support to religious causes. She reported back that there were two sides to the stories and she would tell them all about it when she saw them. Evidently she had not swung over completely to the side of the missionaries. In addition to her findings on tea Susan studied the social, political and religious ways of the people.

Again she hired a sedan chair with coolies and traveled far beyond the treaty limits, expecting to have her head cut off, she cheerfully wrote. But the reception she got surprised her. "I was treated with more respect than the Queen of England would be if she came to our country" was her way of putting it. Rightly or wrongly, Susan believed herself to be the first American woman that many of the country people had seen. As they penetrated far beyond the limits her coolies grew nervous and wished to turn back, but Susan persisted. Crowds followed her wherever she went but she knew no fear for, in her own words: "I do not believe I shall die until my time comes; and I have faith to believe that I shall live to see Mme. Demorest's Tea Club employing thousands of women, and giving people *good* tea to drink."

Writing from Swatow on December 8, 1870, Miss King gave her impressions of the people, the joss houses, the tombs on the hillsides, the stone gods, the intensively cultivated soil, the junks, the narrow streets, the running sewage. She was struck by the fact that no women were seen in the streets and that a man seldom spoke of his wife. He did not think she knew or should know anything. Nor would a Chinese man eat with a woman or have her enter his house. She must live with the girls in the rear. She thought the plight of the women sad. When a man married he could take his wife home but the wife could never take her husband home. She discussed the binding of feet and warned Mme. Demorest that the "Woman's Rights Women" should be careful lest they wind up in the same manner, for the idea behind the binding was to keep women at home, so that they would be powerless and could do no harm. "It would make your heart ache to see the poor farmers' wives work with such little feet," she wrote. "They say they suffer pain till they die. But it is a law, and it has to be done."

She was flabbergasted when one of her coolies said one morning that his wife, who was her personal attendant, had just given birth to a baby but would be on duty within an hour, after she had had time to plunge in the river with the infant. She arrived within the hour, calm, dutiful, and utterly baffling to Miss King. Life on the Chinese junks seemed equally depressing. A good healthy man earned eight cents a day and did six times as much work as a laborer in America.

Miss King was frank in saying that the Orientals were delighted with her. They feasted, honored and welcomed her. They inducted her into their "social gossips," their weddings, betrothals and funerals. She picked up a patois that she called "Piggie English" for purposes of communication. On all her trips she carried copper coins to buy candles, incense and fireworks at the temples. "I was chin-chinned wherever I went, and treated as if I was the spirit of their Mother God," she wrote. They prepared their most epicurean dishes for her. She feasted on shark's fins and bird's-nest puddings, sweetmeats and potted chicken. In the Tartar country some of the great dogs that infested the mountain fastnesses were slaughtered to make her a robe and a rug of their rich dark fur. When she was leaving they gave her a magnificent lacquered chest stuffed with chowchow for her journey.

But when she toured the tea plantations on her way to Hong Kong Susan, the master bargainer, met her match and acknowledged it. She pronounced the Chinese curiously immune to invention or improvement. What was good enough for their fathers was good enough for them, and they feared that changes of any sort might displease their ancestors. Before leaving China she decided that there was a strong scent of the Tammany ring about the whole tea business. "First, the natives cheat while growing the plant, then the buyers have a hand at adulteration, then the jobbers, and then the small merchants come into it," she wrote. "By the time the consumer gets his cup of tea the native grower of the plant would not recognize the article." However, that would be rectified when the Woman's Tea Company put its fine quality tea on the market, Miss King assured Mme. Demorest. Americans simply did not know what good tea was.

They had an excellent chance to find out when the first cargo of 17,000 tons ordered by Miss King had got back to the United States and was being sold at the Demorest Emporium, 838 Broadway. It was named Mandarin Tea and was advertised by a Mandarin figure holding up sealed packages. Chop No. 1 sold for $1.50 a pound, Chop No. 2 for $1, Chop No. 3 for 75 cents. Eight-pound chests at $7 were put up for hotels and clubs. Promotion for this new product was conducted with Mr. Demorest's usual aptitude for such matters.

Mandarin Tea was guaranteed to be equal, if not superior, to any tea ever imported into America. It was pure, fragrant, exquisite in flavor, quite different from the concoctions composed of the refuse, and sometimes the leaves, of American shrubs that were accepted as tea because they sold so cheaply. Mandarin Tea was the first picking of choice leaves, grown in favorable localities, of the kind used only by Daimios and Mandarins in the Orient. Thus ran the advertisements that helped to make Mandarin Tea a favorite brew in the 1870's. By the spring of 1872 Mme. Demorest felt that they were on their way to providing lucrative employment for many women across the country. "Lady agents wanted in every section of the Union," "Enterprising and responsible ladies wanted in every city"—so ran the advertisements.

But women did not dash in to sell tea with quite the enthusiasm they had shown for paper patterns. However, the movement grew and Miss King's second departure—this time in the clipper ship—was a master stroke. Families, clubs and hotels began stocking up, and $1,000 orders came in. The tea was shipped in all directions by express. After Miss King's return in 1873 the company was declared a success. They had bought and paid for their clipper ship. They had many agents throughout the country, but they conceded that the business would have developed more quickly but for their determination to have women only handle the tea. This slowed them up. Thousands eager to do business were destitute of resources, the common complaint of the nineteenth-century woman. Mme. Demorest saw that they had to be helped, and allowed to work at their own pace. Philanthropy and commerce made a difficult combination.

It became the fashion to drop in on the ground floor of the emporium and have a cup of Mandarin Tea, in addition to looking at gowns and paper patterns. The décor was seductive. Silk-embroidered panels brought home by Miss King hung on the walls. Lacquer, images and all kinds of curios were displayed. Tea was quietly served by attractive attendants.

After her travels in the Orient Miss King settled down again in the large rambling house on West 105th Street where she lived with her mother and sister. It had double turrets and on either side of the front steps were flower pots given her by the Tartars. She had filled them with wild ginger. Her rooms were stuffed with treasures from the East. Rare embroidered silks hung on the walls. She had relics from pagodas, idols, Japanese and Chinese teapots of all kinds, a lacquer tray eight hundred years old given her by a Japanese Prince, a bowl with the Chinese Emperor's crest, toys, games, Oriental money, Buddhist tracts, tortoise shell from the Palau Islands and innumerable pieces of lacquer.

When a reporter from *Pomeroy's Democrat* visited her, she served him Mandarin Tea from the lacquered tea chest she had brought for her own use on the ship. She explained that she had nothing to do with the established tea importing houses and that she expected to retire from the business when it was in full operation. She believed the women must run it themselves. "I've been to China to show them what they can do," she announced in her resonant voice. "They can make up great American tea companies for women just as for men, and control trade just like men, and if we can make the money what do we care for the ballot?"

In the calico dress and the same pair of heavy shoes that she had worn on all her travels, Susan walked briskly about in her old-fashioned garden. She led the way to the carriage house where two small Javanese monkeys chattered as she entered. She had brought home scores but some had died; others had been given away. A room in her house was hung with cages where parrots, mynah birds, Javanese sparrows and Japanese wrens kept up a chorus. Some of the celebrated Tsin-Tsin larks were imprisoned in one cage and a few of the fighting quail of Chinese Tartary in another.

Susan's iron-gray hair was brushed severely down from a center part and coiled in a small bun at the back. Her skin was tanned and weather-beaten from her travels. She spoke rapidly in a loud, ringing voice and there was no artifice about her. It was obvious that Mme. Demorest's patterns had done nothing for her. With the utmost solemnity she did gyrations, prostrating herself on the floor to show how the Chinese did it. Mr. Demorest, her old friend, had driven the reporter out to the country to meet her. Mark M. Pomeroy's *Democrat* had the largest circulation of any paper in the Northwest. Together with the La Crosse *Democrat*, which he also owned, a quarter of a million readers were reached. And the Demorests always liked to speak to the country as a whole. Their business was national in scope.

CHAPTER IX

Questions and Answers

O N AN AUGUST DAY in 1872 Mr. Demorest celebrated his
fiftieth birthday with a party at the family home. The
parlors were crowded with well-known New Yorkers gathered
to do him honor. Lawyers, editors and clergymen predominated
and the toasts were in the family tradition—nonalcoholic. There
were times when his impish son Will played tricks on Mr.
Demorest. When he induced Vaughan, the butler, to spike a
mince pie with rum his father unwittingly thought it delicious.
Mr. Demorest's preferred punch was milk with bananas and
red Antwerp raspberries with pulled French roll added. In the
country he often drank a mixture of milk and molasses. He
favored his wife's Indian huckleberry pudding, Phoebe Cary's
compote of apples and Alice Cary's plum pudding.

As usual, Mr. Demorest had an announcement of business
change or progress to make. Nothing ever lagged in his emporium, and the *Telegram* next day noted that he "stood at the
head of fashionable journalism." In answering a toast he said
that the year's chief innovation had been a change in the

method of supplying patterns. They were now folded flat and
enclosed in envelopes, with the design on the cover, thus making
them as identifiable as spools of thread or papers of pins. He
described 838 Broadway as a "radiating center of influences
representing many departments of the world's progressive ideas."
And in more than one respect Madame should come in for the
lion's share of the credit, he added. His own inventive gifts
were lauded by one of the speakers, who recalled that even as a
schoolboy he was known for his boats, his kites, his models of
one kind and another.

Mme. Clara Brinkerhoff sang operatic selections before the
evening was over. Vienna, dark and sparkling, did the "Echo
Song" and Henry gave one of his standard recitations. By this
time he was an enthusiastic oarsman, as well as a trained elocutionist, and he had all the family verve and personality. His
customary recitations were *Death-Doomed*, *The Gambler's
Wife*, *The Raven* and *The Bells*. All four of the Demorest
children shared in a warm family life and their gifts were encouraged by both parents. Mme. Demorest loved to see them all
enjoying themselves. She took them driving with her, to the
shops, to concerts, to festivals of all kinds. Both parents kept
them up to the mark in their studies and had strong ideas about
the educational practices of the day. They were encouraged to
keep all manner of pets and their country life was abundant.
Although so urban in her experience, Nell never lost her deep-
rooted love for the outdoors. But there were many jolly parties
at the Demorest city home—great family gatherings at Christmas, birthday parties for everyone, and a New Year's Day reception at which formally dressed men stopped in for the mild
punch that took the place of the glass of wine or mug of rum
they got elsewhere.

Mme. Demorest's autumn showing that year again revolved
around a prima donna—this time Mme. Pauline Lucca, the
Viennese singer who had drawn crowds to the Academy of
Music. She had the added aura of being a war heroine, for she
had joined her husband, Baron Rahden, at the battle front and

nursed him after he had been wounded in the Franco-Prussian War. She arrived at the fashion emporium with an entourage, and the customers stopped in their tracks to observe the well-known singer. She spoke little or no English and Mme. Demorest tried painstakingly to explain to her the fashion techniques of the house. Gay and easygoing, Mme. Lucca toured the show-rooms, was shown a picture of Jenny Lind on the walls, and kissed little Evelyn Demorest, who stood beside her mother. It amused her to finger the Lucca train that had been named specially for her.

In this same showing were the Lucca polonaise, the Vienna train, and the Princess pelisse. The Vienna Polonaise, named for the Demorest daughter, later turned up in a little Welsh church and in various parts of Europe. The Demorest patterns, with their identifying names, had a way of traveling around. The *Mirror of Fashions* at this time added to its cover embellishments a few more exclamatory points, in the mood of the era. It was now subtitled: *The Ladies Literary Conservator of the Novel, the Entertaining, the Artistic, the Useful and the Beautiful, Comprising Elegant Engravings, Reliable Fashions, Original Stories, Poems, Household, Music, Fashion. Its Utility and Beauty, rather than its Frivolity and Extravagance.*

But Alice Cary's name had appeared for the last time in its pages, a matter of deep regret to both the Demorests. She had died in the spring of 1871. For years her name had appeared with regularity in their magazine. "Her sympathies were all on the side of humanity," commented Mr. Demorest, "and particularly with women, and her influence was unmarred by any of those personal failings which so often have to be excused as the 'eccentricities of genius.' . . . To miss her, is to miss some of the sunshine which we have endeavored to infuse into its pages." Phoebe died in Newport five months later. When Alice was gone, all was gone, said her friends, declaring in the language of the day that she had died of a broken heart. She wore bright-colored clothes after Alice died and opened their house to friends. She kept her sister's room filled with fresh flowers.

Finally she took to her bed, saying, "There is nothing the matter with me; I shall be better tomorrow." And then amiable Phoebe, who had always been part of the literary salon, quietly went to sleep.

A few months later a frequent visitor at the Cary home had also slipped away—Horace Greeley. Both he and James Gordon Bennett, the most famous editors of the period, died in 1872. "It is done! I have fought the good fight. I know that My Redeemer Liveth," said Greeley at the end. The wife who had tormented him for years had died a month earlier. Dr. Beecher, whom he had both admired and condemned, paid tribute to the powerful and lonely man who had helped to build his fame and fortune. Broadway and Fifth Avenue were dense with attentive citizens who had always been interested in Greeley but had never understood him. Mr. Demorest attended the impressive funeral of his old friend. The town missed his awkward, hurrying figure lunging along with an absent-minded look, his soft wide hat pushed back from his bulbous forehead, his small glasses resting crookedly on his nose. Lauded, maligned, jeered at and cheered, he had died a broken and confused man. But he had set his mark on journalism.

Whitelaw Reid took over the *Tribune*. By 1876 a tall new tower had risen at Nassau and Spruce Streets. At the time it was the highest building on Manhattan Island and was well within sight of the ancient spire of Trinity. Charles A. Dana hailed Reid one day as the "Young Editor of the Tall Tower," a phrase that stuck and became a Park Row legend. Bennett, the stormy, erratic Scot, no less of an inflammatory force than Greeley, had handed on the *Herald* to a son of his own name who would widen the scope of the paper and bring innovations into the field. Like Mr. Demorest, the elder Bennett did not smoke or drink. But he dug with fierce delight into the scandals of his time.

William Cullen Bryant, another of Mr. Demorest's friends, had given stature to the New York *Evening Post*, and his aphorisms were finding their way into the English language. Reserved, shrinking always from self-assertion, he could frequently be seen browsing in Brentano's, the bookstore that had begun with a single table in the hallway of the old Revere House at Broadway and Houston Street, and was now the most flourishing establishment of its kind in America. When August Brentano, fresh from Austria, opened his first shop he called it Brentano's Literary Emporium and for a time he shared a building at 708 Broadway with the father of Charles and Daniel Frohman, who ran a tobacco business. Visitors from abroad who stayed at the New York Hotel across the street dropped in and asked for foreign periodicals. Brentano began ordering them and thus learned to feed a cosmopolitan trade. By 1870 he was a neighbor of the Demorests on Union Square. His emporium was next to the Goelet mansion and Tiffany's was down the block.

Demorest's at this time kept reminding its readers to study the newspapers and periodicals. They were urged to read everything good they could lay hands on, and Jenny June held out for the English stand-bys. "For studies take Mrs. Browning, Ruskin, John Stuart Mill and Shakespeare," she advised. "Don't waste time and strength on 'society novels.'" She might as well have spoken to the wind, for society novels were doing well. But so were the Brownings. Amid the Persian hangings and Nottingham lace curtains, the girls read *Pippa Passes* and dreamed a little over *Sonnets from the Portuguese.* The nineteenth-century authors who would become world classics had found a gold mine in American periodicals and for small sums the public could keep up with the latest installment from Dickens or Thackeray. In fact, there often was breathless suspense from one issue to the next. *Harper's* went in heavily for these importations that helped to shape the American reading taste of the period. But while the Victorians wrote with tremendous fecundity, American books were becoming more realistic, with the work of such men as Emerson and Whitman. A regional consciousness was beginning to show. Mark Twain had come up with truly native humor in *The Innocents Abroad* and the vogue for Western adventure was encouraged by such writers as Bret Harte.

Concerned with the lack of realism in children's reading, *Demorest's* was trying to give them something meaty in their magazine, *Young America*, which had first appeared in 1866. Children had found fresh wonder in the books of Louisa May Alcott. In 1871 *Little Men* had been added to *Little Women* to round out the delectable picture she had created. *Through the Looking Glass* came out in the following year so that the children of the early 1870's were the firsthand recipients of some deathless classics. In a lesser way Susan Coolidge's *What Katy Did* entertained a generation of girls and *Dotty Dimple*, a Southern favorite, was serialized in *Young America*. But the dime novels were worrying many parents. They were lurid inside and out, with flaming red, green and yellow covers. Houses in flames and murderers on gallows made popular illustrations and the text rambled through a forest of fantastic crime. Deadwood Dick and Cap Collier preceded Nick Carter and Frank Merriwell. The Horatio Alger touch came in with *Ragged Dick* in 1867 and the *Luck and Pluck* series was going strong by 1871.

The Demorests sought to counteract this with a magazine that would be free of the falsities and exaggerations common to children's books. They used stories and sketches that were both natural and truthful, together with practical information that could be turned to account. They felt that children needed tales that they could identify with their own lives—stories about pet dogs and kittens and the lore of the woods rather than the "wonderful, lying stories that excited childish fear and wonder and the dreadful ogres and wicked giants, the gaudy coloring, abominable caricatures and atrocious falsehoods" of some of the fairy stories. Nor did they think well of the tendency to doom to an early death the truthful and pious child, with the inevitable mournful litany of the day. Truthfulness, naturalness and simplicity were urged on mothers in this, as in all else.

Harper's Weekly described *Young America* as the "most

sparkling Juvenile Magazine ever issued." It carried stories, poems, music, games, puzzles, enigmas, riddles, and billed itself as the "Children's Museum of Philosophy, Art, Science, Literature and Fun," for it dealt with all these subjects in a simple way. History, biography, astronomy, chemistry, all had their innings. It carried dissected maps, puzzle pictures and toys. The cost was 15 cents an issue or $1.50 a year and the premiums cheered many a farm boy on his own way to fame. The gold pens were as popular as the spyglasses, the harmonica as the magic lantern with twelve slides, the box of paints as the photo album, the large wax doll as the china tea set, the compass as the telescope. The Bible was often one of the premiums although nearly every home already had one at that time. The scientific notes and the animal lore were accurate and not blown up to feed a child's imagination. There were simple biographies of men like Mozart and Lincoln. The sketches were packed with information on whale fishing, hunting and other outdoor subjects. The names of great men were buried in puzzles, and anagrams were built around greenhouse plants. Historical essays on foreign countries ran in every issue. The "how to make something" theme was highly developed, from how to make a coasting sled to how to make a brush and comb box. A pet item was the *Miniature Magazine*, a tiny handful which sold for 5 cents and was a reproduction of the large one.

The children loved these novelties and for a time it seemed an asset to the house. Having brought up four children of her own Mme. Demorest took a keen personal interest in *Young America*. In a "Chat with Girls" in an issue of 1872 she had diagrammed a pattern sheet for a tiny suit that any clever little girl could cut for her dolls. It was simple, she explained, getting across her own clue to style, "because children and dollies really look better dressed simply than when tricked out with finery which crushes and musses, and makes them look fit only for the ragman." In a roundabout way Mme. Demorest preached hygiene, style and good eating habits to her young readers. She warned them that cake, candy, fats and overeating would destroy their teeth and complexions, so that later on they would have to use paint, powder, false hair, and false teeth, "which render them hideous old women."

Soon there were copyists and juvenile magazines were added to the great spate of publications. But the winner came into the field when *Scribner's* brought out *St. Nicholas* in 1873 with Mary Mapes Dodge, author of the popular *Hans Brinker*, as editor. After nine years the Demorests in 1875 decided to discontinue *Young America* and incorporate some of its features in the parent magazine. They announced that a juvenile magazine "never did, and never could, be profitable," and they gave as one reason their belief that American children were no longer simple at heart.

They are young men and young women by the time they leave the nursery, and want grown papers, and grown books, and grown magazines . . . They imbibe a taste for the horrible, the exaggerated, and marvelous, which is catered to by unscrupulous persons, and which makes all else seem insipid and namby-pamby to them.

The same conclusion came to the surface again when *The Adventures of Tom Sawyer* was published in 1876. A reviewer in the New York *Times* observed that "both East and West our little people are getting to be men and women before their time," and suggested that a milder type of book than *Tom Sawyer* might seem to be preferable for them. The critic did not think they should be encouraged in their cravings for cayenne and mustard, since "without advocating the utter suppression of that wild disposition which is natural in many a fine lad, we think our American boys require no extra promptings." But the premiums for children continued merrily through *Demorest's* and the family flame did not falter when *Young America* was dropped. Meanwhile Jenny June was pursuing her earnest way and was checking up on educational advances, which she knew to be of primary interest to her employers. She recorded a change of attitude toward well-educated women. "It is not so many years since scholarship was supposed to unfit, rather than fit, a woman for the performance of a society role," she wrote. "A learned woman was one to be avoided. She was an unnatural monster for whom there was no place in the world. . . . She was something disliked by gods and men, and required only age and ugliness to be treated as a witch." But she found that men of liberal viewpoint at last were willing to give women a chance for education and even, under certain restrictions, an opportunity to earn a living. However, they were still afraid that the girls would overstep the boundaries marked out for them. The brightest sign of the times, she thought, was the effort being made by the girls themselves to individualize women, to erect a standard of womanhood rather than wifehood, to make them self-sustaining, self-reliant and respected, whether or not they became wives and mothers.

Jenny went seriously into the subject in 1873 in a talk to the Brooklyn Woman's Club, an outgrowth of Sorosis. Higher education for women was under hot discussion at the time, with the women's colleges opening up fresh avenues of intellectual endeavor. Yet she did not believe that such institutions as Vassar would necessarily better the condition of girls in the future. The plan was too general, the ideas too transcendental. The instruments which it put into their hands were not sufficiently practical or available. As she saw it, their education should fit them directly for kitchen, parlor, schoolroom or workshop. She proposed a dress professorship as a step in the right direction. But, however dubious she was about the Vassar method, as she looked around she wished that she might have been one of its students. Its art gallery by this time had from 400 to 500 paintings. Its library housed a thousand volumes. The girls dressed plainly and had little pocket money. The fees were $400 a year.

The fashionable schools of the period did not please Jenny at all. Seeking health, vigor and knowledge in the girls, she found instead a "slender bunch of vanity and affectation, with a smattering of various accomplishments, a superficial knowledge of society, a contempt of anything useful, an immense realization of their own claims, and a general disregard of those of

Ellen Louise Curtis Demorest

William Jennings Demorest

Mrs. Jane C. Croly (Jenny June)
wearing the emblem of the Sorosis Club

Vienna Demorest

Mr. and Mrs. Demorest. She is wearing
the gold scissors symbolic of her paper-
pattern business.

Miss Julia Gardiner—known as "the Rose of Long Island" and later to become the wife of President John Tyler—is pictured displaying an endorsement of the dress shop in the background. (Courtesy, Museum of the City of New York)

Castle Garden in 1848 (Currier print, courtesy of the Library of Congress)

Brooklyn Bridge, which was officially opened in 1883 (Courtesy, the Library of Congress)

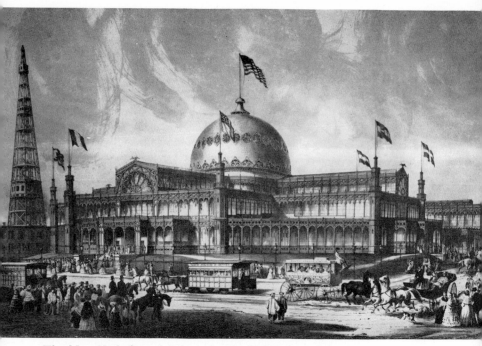

The New York Crystal Palace, for the Exhibition of the Industry of All Nations, built in 1853 (The J. Clarence Davies Collection, Museum of the City of New York)

Washington Square in 1851, then used as a parade ground (Courtesy, Museum of the City of New York)

St. Paul's Church in 1850, between Barnum's Museum and the Astor House (Courtesy, Library of Congress)

Croton Reservoir, opened in 1842 and torn down in 1900 to make way for The New York Public Library on Fifth Avenue at 42nd Street (The J. Clarence Davies Collection, Museum of the City of New York)

Washington, Madison and Union squares in the 1870's (Courtesy, Library of Congress)

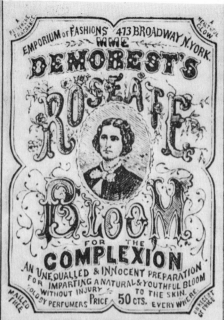

An advertisement for a Mme. Demorest beauty preparation

AMINA POLONAISE.

THE polonaise, illustrated above, is very handsomely made up in thin whi goods trimmed with "Standard" double-edged plaiting trimmings. Nos. 1 and with Valenciennes edge. One style of these trimmings is illustrated on page 2 Pattern of polonaise No. 1372.

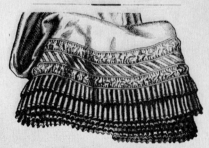

LADY'S TRAIN PETTICOAT.

To insure a gracefully hanging skirt, quite as much care and attention should b bestowed upon the cut and mounting of the petticoat to be worn underneath it, a upon the style of the skirt itself. Especially is this necessary with a train skirt which requires the support of a petticoat not quite as full, but very nearly as long a the skirt, with a full trimming at the bottom, which should extend only across the back and sides if the skirt is very much gored in front. The petticoat illustrated cut after pattern No. 552, is made of fine cambric, trimmed on the bottom with two rows of "Standard" fluting, Nos. 2 and 3—headed by a band of "Standard" alter nate insertion. This makes the entire trimming an excellent depth for a train petti coat, nine inches. The same style of trimming, in narrower widths, is very pretty for shorter skirts.

Part of a page in *Demorest's Monthly Magazine* showing the use of trimmings

Elaborately dressed children in front of Mme. Demorest's fashion emporium on East 14th Street in 1876 (Courtesy, New York Public Library)

Medals awarded to young people by William Jennings Demorest for excellence in the delivery of prohibition essays

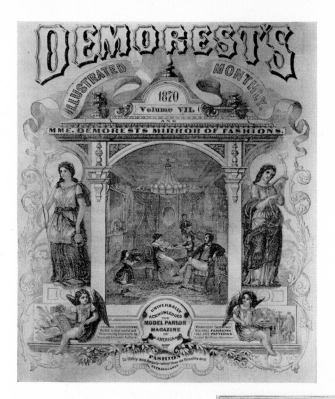

Covers of *Demorest's Illustrated Monthly* and *Mme. Demorests Mirror of Fashions* and of *Demorest's Young America*

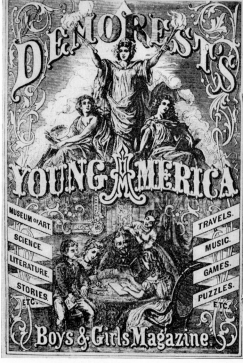

san A. King, who sailed to
e Orient in 1872 in the
pper ship she and Mme.
emorest chartered to bring
ck tea

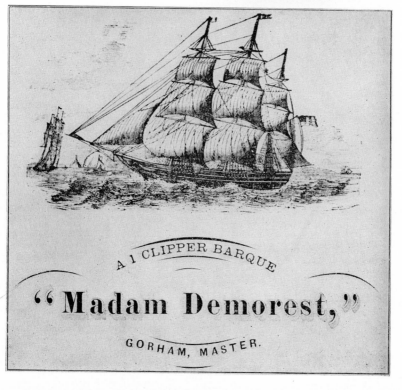

A 1 CLIPPER BARQUE

"Madam Demorest,"

GORHAM, MASTER.

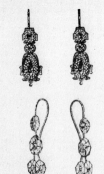

THE DIAMOND NECKLACE.

The necklace is magnificent, formed in clusters of diamonds of the finest water, with tiny and graceful pendants of the same exquisite jewels.

THE DIAMOND HAIR-PINS.

The Diamond Hair-pins must create a sensation wherever they are worn, being composed of a cluster of diamonds, set in the most superb style, the form is so fully illustrated, that they require no further description.

THE DIAMOND EAR-RINGS.

Beautiful clusters of diamonds, arranged style that would form exquisite models.

CORAL SET.

An inexpensive style of ornament, but and arranged in a very chaste and unique des

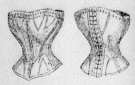

BRIDAL CORSET.

This exquisite specimen of miniature co making was of rich white satin, shaped on new French model, and beautifully stitched top of the corset was mitred, and embroid with shaded stars.

MRS. GEN. TOM THUMB IN HER RECEPTION DRESS.

The material is a superb quality of taffetas, changing from pale amber to a silvery white, and producing a peculiarly rich and delicate tint. The skirt, cut *en traine*, is ornamented to represent the emblems of different nationalities on each separate breadth, connected at each seam by marabout feathers and lace, altogether forming an elegant border round the skirt. The design in front of the dress represents Growing Corn for America; on the right a Rose for England, encircled by buds and leaves; on the left, Laurel, for France; and on the remaining breadths are exhibited an Acorn in oak leaves, for Germany; a Shamrock, for Ireland; the Thistle, for Scotland; and a Vine with clusters of grapes, for Italy. The designs are traced in very narrow folds of white satin, their effect being heightened, where it is necessary to their full representation and raised appearance, with narrow *point applique*. The left side is looped up nearly to the waist in regal style, over a petticoat of white glace silk, covered with puffings of fine tulle, the divisions being traced with seed pearls.

The corsage is arranged with tiny folds of white satin, edged with *point applique*, describing a little jacket, rounded off from the stomacher. The sleeves are short and trimmed to match the corsage.

This dress was also arranged with reference to being worn by the little Bride on the occasion of her presentations at the Courts of Queen Victoria and the Empress Eugenie, etc., and is altogether acknowledged a great success.

It was ordered by Mr. BARNUM at the request of Miss LAVINIA WARREN (now Mrs. Stratton), who gave *carte blanche*, as to style and cost, and was designed and made at our establishment, 473 Broadway.

BRIDAL SKIRT.

Mrs. General Tom Thumb in her reception dress made in the Demorest establishment, and some of her bridal accessories (From *Mme. Demorest's Quarterly Mirror of Fashions*)

Ball gowns of the 1870's (*Frank Leslie's Lady's Magazine*, courtesy New York Public Library)

The dry goods district on lower Broadway in the 1870's (Courtesy, Library of Congress)

Union Park in 1878 (Courtesy, Library of Congress)

Delmonico's in 1875, at Fifth Avenue and 14th Street (The J. Clarence
Davies Collection, Museum of the City of New York)

New York City Hall in the 1870's (Courtesy, Library of Congress)

The Drive in Central Park, a fashionable thoroughfare in the 1870's
(Courtesy, Library of Congress)

Fashionably dressed ladies—one ready to ride in Central Park

anybody else." It did not surprise her that women thus trained
should break down at the first taste of hardship and turn to
marriage. Jenny was enthusiastic about Elizabeth Peabody's
kindergartens and urged girls to take up this type of teaching.

She was pounding hard as she launched a series of talks on
the businesswoman, author, artist, philanthropist, educator, social leader, committee woman, journalist and clergyman, as well
as mother, cook, housekeeper and seamstress. None was overlooked. She was particularly scathing about the society woman
who did nothing but dress, run around and plan parties. The
woman in business, as Jenny viewed her in the 1870's, was not
an inspiring sight. She shrewdly surmised that she was only a
dismal parody of the businesswoman to be. "You can see them
in Bleecker Street and some of the avenues, in dark little dens
of shops—holding one baby in their arms, while another tugs
at their skirts. You can see another class acting as runners, or
agents, for men, wearing dingy alpaca, their faces gradually ac-
quiring a hard, dry, anxious look, which settles upon them, and
takes out all traces of youth, freshness and beauty."

But Jenny still saw hope for the future in this area. "It will
not be long before the age will develop some women of business," she predicted, "and when it does, be sure they will take
a high place in the estimation of men, and in general society."
Wonders had been accomplished in the previous twenty years
and the next ten would see the establishment of women's banks,
manufactories, real estate offices, wholesale houses and, she
hoped, a prosperous woman's clubhouse. She listed the special
qualifications needed for the good businesswoman as conscience,
clearheadedness, power of taking in details, stick-to-itiveness,
judgment and insight. To become a woman of business the girl
should begin early and, like a boy, start on the lowest rung of
the ladder. Men had been chivalrous to women, humane to
women, generous to women, devoted to women, almost everything but just to women.

As she moved around she never forgot the main props of the
Demorest empire. She argued strongly in favor of uniforms for

all schoolgirls. She advised college girls to have few, simple and good clothes, with five changes in dress altogether. She reminded them that the Demorest "reform" pattern for underwear was well adapted to school purposes. It did away with superfluous garments and substituted one piece shaped to the form, which took the place of chemise, drawers and underwaist. She campaigned for better clothes for the working-girl—simple, tasteful garments instead of the cheap fabrics and showy trimmings that they wore with a "Fifth Avenue-on-Sunday idea of style." In all her advocacy of correct attire Jenny's stand was firmly stated—that woman's physical life was the "ladder by which she descended below the earth or mounted to heaven." What she demanded was not so much technique as full understanding of the principles underlying good health and sound motherhood.

The reforming note broke through at every point. Mme. Demorest's strong philanthropic interests were often visible in Jenny's writings, for Nell rarely wrote herself. She cited the debatable fact that with indefatigable spirit women had created all the homes, asylums and charitable institutions in the country. She believed that women should serve as school commissioners and school trustees, as prison inspectors and poor-law guardians. "It is idle to say women are not trained to govern and control," said Jenny. "Train them, then. History shows that they make excellent rulers."

Discussing women doctors, with the sterling examples of Dr. Elizabeth Blackwell and Dr. Mary Putnam Jacobi before her, Jenny advised girls not to take up medicine unless their fitness for the work presented itself as an unanswerable argument. "It is not women-doctors, after all, that we want," she wrote, "but women who will so live and teach others to live, that we shall have no necessity for doctors. The successful women doctors can be counted upon the fingers." A severe epidemic of children's diseases was raging at the time, particularly scarlet fever. Vaccination and kindergartens for small children were being advocated in Demorest's.

To show what women could do in the way of work Jenny, who was not given to boasting, recalled her own efforts as wife and journalist. In nearly twenty years she had not had one entire week of leisure and had often waited for months to call on a friend. She had risen at seven each morning and worked until midnight, writing at home, in her office, wherever she happened to be—once behind a bar counter in Chicago before running after a train to deliver her copy to the baggage master. She had been called on to fill nearly every type of newspaper job— writing editorials, market reports, gossip from Paris and letters from London, book reviews and dramatic criticism, fashion and household hints. She had edited telegraph reports, written heads and made up the paper. More important, although she would not have mentioned it, Jenny had borne five children and made life pleasant for an exacting and brilliant man.

At this point she urged a woman's paper for women—"bright, newsy, intelligent but not pretentious, cheap but not vulgar, honest, fair, impartial." Jenny June was the woman who could have run it. As it was, she acted as adviser in chief for the Demorests to the thousands of women who bombarded the magazine with questions. But Mme. Demorest was always there with her sage advice and practical outlook. They agreed completely on nearly every given point, except that Jenny was less concerned with style. She continually projected for her readers her belief in the influence of the mind over the body and tried to put iron into the souls of her correspondents. She told them that their purposeless lives were responsible for nine tenths of the nerves, low spirits, and general debility of which they complained. She thought their heavy breakfasts of oatmeal with beefsteak, fried potatoes, eggs, chops, fish, corn bread and hot biscuits, might have something to do with it, too.

Jenny advised them how to dress for church, how to launch a club, how to guide an erring husband, how to garnish the dinner table, how to hang pictures, from the "Old Oaken Bucket" chromo to a Ryder or Eakins; whether a girl should do round dances with a strange man met at a ball, where to find poetry suitable for an autograph album, how to make calf's-foot jelly, how to cure a jealous temper or pinpoint Heliogabalus' dates as Emperor of Rome; whether a pink satin bodice would be good over a white tulle dress, whether bunting would be right for lambrequins, whether or not to do fancywork in the parlor when a gentleman called to spend the evening, and what George Sand's marital status chanced to be at the moment.

Thus the girls of the Age of Innocence worked out their problems, while a drive was on in *Demorest's* against the free and easy ways of the younger generation and the glib use of first names. As women in the home coped with boiled whortleberry pudding, crabapple marmalade, plum syrup and lemon sponge, they got their beauty hints on the side and tried them out in the kitchen. Tired businessmen returning home to bright-eyed wives never knew that they had been squeezing orange juice, lemon juice or soapsuds into their eyes to make them sting and shine; or had been eating lump sugar wet with cologne for the same purpose. Nor dared they rumple the elaborate puffs of hair that had taken hours to arrange, with ringlets down the back, or done up in the Grecian coil and crimped in front before being drawn back in bands.

The love problems with which Jenny coped in the Ladies Club were symptomatic of the age, or perhaps of the eternal male and female. The theme of the siren versus the chaste woman came up repeatedly. Jenny speciously argued: "The virtue that good women want is toleration. Out of their own circumscribed sphere, everything to them is probable evil. Let them learn to look upon it as probable good, and they will find in simple charity a philosopher's stone that transmutes all it touches into gold." A bride wrote in anguish a few months after marriage that her husband went out every night and stayed away until two in the morning. Jenny advised her to stick it out. Anything was better than separation from her husband. A good wife could sometimes make a good husband out of indifferent raw material.

The oracle listed what she considered the qualities needed for success in marriage: health, self-reliance, judgment, truth, mutual consideration, forbearance and industry. Glamour did not come into view, although Mme. Demorest did everything to give women outward charm, from her cosmetics to her hats and gowns. Beginning in March, 1871, Jenny ran a series of papers on marriage that were devoutly followed by *Demorest's* readers and evoked much comment. In addition, she gave reams of advice on how to entertain a suitor, what gifts to give him, how to cater to his vanity by discussing the things that interested him, how to treat him with affection and confidence, but also with maidenly reserve; how to improve the complexion with sulphur pills, Turkish baths and boiled oatmeal with cranberry sauce for breakfast. Women then, as later, were concerned about their weight. Jenny supplied the answer that did not change materially in the next ninety years: "Live on lean meat, and acid fruits, drink little water, tea or coffee—eat no sugar, or farinaceous food."

She was doubtful of the lasting quality of boy and girl love and early marriage, feeling that if girls had work there would be less of this. "The idleness of girls is undoubtedly one of the causes of depravity in boys," said Jenny. The wild ways of the 1870's had resulted in severe attacks abroad on the morals and manners of the American people. The girls were accused of being loud in public and of being much too free in picking up chance acquaintances. Jenny took note of this when she wrote:

Let us, then, cultivate manners, and thereby improve our morals, which seem of late to have been made to fit them—or it may be are only the result of them—that we may get rid of the stigma of being the worst-mannered people in the world, and win the more honorable distinction of being as gentle in manners as irreproachable in morals.

She considered woman's long confinement before and after childbirth as nonsense and quite unnecessary. She had taken only a minimum of time off herself to have her babies. She believed in the diffusion of sex knowledge through good scientific books. She backed up the growing desire in the South for women's clubs. She urged the women to organize without delay, to cultivate discussion and extemporaneous thinking, to draw up memorials to municipal bodies, to fight tobacco and to keep a sharp lookout for those who tried to run the local political machines for their own benefit. She thought that husbands should encourage their wives to read the daily papers and that men who married with the idea of being masters in their homes were not fit to marry at all. Thus *Demorest's* kept pounding away at the social order. Although Jenny argued from every possible angle, her judgment often was based on common sense.

New Yorkers brushed their teeth with Sozodont in the early 1870's. They used silver napkin rings, had their clothes cleaned with Sapoline, enjoyed conversaziones, sewed with Eureka spool silk, cut cloth with Seymour's shears, drank Mandarin Tea, had deep gilt frames with arabasques for their chromos, played chess, backgammon or bezique and, of course, bought Mme. Demorest's patterns. The list of wedding presents they could give was formidable, ranging from Tiffany diamonds and Steinway pianos to lacy parasols with jeweled handles and white china menu stands. Silver salt cellars and spoons came in the shape of wheelbarrows, shells and tubs. Silver sardine boxes and spoon warmers were always welcomed by the bride. Silver cake baskets and épergnes were standard choices. There were silver egg boilers and gypsy kettles, tankards and mugs, silver biscuit boxes and water coolers, Dresden candelabra, game pie dishes, nautilus shells for flowers, cuckoo clocks, Venetian mirrors and antimacassars, bed quilts, cushions, footstools and handscreens all ready for the bride to sew.

The favorite forms of entertaining at that time were formal and informal receptions, breakfasts, state dinners, high teas and luncheons. Breakfasts were usually given by single women or bachelors, with a fruit stand in the middle of the table and a silver service from which hot chocolate was poured. Cold game pie, broiled partridge, little chops with frills, waffles, fresh eggs cooked at the table, bacon and jam rounded out the meal. The guests dawdled over the table for two or three hours, winding up with Chartreuse or Maraschino in Venetian glasses. Then they went riding, shopping or calling.

Dinners were usually limited to twelve persons in the average home, and increasingly the carving was done by servants from great joints on the sideboard. Breakfast at eight or nine, luncheon at two, dinner at six or seven, left no margin for tea, so that the fashionable five-o'clock English tea did not penetrate New York homes as a whole, although the traveled found time for it. Women had come to prefer the two-o'clock luncheon for entertaining, either at home or away from home. The menu was uniform—fried oysters, cold ham, cold tongue, cold chicken, sardines or a salad, fruit, cake, tarts and ice cream. This was the favorite form of entertaining by women living in boardinghouses or hotels, of which there were many in the 1870's. High teas on Sunday evenings were considered smart. These involved cold meats, charlotte russe, jelly shapes, sardines and ice cream, with music afterward. The gourmet feasts at Delmonico's, the hotels and men's clubs that made lively newspaper reading half a century later were reflected only in a moderate way in the average home.

But the home setting was changing in all respects. Five or six period styles were in vogue for drawing-room furniture, with the greatest emphasis on Louis XIV. The more discriminating blended their pieces. Rosewood flourished throughout the Age of Innocence. A Voltaire easy chair stood cheek by jowl with a Louis XIV divan with heavy fringe and tassels. Horsehair was on the decline and plush had taken its place. The more elaborate upholstery was of satin brocade or brocatelle, sometimes woven in gold and imported from Paris. A black satin of great popularity brocaded with gold vines and blossoms was flooding the market. Cabinets, pedestals, tables and easels of marqueterie, or of rosewood and ebony inlaid with ivory, were scattered around the drawing rooms. A painting displayed on an easel was considered a graceful touch. There was not yet either the clutter or the magnificence of the 1890's but things were moving in that direction and far away from the austere simplicity of the colonial tradition. Persian suites were used for reception rooms, boudoirs and libraries, their frames completely hidden by upholstery brilliant with giant-sized flowers.

Black furniture had led to black carpets, usually patterned with golden arabesques, snowy bells, emerald moss and foliage, or scarlet geraniums and carnation pinks. Axminster and Moquettes were used for parlor-floor coverings, with medallion patterns and bouquets of splashy flowers. At the Centennial Exposition in Philadelphia, William Sloane bought a superb collection of Oriental rugs for more than a million dollars, and soon they showed up in the more elaborate homes of the East. Brussels carpeting, Royal Wiltons and Axminsters sold at Stewart's for less than $5 a yard. Huge rugs were ordered for the hotel trade and Richard Canfield, the gambler, bought one at Sloane's that required three flatcars for shipment. Alexander Smith Cochran paid $75,000 for a Persian rug. The era of lush Oriental carpets had arrived. And Aubusson tapestries hung in many of the more affluent homes. Dining rooms and libraries were carpeted with Persian or Smyrna rugs. Marqueterie and Florentine gilt were used in bedroom furniture. The beds had porcelain medallions in the headboards, repeated also in tables and the backs of chairs.

This was New York. But Jenny thought of the humbler homes across the country where many of her readers lived. "By all means use that idle parlor," she wrote. "What good are parlors whose seats are covered with pale satin, wrought with silken roses, and trailing foliage? The children should play freely. Everyone should enjoy it." Her own house was a cheerful blend of good taste, good living and good furniture.

CHAPTER X

❦

Panic on Wall Street

THE CRASH OF 1873 caught the nation unawares and cut deep into the world of the merchant. When the house of Jay Cooke suspended on a September day, followed quickly by other collapses and the closing of the Stock Exchange for the first time in its history, panic spread across the country. The Gold Room, with all its dazzle and excitement, was hushed. The churches were empty and women stayed at home. No one was in the mood to shop or pay calls. The lobby of the Fifth Avenue Hotel was jammed with restless, dazed men debating what they should do. President Grant came in hurriedly from Long Branch. Fifty millions were quickly raised to support the market. The government, the banks and Western interests threw money into the breach, but established firms toppled and famous names faced ruin.

Jay Cooke's banking house had been growing in power ever since his start in Philadelphia in 1861. Time and again it had given support to Salmon Portland Chase in his operations as Secretary of the Treasury during the Civil War. The white-bearded banker, who looked like a patriarch in his great cape cloak and wide-brimmed soft gray hat, and was genial and devout, worldly and simple all at the same time, had a mansion near Philadelphia and a country seat at Put-in-Bay on Lake Erie, where he was visited by clergymen, missionaries and reformers as well as bankers and men of affairs. But when he tied his fortunes to the Northern Pacific Railroad and Oakes Ames came to grief, ruin stared him in the face. As other banks suspended and trust companies failed, defalcations of various kinds came to light and the Crédit Mobilier scandal burst wide open, to the embarrassment of President Grant. At that moment Wall Street came to a shuddering standstill. The merchants suffered along with others but the Demorest fortunes were close to their peak at this time. Their business had increased fifteen-fold in four years and two million patterns were shipped out from their plant each year, making the largest express delivery from any single house of business in the country.

In 1874 they moved from the three adjoining houses they occupied on Broadway to one of the city's fine old mansions at 17 East Fourteenth Street and, in addition, Mr. Demorest backed the erection of the seven-story printing house of Lange, Little & Company at the corner of Astor Place and Lafayette, site of the home and gardens of John Jacob Astor. The Astor Library and the Mercantile Library faced the new printing house, which had sixty Adams presses and miles of vaults, and was rated one of the best equipped in the world. Cooper Union stood to the right, Scribner's to the left, and other publishing houses girdled the area, on Broadway, Ninth Street and the Bible Society block. Lange, Little & Company did the printing of the City Directory, of the Erie Railroad, of almanacs, periodicals, books and other jobs, not the least of which was Mr. Demorest's own printing bill of more than a quarter of a million dollars a year. He was one of the three partners in the firm. The other two were Edward Lange, a German, and Joseph J. Little from New York State, two men who had come to New York seventeen years earlier with nothing, had worked as print-shop jobbers and had joined forces to form a powerful house before they were thirty-five.

Mme. Demorest did not visit the printing house. She had her own sanctum—described by the *World* as a boudoir frescoed in lavender and gilt—where she sat, stiff-backed and alert, close to the wide windows that gave an oblique view of the fashionable promenade on Union Square. Opening off this salon, where she interviewed philanthropists about wayward girls and discussed costumes with opera singers, was Jenny June's office with a bright carpet, a lounge and a well-appointed desk. Together these two women were a more potent force than an army of noisy feminists.

The Demorest showroom ran the entire length of the mansion on Fourteenth Street, with deep bay windows fronting on the street. The wisteria vine and delicate iron tracing that had given charm to the house had been torn down with reluctance by the Demorests to give them a modern business front. They were now close to Delmonico's, and Chickering Hall was one door away. They were opposite Wheeler & Wilson, the sewing machine company that had taken the building just vacated by Brooks Brothers. The Woman's Tea Company occupied the basement floor of their new home. Salesrooms and the business office were on the ground floor. The editorial rooms were on the second floor and the designing and manufacturing departments occupied the third and fourth floors. They had three times as much room as in their Broadway place, for the house was wide and high-ceilinged. It was one of the more famous mansions of the city until trade crowded it on all sides on Union Square. Mme. Lucca had been living in it when they took it over.

Behind the plate glass were the small carved desks of the "lady assistants," set with vases of flowers. The walls were lined with pigeonholes filled with patterns. The *World* considered their showrooms the handsomest in the city. There were mirrors everywhere, reflecting back the dummies arrayed in their illusive garb of tinted paper. "The great bay-window, with mirrors upon each side, reflecting the promenade and gay moving panorama of Fourteenth Street, all of the other mirrors reflecting the equally bright panorama inside, united to the savoir faire of Madame herself, making a most charming ensemble," said a newspaper observer.

The large cutting room had a dozen tables with slabs of planed wood on which were spread uncreased sheets of manila paper—elephant folio, in layers of 120 to 150 sheets. Using a sharp-pointed knife with loaded handle, the girls cut 120 patterns at a time. Others folded the patterns and put them into envelopes. Writers, translators, designers, artists, engravers, compositors, printers, cutters, clerks and paper mill operatives all worked for the Demorest interests. Dressmakers liked to have both the trimmed and the untrimmed varieties of patterns. Every season there were a hundred new designs of improved fit and style. The originals were kept on exhibition in the showroom, so that the public could study the precision with which they had been copied.

The colored tissue paper for the trimmings was imported in special sizes and in great quantity from Europe. The thin, tough manila paper from which the plain patterns were cut was made expressly for the Demorests. It came in mammoth sheets, almost carpet size, and 5,000 reams were ordered at a time. One entire floor was devoted to large illustrated envelopes with the patterns in boxes of a thousand each. The pattern albums made a library in themselves, loaded with promise for women in lonely spots. Bales of patterns and journals were piled in the basement, waiting to be shipped in all directions. "A paper juggernaut," commented the New York *Graphic*. A million catalogues and a million copies of the *Journal of Fashions* were distributed every six months. Mme. Demorest's mammoth *Bulletin of Fashion* and her semiannual *What to Wear* were addressed to agents with their own names and advertisements printed on them, linking them to the central emporium. Mr. Demorest thought of everything.

In two decades the pattern business had grown from nothing.

Its commercial value doubled and redoubled each year. By this time France had two or three houses where patterns were made, but the volume of trade was insignificant. England had several inconsequential emporiums. But in the United States the pattern business had reached the proportions of an industry. Demorest's now had 1,500 agencies in operation. There were forty in Brooklyn alone. Rival interests were multiplying around them by this time. The new building gave greater scope for their operations. The demand from abroad induced them to issue their styles simultaneously in Paris, London and New York, accompanied by full directions in French and English. By 1876 the Demorest imprimatur had become international in range. One steamer alone carried a ton of patterns to a single sewing-machine company in England—more than was turned out by all the London and Paris houses put together. From one small trial order it had become a landslide.

Mme. Demorest's autumn opening that year had particular prestige. As basques, polonaises, paletots and pelisses went on display she got much personal attention as the key figure in the world of paper patterns. "They are a power little apprehended or appreciated," commented the Baltimore *American*. "They promise shortly to *form* the world, if they do not reform it. Imagine two millions of them turned out at once to be distributed over Europe and America; from New York to Chile and the City of Mexico on the one side, and from New York to London, Edinburgh, Glasgow, Paris and Berlin on the other." And Matthew Hale Smith, a contemporary author, gave his own rather flowery picture of Mme. Demorest at work:

She is one of the best known ladies in America. She is the acknowledged leader of fashions in this country and in Europe. Stylish in dress, faultless in taste, she exhibits her artistic ability as truly as Lawrence with his pencil, Chantrey with his chisel, or Leitz with his mystic touch. Twice a year Mme. Demorest throws open her elegant salons for the crowd composed of the élite. The artist herself, amid her stylish and showy goods, is worth looking at. A lady, tall, slim, with a graceful bearing; tresses black as a raven's; eyes black and sparkling like diamonds; with a complexion reminding one of an Italian countess; her robe simple but elegant. In any company Madame would be pronounced the best dressed lady in view.

The style, accuracy and cheapness of the patterns had worked a revolution in society as complete and beneficent as that of the sewing machine or the piano, Mr. Smith went on. Mme. Demorest's position in the world of fashion was conceded everywhere so that she stood without a rival. All told, she had received twenty-five diplomas and medals of honor. But Mme. Demorest also had common sense and a lively sense of humor, and she would have been the last to take all that credit to herself. There was the head of the house, the dynamo behind the whole operation. There was her sister Kate, who had everything to do with the patterns. There was Jenny June, whose writings had depth and sagacity and who was a host in herself. But Madame was the figurehead and she fulfilled her role with dignity.

However, another fashion empress, more daring and dashing than Mme. Demorest, was seated in a more glamorous sanctum, where the ink was like vin rosé and the hangings were of heavy satin. There were reverberations all through the fashion world in the 1870's as Miriam Folline Squier, divorced in 1873, married Frank Leslie in St. Thomas's Church the following July. A bronze-haired beauty, originally from New Orleans, Mrs. Leslie had a history behind her and ahead of her. Earlier she was known as Minnie Montez and had toured the country as the sister of Lola Montez. She had two husbands before she married Frank Leslie and her fourth would be Willie Wilde, the brother of Oscar Wilde.

She loomed large in Leslie's publishing empire before she became his bride. She edited *Frank Leslie's Ladies' Gazette of Paris, London, and New York Fashions* and did it with style. She exercised both taste and editorial judgment as she presided from a comfortable armchair in Leslie's five-story publishing house at 537 Pearl Street. While she was still Mrs. Ephraim George Squier she had attended the Lincoln inaugural ball, wearing diamonds and opals. Again she was conspicuous at the Paris Exposition of 1867, appearing on the platform wearing a $20,000 purple gown from Worth. She picked up her bonnets at Barenne's in Paris and combined her personal splash with dispatches sent back to the magazine. She did the grand tour, from the gondolas of Venice to a Fourth of July fete at the Grand Hotel in Paris, where she was toasted as the most beautiful woman in France. She next turned up at Saratoga to attend the wedding of Frank Leslie's son, Alfred, and to appear from time to time having game dinners with her employer at Moon's Lake House. Eventually she married him and helped to run his properties. The Demorest and Leslie paths inevitably crossed, since both summered in Saratoga and their editorial functions had kinship. Leslie's, too, established a purchasing department for the convenience of out-of-town subscribers. They, too, dealt heavily in patterns in the 1870's, although in actual fact some Leslie tracing patterns had been floating about on the market as far back as the fifties.

Mrs. Leslie covered the openings and charity balls. She moved about in the world of fashion and high living. The Leslies were as worldly as the Demorests were austere in their personal lives. The celebrities of the hour flocked to their home on Fifth Avenue. Their guests were not the reformers and people with causes who haunted the Demorest home. But she made her biggest splash at Saratoga, where her doting husband built Interlaken, a twelve-room house with stables, arbors, rustic summerhouses, conservatories and terraced lawns rolling down to the lake. Together they watched the International Amateur Regatta Race of 1874 from a grandstand at the edge of the lake, and Leslie presented a $1,000 challenge cup by Tiffany in silver, representing Cleopatra's barge. The next year Miriam had her own barge, the family yacht, to take her around the lake. Mme. Demorest would not have been human had she not observed the growing power of Mrs. Leslie, her success as she managed the intricate properties of her husband's publishing empire after his death, her travels, her books, her support of the suffrage cause, the place she carved for herself in public life. Nell did not live to learn that when Mrs. Leslie died in 1914 she left a fortune to Mrs. Carrie Chapman Catt.

But the lively lady who really tore the town apart in 1874 was Victoria Woodhull, who had been whipping up a storm ever since she and her sister, Tennessee Claflin, arrived in town in 1868 and charmed Commodore Vanderbilt, Jim Fisk and Jay Gould. The sisters dabbled in journalism, suffrage and clairvoyance. They launched their own paper. They hobnobbed with Wall Street's best. The first issue of *Woodhull and Claflin's Weekly* in the spring of 1870 was an eye opener in itself: "Upward and Onward. Progress! Free Thought. Untrammeled Lives. Breaking the Way for Future Generations."

Although Victoria lived in the world of journalism she was not of it. Two masculine ghosts functioned in the background, but she brought all her native dash to bear on the subject. No fashions for her, but women's rights when circulation lagged or, better still, the scandal of the day. She was magnetic, raffish, eerie, heralding the freedom of women, preaching free love, basking in the counsels of the great financiers and using the honest craft of journalism for her own strange ends. Tennessee communed with the spirits. Victoria got her inspiration from man. Her editorials urged independence in woman. All manifestations of feminism were applauded. Finally her paper conducted a hot campaign to make Victoria President. But, like Horace Greeley, she took a bad beating from Ulysses S. Grant. She accepted her defeat serenely, although suggestions of blackmail had begun to give her trouble, and she was forced to suspend publication in the summer of 1872. But she continued to lecture on free love and the impending revolution. She was an effective figure on the platform with the strong glow of her dynamic personality. And soon she humbled the most notable preacher in American history—Dr. Henry Ward Beecher.

His sister, Harriet Beecher Stowe, had made the mistake of satirizing Vickie in *The Christian Union*. Catharine Beecher, who was opposed to her suffrage tactics, also had attacked her.

But his half sister, Mrs. Isabelle Beecher Hooker, who championed votes for women, defended her. In any event, Victoria launched one of the major social scandals of the era by spreading on the record the story of Dr. Beecher's devotion to Elizabeth Tilton, the tiny, fair-haired wife of Theodore Tilton. She had been a Sunday-school teacher at Plymouth Church, seemingly devoted to Tilton until she came under Dr. Beecher's spell. Tilton was a blond giant magnetic to women and joyous in manner to everyone. He cared little for tradition and edited the New York *Independent* with an able touch.

Victoria revived her defunct journal in order to print eleven columns of lurid detail. The triangle had been dinner-table gossip for months but she transmuted it into the unbeatable clarity of print, and copies of her paper sold for $40 each. Anthony Comstock slapped the sisters into Ludlow Street Jail. But the paper resumed publication in December, 1872, and in January Vickie crashed a meeting at Cooper Union in the disguise of an old woman—while a marshal waited to rearrest her—and told the story all over again before anyone could stop her. The tempest of revelation kept the audience transfixed. Tilton sued for alienation of affection and Dr. Beecher had to face trial in 1875. The aging pastor with the magnetic voice and powerful personality made a poor witness for himself, and Elizabeth shilly-shallied on all issues, but after it was over admitted the justice of the charges.

The courtroom was jammed with celebrities and flowers arrived each day for Dr. Beecher from his congregation. The case ran on for six months and the testimony was read with interest around the world. The jury finally disagreed and Plymouth Church, as well as Dr. Beecher, interpreted this as an acquittal. He flourished again as lecturer, preacher, pontificator, but a shadow had passed across his sun. Things would never again be quite the same for him. Having done her worst, the suffragists were riven apart over Vickie. In a sense she had become their most dramatic leader since presenting her famous memorial to Congress demanding equal rights. Susan B. Anthony and Mrs.

Elizabeth Cady Stanton did not approve of her, but they defended her because their suffrage principles came first, and Vickie had come up with a clever device in her approach to Congress. In 1871 the National Woman Suffrage Association had backed her memorial, demanding the enactment of legislation that would enable women to exercise the right of suffrage already assured under the Fourteenth Amendment. This sidestepped the issue of a new amendment. Vickie could wear a bonnet as well as make a speech but the articles she ran on prostitution, abortion and free love were hard for those two worthy citizens to take. And with Dr. Beecher she had gone too far. Disaster seemed to surround her until she and Tennie moved to England, the suffrage queens from across the sea. Both married well and finished life with honor and wealth. Tennie, as Lady Cook, was the moving spirit in the purchase of Sulgrave Manor.

Mrs. Woodhull was not a popular figure in the Demorest home, which Dr. Beecher had often visited. Mr. Demorest chilled off to Theodore Tilton, too, and no longer ran his poems in his magazine. Crusades were in the air, the logical sequel to the high-powered villainy and scandal of the 1870's. The Rev. T. De Witt Talmage, of Brooklyn Tabernacle, stepped into the breach as Dr. Beecher fell from grace. He preached lustily and wrote extensively on the "abominations of modern society." He searched for sin in the obvious places and found it. Tall, red-whiskered, ungainly as he went along with arms swinging like windmills, he toured the brothels, gambling houses and concert saloons. His blistering sermons on "The Night Side of New York" took the town by storm and packed the Tabernacle, which seated 5,000 persons. It was fire and brimstone preaching, focusing on vice, crime, and civic scandals. But *Demorest's* took him to task when he charged in a book published in 1872 that women oppressed women as much as men did. They beat them down to the lowest figure as milliners, seamstresses, mantua makers, said Dr. Talmage, with the added jab: "If a woman steps aside from the path of virtue, men may forgive—women never!"

This did not go unobserved in the private sanctums of Mme. Demorest and Jenny June. "Who is it that doles out the money for washerwomen, milliners, seamstresses, and dressmakers?" an editorial in the family magazine demanded. "Not women, but men. Who arrogate the right to control the income, and speculate or spend upon their own devices ten dollars to the one that is appropriated to woman's work in the family? *Men.* Who place the ban upon women? Who refuse to marry them when they have fallen through their means? Why, men."

But in the midst of all the commotion one sinful soul who had been riding high for a good many years was shot down cold on one of the five stairways of the Grand Central Hotel on Broadway, a newly finished marvel, eight stories high, crowned by three flagstaffed domes and advertised as the largest hotel in the world. The victim was Jim Fisk. The killer was Edward S. Stokes, who had appropriated Josie Mansfield, Fisk's mistress. Dark-eyed, softly rounded, flashy and fearless, Josie had been seen for years with the Prince of Erie, heading for the races in his six-in-hand, driving through the park in his Clarence, a vehicle upholstered with gold cloth; sailing in the *Plymouth Rock*, with its gilded dining room and marble barroom; marching into Delmonico's in a dazzle of diamonds and feathers; acting as hostess to his friends in her brownstone house on Twenty-third Street. Fisk's days of driving to the races in a drag loaded with chorus girls and drawn by black and white horses with gold-plated harness and Negro postillions in white livery were over forever.

His star had been falling with the exposure of the Tweed Ring. By this time Thomas Nast was lecturing in New York. With *Harper's* and the *Times*, he had played the key role in the collapse of the Tammany forces. He had left his mark on the history and nomenclature of the land by pinpointing the Tammany Tiger, the Republican Elephant, the Democratic

Donkey. *Harper's* had stood firmly behind him even when the house's publications were boycotted by the public schools. The Erie Ring and the Tweed Ring had interlocked. In the final stages Jay Gould, who had tried with Fisk to corner gold in 1869, deserted his old ally. The tall circus hostler, the Vermont peddler with waxed mustache, whose flashy looks and ways had been making history for years, was gone and his enemies as well as his friends stood by his bier. Gruff Tweed and suave Mayor Oakey Hall were under indictment. One would retire to write. The other, Tweed, would die in jail in 1878. The ring had plundered the city for untold millions.

But New York, with its growing wealth and sophistication, had pirates at both ends of the social scale. Bank messengers carrying gold and greenbacks through dark alleys and up narrow stairs were sometimes garroted by thugs who worked in teams. Some of the banks had carriages with police officers to ensure the safe transfer of funds. The fashionable regions were the most dangerous for the citizen. There were many robberies on Murray Hill. An entire row of houses was sacked in one night, and neither bulldogs nor private watchmen were able to prevent these depredations. The thieves worked with skeleton keys, revolvers and bowie knives. Few people would walk the fashionable streets alone at night, lest someone leap out at them from dark porticoes or badly lighted basement steps. One wealthy man gave up his home after being chased into it on several occasions.

Fine old trees still stood around the wharves where outdated ships discharged their cargoes. The spire of Trinity was the downtown landmark and birds still wheeled around it. The Fifth Avenue Bank opened in the Sherwood House at Forty-fourth Street and Fifth Avenue in 1875. A special parlor had been fitted up to draw in feminine trade. It was richly carpeted and discreetly furnished, and the whiskered men in the cages had been instructed to make everything crystal clear to the bewildered ladies entrusting their fortunes to the bank's care. Nearby, trains puffed in and out of the Grand Central Depot, with its red-brick walls and cast-iron trimming, painted white to suggest marble. The tracks were sunk below surface level in 1872, forcing squatters to move on. Steel locomotives had been banned south of Forty-seventh Street in 1857. But there were plenty of accidents while the trains still ran above-ground.

Central Park was finally completed in 1876, although New Yorkers had been enjoying rambles and drives in the general area for years. It was first envisioned by Andrew J. Downing, drawing his inspiration from the parks of Europe. In 1858 prizes were offered for the best design. Out of thirty-three that of Frederick Law Olmsted and Calvert Vaux was chosen. Richard M. Hunt, responsible for many of the great mansions of the day, went to work on it. At first it covered an area of 776 acres. Eventually it embraced 843 acres, with walks, terraces, gardens, bridle paths and lakes. It was necessary to buy 7,000 lots and settle many claims before the work could go ahead. Half a million trees, shrubs and vines were planted. Squatters were evicted. Property values soared. Those who could afford it moved northward to bask in the verdancy of the great new Park.

Soon there were seven miles of carriage roads, six miles of bridle paths and twenty miles of walks. Dodworth's band played in an ornate Oriental pagoda, and no carriage could drive past in the middle of a musical number. All classes enjoyed the shade, the verdancy, the grottoes and rustic houses, the bridges and picturesque nooks. Awnings made shady spots for resting. There were nurseries and goat carriages, camel rides and swings to keep the children busy, and they fed the swans or sailed in small boats on the lakes. Driving and trotting flourished through the 1870's until this craze declined and polo ponies, hunters and hackney cobs gained in grace. Soon tandems and dogcarts supplanted the sulkies and buggies, although dogcarts were frowned on at first. Every kind of equipage ambled through Central Park with every sort of citizen in it. The young pre-

ferred the phaeton. Their elders were disposed to ride in spacious barouches or to shut themselves up in closed broughams.
Mrs. August Belmont startled spectators whenever she appeared
in her curious demi-d'Aumont, an import from Paris. By
this time New York had acquired its own Rotten Row and
plumed ladies cantered sidesaddle in groups or with liveried
attendants, usually before breakfast. But English sparrows were
in disgrace and New York State had made it a misdemeanor to
feed or harbor them. Within twenty years they had spread from
the parks of New York to the Rocky Mountains and had become a public nuisance. They drove away the songbirds, almost
exterminating the robins.

As Central Park developed, the affluent built their houses on
either side of it. A. T. Stewart died in 1876, the year in which
the Park was officially opened. His neighbor, William Back-
house Astor, whose real estate holdings by this time were vast,
had died the year before. A number of the merchants who had
long clung to lower Fifth Avenue began moving uptown. To
get away from the brownstone tradition Mrs. Mary Mason
Jones, daughter of banker John Mason, put up Marble Row between Fifty-seventh and Fifty-eighth Streets on the East Side
and settled there herself. Here the spectacular Mrs. Paran
Stevens, wife of the owner of the Fifth Avenue and other hotels,
was reluctantly received into the fold. Soon the wilderness above
Fifty-ninth Street became the area of mansions owned by men
with great fortunes. Henry Phipps, Charles T. Yerkes, William
A. Clark, Daniel G. Reid, William B. Leeds and Andrew
Carnegie settled eventually on the strip that came to be known
as Millionaires' Row. The Demorests joined in the early exodus
uptown and settled close to the Park. They took a mansion at
21 East Fifty-seventh Street, and soon Mme. Demorest could
be seen in her landau driving down to her emporium over the
Belgian paving blocks. Kate lived with her and had a large room
upstairs, where she worked over her pattern designs. The new
house was a four-story building with an English basement.
There was plenty of room for the young people who came and

went, and for Mme. Demorest's receptions. They soon bought a
farm at Claremont and drove out there on Sundays for chicken
dinners.

Because of her deep interest in all philanthropic organizations
affecting women and children, Mme. Demorest was gratified by
the establishment of the Society for the Prevention of Cruelty
to Children in 1875. It sprang from the earlier organization of
the same name for the protection of animals. Henry Bergh, who
inspired this protective move for children, called on the Demorests and gave them the Society seal, which they had engraved to
use with their editorial comment: "The question of cruelty to
children is as capable of solution as the question of wife-beating,
and one can be made as rare and disreputable as the other."
Both were in frequent usage at this time and children were the
victims of drunken parents, strange punishments and forced
child labor. The ragged, starving child of the slums was not a
myth in the 1870's. The Demorests thought that the moral
effect of public opinion in this instance would serve to prevent,
even more than to cure.

Demorest's took a firm stand on questions of prison reform,
the treatment of the insane as advocated by Dorothea Dix, and
other experiments in the social science field. It welcomed the
establishment of the Young Ladies' Christian Association, the
Working Women's Unions, the United Grangers and the National Conference of Charities and Correction. Jenny June
warned the women's clubs not to limit themselves to the narrow
channels of sewing, philanthropy and small ideas but to drive
for intellectual goals and organizations designed to train women
for public affairs. Sometimes opposing voices spoke out quite
loudly in the pages of *Demorest's*. Lady Burdett-Coutts, England's wealthiest and most philanthropic woman, was protesting
the use of the plumage of hummingbirds as feminine ornaments
at this time. At a ball given in Paris by the Duc de la Roche-
foucauld for the heir to the British throne, one woman had
appeared in a dress made up entirely of the skins of canaries.
Another wore a robe quilted with the tiny blue feathers of the

jay, and a third wore a costume powdered over with hundreds of minute ruby hummingbirds. Lady Burdett-Coutts' good works were legendary, out of the bottomless reserve of $65 million. She always chose the unusual way of spending her money and was an object of great interest to the suffrage pioneers of America. She liked to build churches, endow missionary dioceses, lace London with improved tenement dwellings for the poor, back small industries, and wage her own campaigns in her own unusual way. In 1881 at the age of sixty-seven she married William Ashmead-Bartlett, a Philadelphian of twenty-nine, who took the name Burdett-Coutts.

The rise of Italian opera and ballet in America was closely observed in the columns of *Demorest's*. Patti, after being sensationally presented in 1859 by her brother-in-law Maurice Strakosch, had decided to stay in Europe and it was long before Americans heard her again. Clara Louise Kellogg, a native American singer, was coming into view. Louis Moreau Gottschalk, pianist and composer from Louisiana who had worked in Europe with Chopin, was a matinee idol who was all but torn asunder by his worshipers when he made public appearances. Singers and instrumentalists performed regularly in Steinway Hall, and the Philharmonic Society had five or six symphony concerts a year. The tempestuous Theodore Thomas charmed and instructed his audiences in New York and Chicago with his symphony concerts. For popular music the crowds flocked to Terrace Garden at Fifty-eighth Street and Third Avenue, to the Central Park Gardens, or to the Belvedere, far out in the country. Variety drew hearty audiences and a family trade to Tony Pastor's Opera House on the Bowery, where much musical comedy talent was developed that later fed the stage. There was a decline in the number of theaters as variety gained ground.

The year 1874 was a significant one in the theater, with Charlotte Cushman bowing out at last at the Booth two years before her death. "Never did the star of any tragedienne set in a blaze of glory more resplendent," commented *Demorest's*.

Mark Twain's *The Gilded Age* was a success. Boucicault had written a new play for Wallack's. Twenty-three girls dancing the can-can were arrested at the Metropolitan Theatre early in 1875. The audience jumped up and headed for the street, and the girls, hiding behind the scenes, were dragged out in their spangled tights from behind barrels and boxes. It was all in the spirit of the 1870's. Albani was singing in New York that winter, having been engaged by Strakosch for the Italian Opera Company. Among his other stars at the time were Christine Nilsson, Clara Kellogg, Pauline Lucca, Campanini and Maurel. Meanwhile, Wilkie Collins, Anna Dickinson and Mary A. Livermore were stirring things up on the Lyceum circuit.

It was a period of restless groping by Americans for better things. Their homes reflected their changing values. They cultivated the foreign artist. Their taste in music was becoming more sophisticated. They traveled more. And among the most zealous of travelers were Mr. and Mrs. Demorest. In the spring of 1875 Mme. Demorest set off for Mexico with Susan King and sent back her impressions to the magazine. She did not often write for it, but when she did she gave a practical account, quite typical of her nature, of what she saw and did. Both women were taken into the official fold and received honors not usually accorded to their sex in Mexico. They attended the opening of the National Congress and were entertained by President Lerdo. Mme. Demorest was made a member of the Geographical and Statistical Society of the City of Mexico. She visited the School of Mines and in particular studied the educational methods in Mexico, another of her major interests. She appraised the orphan asylums, took stock of the food in their storerooms and the clothing the children wore.

There was business to conduct, too, as she traveled, and she visited two mercantile clubhouses in Vera Cruz and talked fashions to many merchants there and in Mexico City, where she had an agency. Mme. Demorest decided that the women's dress was completely Europeanized but that the fashions were several years behind the times. She was interested in the fine linens, silks, laces, embroidery and native jewelry in the shops. The more fashionable women rarely entered stores, she observed. Usually the wares were brought to their carriages for examination. The two tourists visited Havana also on this trip, where another agency was established, and Mme. Demorest, an excellent sailor, wrote graphically of their experiences at sea.

After her return home, Mr. Demorest set off for Europe. By August he was in Lucerne and as he traveled through Switzerland he was struck by the thought that it was strange "a country so rich in natural gifts should be so poor in its evidences of human life and progress." It seemed a paradise of a country but "the people needed reconstructing with some of our enterprise." He watched the women pounding their washing at the river's edge and thought this primitive. The luxury hotels compared favorably with those of Saratoga. But as he traveled through Berne, Strasbourg, Mayence and Cologne (with the fragrance of its toilet water pervading the air) he observed women working on the roads, in clay pits, in coal mines, digging and planting and "wherever hard labor is to be done, all over Europe." He longed to help the women who carried loads on their heads and to rescue them from the babies strapped to their backs.

The railroad cars in Switzerland struck him as being "democratic" and the Channel boats wretched—"mere tugs, decks lined with wooden benches, ladies in shawls and waterproofs, men to neck and ears in their mufflers, nothing like the magnificent Sound or North River steamboats." The coaches from Dieppe to Paris were uncomfortable but the scene outside was engaging—red poppies mingling with the grain, thatched cottages and peaked roofs, land cultivated to perfection. In Paris he went sightseeing by night and by day. After viewing miles of pictures, of statuary, of shops, he wrote: "Who could imagine that, under this brilliant exterior, so much of vice, and misery, and wretchedness, lie concealed?"

But he thought it extraordinary that Paris should have recovered so quickly from the siege. "The destruction in palaces and monuments burned, in damaged houses, in commerce and business lost, and in various other ways was about . . . $125,000,-000," he wrote for his magazine of January, 1876. "But the debts have been nearly paid, the buildings mostly restored, and hardly any evidence now exists of the siege or the fearful days that followed." He paid tribute to the genuine thrift and industry of the French and thought the price of their exports stupendous. Wherever he went Mr. Demorest took note of inventive or scientific touches. The French had recovered and the Demorest office on the Rue Scribe was ready for operation. The pattern business was flourishing on all fronts. So was the magazine.

From this time on Madame Demorest devoted more and more of her time to social life, travel and philanthropy and less to the emporium. With things running well she confined her interest largely to the creative side of fashion but she always appeared for showings and important occasions, and her name continued to symbolize the house. She no longer wore the little gold scissors attached to her bodice, a bauble suggesting her trade.

CHAPTER XI

Centennial Exposition

THE CENTENNIAL EXPOSITION of 1876 was a landmark in Demorest history, for the celebrated pair were revisiting Philadelphia, the city in which their first paper patterns were cut and exhibited. They returned to New York with two medals of honor and two diplomas of merit, adding to the awards that the patterns had been picking up for twenty years. In 1875 they had distributed three million patterns around the world. Mme. Demorest's display in the main building was one of the chief attractions of the fair for women, and correspondents from abroad pounced on it as they did on America's new machines and domestic improvements.

Bronze figures of nymphs stood at the four corners of a pavilion with a raised platform covered with an Aubusson carpet. Inside six wax figures displayed model gowns. One was a costly model of the Empress Eugénie. All were dressed in the latest mode. Two display cases of polished walnut with medallion monograms on the panels held patterns. Bound copies of the Demorest magazine stood on easels, and current numbers of the *Portfolio of Fashion* were displayed on music racks. A special case held Mme. Demorest's famous corsets in cardinal, cream, pale blue, black and pink, as well as her skirt suspenders and shoulder braces. The display summed up the Demorest history for all to see.

Both President Grant and General Sheridan were present for the opening and wherever these famous generals moved the crowd gathered and the applause was deafening. The Civil War was still a burning memory. Whittier's "Centennial Hymn," conducted by Theodore Thomas, was followed by the Grand March. Dom Pedro, Emperor of Brazil, was a feted guest, to the delight of Mr. and Mrs. Frank Leslie, who entertained him at Saratoga and functioned importantly at the Exposition. The Frank Leslie Pavilion advertised the family wares and Miriam was perhaps the most dazzling feminine figure there. That same year her husband founded a new periodical which he named *Frank Leslie's Popular Monthly*. It was cheaper in price and quality than *Harper's* and *Scribner's* and it quickly built up a large circulation. But two years later Leslie was bankrupt.

The great Corliss engine, 1,400 horsepower, that drove all the exhibits in the Machinery Hall, was the chief mechanical wonder of the Exposition. But among the minor novelties were a dishwashing machine resembling a squirrel cage, a life-preserving mattress, a handy little spring step adjusted to upper berths in steamships, the curious displays of the sewing-machine companies, American looms making ribbons, carpets and damask, cottons, pins and paper. In the century since the Declaration of Independence the railroad, the steamship, the telegraph, the sewing machine, gas for illumination, and countless other advances had come to pass, and much of it was illustrated at the Exposition. The telephone was just coming into use. Typewriters were on the market, although still regarded as curiosities. George M. Pullman was revolutionizing railroad travel.

Mme. Demorest moved about in regal fashion, viewing the Queen of Belgium's lace, mosaics from Italy, Dutch tiles and carpets, copies of the art treasures in the South Kensington Museum, stained glass, and the needlework in the Woman's Pavilion. Her own exhibit had been ruled out of this pavilion but had found an even greater following in the Main Hall. There had been a rumpus in advance about the pattern display. Jenny June had entered the fray when the ladies' committee of the Exposition, which had spent $30,000 on the pavilion, decided that anything out-of-the-way or of the reform order would not be accepted.

"By what right was anything, reformed dress, models of costumes, and ladies' clothing generally, placed under the ban of exclusion?" Jenny June asked indignantly. She felt that the committees of rich women should have been supplemented by working committees representing the labor interests of women. "It is perhaps a matter for congratulation and rejoicing that women are allowed a place in the Centennial at all," she added sarcastically, believing that it would have been better to have their work appear side by side with that of the men. In the end this was how it was with the Demorests' exhibit, although they had asked originally to display at their own expense a series of costumes in paper, illustrative of the fashions of the preceding century. Although eccentric styles such as the bloomer or reformed dress were banned in the Woman's Pavilion no one could accuse Mme. Demorest of trafficking in anything that was not ultrafashionable and feminine. Susan B. Anthony, coping with many problems of her own, took weary note of the feuding in Philadelphia. "I suppose the men will find money, by hook or crook, to visit the Centennial, but the women will have to stay at home." She lectured 120 times that season and had paid off the last of a debt of $10,000 that she had assumed when the *Revolution*, which she edited, failed. *Demorest's* defined this as a "phenomenal exhibition of moral sensitiveness and personal honor," and added that a man in the same spot would simply have gone bankrupt. But both Nell and Jenny June were gratified when the Press Club of Philadelphia let the women journalists of the 76 Club, and their writing guests from around the world, share in all its festivities in connection with the Exposition. This was one step up for the ladies of the press.

Susan's prediction that the women would have to stay at home was scarcely justified as the Exposition got under way and they came trooping in from all quarters, their hair piled high, their bonnets of eccentric and varied shapes worn well back on their heads, with lace strings fastening under their chins. A few sported paradise plumes. They wore double bracelets, one over the sleeve at the elbow, another at the wrist. Ball earrings went with their lace and tulle Fanchon ruffs. The Camellia polonaise, full and draped, topped everything, and the redingote and dolman were on view. They wore bows on their bustles, bows down their flounced and bunched-up skirts. Five-button English thread gloves took the place of kid as they walked through the hot summer haze viewing the wonders of the Exposition. *Demorest's* had warned them:

A quiet style for the street is the first law of good breeding and of true fashion. Let the black be rich, the brown dusky, the purple a veiled haze, and the blue scarce perceptible; but no "warm" or flashy wine-colors; no café-au-lait, no light tea-color for the street. It is not a triumph when the boys turn and comment audibly: "My eye, Jim."

Nevertheless, primrose, straw and salmon, as well as fawns and drabs, appeared in this gay parade. But times were hard. There had been a depression ever since the crash of 1873. The mercantile industry had been much affected, although every effort was made to have a good showing at the Exposition. There were ninety-two Stock Exchange failures in 1876 and the echoes of graft and corruption at national and civic levels would not die down. The South was deeply troubled. The Custer massacre had stirred up national indignation. A bitter fight was on for the Presidency and only Mrs. Grant had much belief that Ulysses would be re-elected for a third term. In the midst of it all Peter Cooper, a good friend of the Demorests, was being proposed for the Presidency by the Greenback party and he advanced considerable money for campaign purposes. Mr. Cooper was the son of a hatter, always a point of interest to Mme. Demorest, and was a born inventor, which appealed to Mr. Demorest. Glue, isinglass, iron and steel were the foundation of his great fortune, and Mr. Demorest heartily approved of the use to which he was putting it, and frequently applauded editorially his work for popular education. Peter Cooper, too, liked to go to Saratoga, and he studied history, religion and art. His favorite writers were Stephen Crane and Thackeray.

But John Bigelow was feeling pessimistic about the New York literary scene at the end of 1876. He wrote to Putnam's: "It looks as if we should have to get New England to do our writing for some time yet." On the social side there were many changes in that significant year in American history. The younger James Gordon Bennett, more dashing than his crabbed father, had introduced polo from England. His friends formed groups to practice in a New York riding academy. Finally he shepherded them out by coach to Jerome Park, and there the first American polo game was played. The introductory public parade of the Coaching Club was held that year in New York, too, with its founders, William Jay, Leonard Jerome and De Lancey Kane presiding in their bottle-green coats and yellow-striped waistcoats. Thereafter the picturesque tally-hos that traveled with a flourish from the Hotel Brunswick at Madison Square to Westchester became one of the city sights. Fox hunting was another imported luxury of the period, so that the noted names and the great fortunes had plenty of outlet in the field of sport and not the least of their pleasures was a magnificent equipage of one sort or another.

The cotillion was in high favor and dancing lessons had become intricate, to put it mildly. *Demorest's* illustrated the new steps with sketches and text. Innumerable girls got up in the family parlors and followed these demonstrations. But the editors, who watched both the social parade and the laboring classes with an impartial eye, put no less emphasis on the fact that there were seventy crafts and occupations open to women in that year. All were listed, from frame gilding to feather curling, from shroud-making to lithography, from press feeders to waxworkers, from pickling to preserving flowers, from silver burnishers to tent and awning makers, from bookbinding to cane seating, from carpetmaking to cigar making, from drawing on glass to making tassels, from harness-making to folding crape. Proofreading, bookkeeping, and ordinary clerical work were providing many openings and saleswomen were increasing in number. In addition *Demorest's* regretfully reported on an army of little girls from seven to ten who picked out bastings, ran errands and acted as cash girls.

Sorosis had a lively Valentine party that year in honor of the wedding anniversary of the Crolys. A large banquet room at Delmonico's was crowded with men as well as women and Jenny June received them all in amiable spirit. Mme. Demorest sent a lifeboat composed entirely of flowers for the occasion, and the Sorosis ladies, who by this time had settled down and were enjoying their success, supplied a bank of scarlet and white camellias. In the following year they had another dinner at which plans were laid to induce Frederick A. P. Barnard, of Columbia, to open the college lectures to women and to let them take the examinations. They thought that Columbia should show as much enlightenment as Harvard in its attitude to women, and at least give them teaching certificates. The Sorosis members kept niggling away until a powerful committee of New York women presented a petition to the college authorities. The trustees pleaded lack of funds and various objections to coeducation, but conceded a point. They would suggest courses of study and test the proficiency of the young women who took them. In the end Dr. Barnard was quite won over but Jenny June and Mme. Demorest were aging and he was six months dead when Barnard College opened in 1889.

Their other point of agitation in 1877 was a protest against women standing for endless hours in the stores without rest. They were also busily at work on the public school system. After eleven years they were prospering but were not letting the grass grow under their eager feet. When Sorosis took up a cause it meant business. Its committees worked on women in art, in the drama, in science and education. But all stood still for a moment in May, 1877, when Alexander Graham Bell electrified an audience in Chickering Hall at Fifth Avenue and Eighteenth Street with a demonstration of the uses of the instrument he had invented. A few days earlier he had introduced the telephone at the St. Denis Hotel, transmitting musical selections played by a cornetist in Brooklyn. That same month the first telephones were installed in the Fifth Avenue section and by 1880 thousands were in use. Dr. Bell's first message was transmitted in Boston in 1876 and his invention was the sensation of the Exposition of that year.

A great fashion figure faded from the scene in 1877 when Mrs. Hale, nearing ninety, retired. Entering the field to support her five children she had been the heart and soul of *Godey's Lady's Book* for forty years and had supplied much of its text, with the ambivalence of one who got her message across while she pushed high fashion. She, too, was a secret drinker at the fountain of emancipation and it sometimes showed in her tactful prose but she never abandoned the ladylike role. From time to time she had run the writings of Irving, Poe, Lowell, Longfellow, Whittier, Emerson and Bryant. Marion Harland was one of her regular stand-bys. Like Jenny June, Mrs. Hale defended spinsters and abhorred bloomerism. She had a distinctive place in the fashion world and there was interest in the Demorest shop when she retired. Two years later she died. By this time Mme. Demorest was in her early fifties. She looked vigorous and young, always preserving her erect carriage and staying slim in a well-padded age.

The magazine, ever mindful of the dedicated worker, devoted some comment in October, 1877, to the quiet garb of the professional woman. Those of "acquired intellectual position" needed little embellishment. A rich black silk with lace served almost as their uniform. "Joke as paragraphists may about the unloveliness of independent professional women," said *Demorest's*, "an unmarried one is rarely to be seen in public without a train of admirers and attendants, while pretty and stylishly dressed girls are neglected, or permitted to waste their sweetness on married men or elderly beaux." Brains were having their innings, or so one might assume from the columns of *Demorest's*. But the sad fact was recorded that these same women wore high button boots with low heels and carried black fans against somewhat muddy complexions. Since Mme. Demorest had just returned from a summer abroad, and had seen fashion at its most flamboyant, this sober sight must have struck her at once.

The year 1877 was an uncommonly festive one at Saratoga. The hundredth anniversary of the battle of Bemis Heights was celebrated in September and the Burgoyne Centennial at Schuylerville in October. The cornerstone of the great monument was laid that October on the centennial anniversary of the surrender. It was the most imposing ceremony in Saratoga's history, with a procession two miles long, civic pageants, orations and patriotic exercises. The Demorest family missed these events because a business trip to Europe was needed to survey their growing interests there and to make arrangements for their exhibit at the Paris Exposition of 1878. Besides, Mme. Demorest wished to cover the openings. The Butterick competition was getting keen. The circulation of the *Delineator* had passed the 25,000 mark and by 1880 it would reach 85,000. New departments were being introduced. The tie-up on patterns was formidable. At the same time the Frank Leslie competition was declining. Miriam did a grand tour of the West with her husband that year, her avowed object being to write a travel book. They had one long, triumphal jaunt from coast to coast, over the prairies, through the canyons, out into the desert. Mrs. Leslie visited Brigham Young in the Lion House. She dined with Senator Sharon in his ornate home Belmont and was reminded of Versailles as she sat beneath the crystal chandeliers. She swept through the rococo splendors of the Palace Hotel in

San Francisco. But the financial crisis of 1877 and the multiplicity of his properties had caught up with Frank Leslie. The circulation of his magazines was dropping. Real estate values were down. His speculations at Saratoga had been disastrous. The Centennial Register was a heavy loss. Miriam's Worth gowns and extravagant ways had not helped. He went bankrupt and assigned his properties. In the spring of 1878 he moved from Pearl Street to Park Place. Meanwhile Miriam's book came out to a mild stir.

Jenny June accompanied the Demorests on their 1877 crossing, as did Vienna and young Will. At the ship concert on the *Britannic* Ole Bull played and his wife accompanied Vienna when she sang. On the way from London to Liverpool they visited Coventry and were shown over Cash's manufactory for the ruffling and trimmings that bore the famous Cash trademark. All were entranced to find the factory in a small village, with gardens and homes for the workers. Men, women and children made ribbons and galloons as well as frilling. Jenny June and Mme. Demorest disapproved of the fact that women were not allowed to share the dining room of this utopian settlement. "They should be," wrote Jenny sharply.

In Paris they found all the women wearing their hair in Mme. de Sévigné style, with rows of straight little curls or with spit curls on their cheeks. The skirts of walking dresses were cut round and at last completely cleared the street. While Mr. Demorest attended to business his wife and Jenny visited the couturiers, and strolled along the Rue de Rivoli and the Palais Royale, admiring the glass, china, lace, lingerie and bijouterie. From three to five they drove in the Bois and at night saw Paris gleaming softly in miles of diffused gaslight arranged in crescent style. But on the fashion end Jenny was disappointed. Where were the smart women outside the salons? After Saratoga, the fashion show was flat and she thought the average Parisienne badly dressed.

After visiting the larger stores—the Louvre, Le Bon Marché, Petit St. Thomas, Le Printemps and Le Pauvre Diable—she decided that even after fittings no one came out looking like the customers of Lord & Taylor, Arnold Constable, or A. T. Stewart. It was different in the scented salons of the big couturiers, but even there she noted that "no wealthy Parisienne, not even one of the grandes dames, would think of indulging in the number of expensive toilettes sported by one of our fashionables at Saratoga. Nor do they so readily follow the caprices of fashion." If one could find a good fast dressmaker in Paris a gown might indeed be run up for half the New York price and with perfect fit and finish, Jenny conceded. The handkerchiefs, stockings, fichus, laces and cravats won her admiration. Lingerie was becoming more form-fitting as gowns narrowed down. Like the impartial observer she was, Jenny noted that a good étage in Paris cost $600 a year and she described in detail the kitchen arrangements in the modest home and the cost of food.

Mr. Demorest and Henry spent considerable time in their offices on the Rue Scribe, for Mr. Demorest was a businessman who worked ceaselessly at his trade. The American Consulate was in the same building. On one side were the offices of the White Star Line. The Grand Opera House was opposite and the Hôtel de l'Athénée to the right. Henry, who had been over for some time, was taking charge of the Paris office. He had inherited his father's business capacity, and he stayed on that winter and helped to complete the arrangements for the coming Exposition. Vienna remained to study music. But Mr. and Mrs. Demorest and Will returned in 1878 on the *Adriatic* to see the Exposition and take in the fashion showings.

Pilgrimages to Europe were becoming an annual event in the Demorest family. On the White Star liners they found the cuisine equal to that of the best hotels. They were also glad to observe that the "steerage accommodations are as superior in their way as those for cabin passengers." In fact, young women could travel with "more safety from intrusion than on some of our great first-class steamboats." The paraphernalia that accompanied the passenger on each trip was formidable. Passengers took their steamer chairs with them and all manner of rugs and valises, as well as the Saratoga trunks that went into the hold. The simplest kind of wardrobe suggested by Mme. Demorest for travel involved a dark walking-length costume with a jacket to complete it, and a shawl or ulster to be thrown over the shoulders at a moment's notice. An old black silk skirt and a couple of blouses, a silk dress and one of black Italian cloth, two thick woolen shawls, a close felt hat and a good gauze veil, would take one comfortably from London to Athens. This was not the way Mme. Demorest traveled, however, for it was her policy never to look anything but her best. Her trunks were well filled.

Mr. Demorest thought that Paris was worse off in the spring of 1878 than on his previous visit. Capital was not being invested and except for the preparations for the Exposition nothing was going on that would provide employment. "The poor are already crying for bread," he wrote, "and as change is the characteristic of the French, this state of things cannot last very long." He did not think well of the arrangements for the Exposition and feared that guests would be treated in the same disgraceful manner as at the Vienna Exposition of 1873. He thought it a pity that the government had decided against erecting an immense statue to the Republic in the center of the grounds, and had settled instead for a cheap, plaster monument of less heroic size. By July Henry was writing back to the family magazine that the American building at the Exposition was the most inferior of the lot. He had been watching the preliminary arrangements with some concern. The British section in the Main Building was four times as large and quite overshadowed the American section. The Austrians had an arcade arched like the Rue de Rivoli. Switzerland had an elaborate chalet with spires and belfry, Tunis a graceful mosque and Holland a fine house in the old patrician style. Spain had an Alhambra effect. The Chinese and Japanese pavilions were gaily colored but Henry thought they looked incongruous in their setting. When the Exposition opened he was even more dismayed. All the smaller countries, even Belgium, had done better than the United States. The Algerian Palace was the largest and one of the most attractive pavilions in the Trocadéro grounds.

Henry, an expert observer in this field, was critical of the fashion section. It was altogether too elaborate and showy, he thought. "Very few *ladies* would make themselves so conspicuous as to wear the gowns." The materials were heavy and rich and women were trying at the moment to look like the subjects of old masters. Brocades were interwoven with silver and gold. Satins had raised-velvet designs. Silk embroidery was encrusted with silver and pearls. Oriental colors were introduced in minute lines and dashes. The total effect was sumptuous and anything but in the American tradition.

A model of the New York Post Office, made up of 284,000 pieces, was on display in the American Building. A Pullman car in steel and copper was all that a train should be, Henry decided. Sarony of New York was represented with charcoal drawings, Mason & Hamlin with its famous organs, and Tiffany with diamonds and silver. The London *Spectator* of September 21, 1878, took special note of the Tiffany silver: "We confess we were surprised to find at the Paris Exposition that a New York firm . . . had beaten the old country and the Old World in domestic silver plate." The famous Tiffany diamond had been found in the Kimberley Mine that same year. But *Demorest's* deplored the American Art Exhibition, saying that it fell as far short of perfect representation as had French art at the Centennial Exposition in Philadelphia.

When the family arrived in force they toured the grounds and drove around in the six-passenger voitures that whizzed from building to building and were even seen on the boulevards, looking like perky little bathing machines. The Grand Cascade at the Trocadéro was less dazzling than they had expected. Four gilded statues guarded the corners of the basin but the water flow was meager and showers of spray were blown in the faces of spectators. The captive balloon of the Tuileries hovered night and day thirty feet higher than the Arc de Triomphe and everyone in Paris was conscious of it. Each ascent cost $4 and Americans sampled it with enthusiasm.

The Demorest exhibit met with its usual success and earned the top fashion award in its class, as was now traditional for them at every world exposition. Theirs was a limited field and Mr. Demorest was an expert and experienced showman. The New York *Graphic* of April 29, 1878, observed that the Demorest operations were breath-taking: "Their harmless little productions are revolutionizing, or rather guiding and directing, fashion all over the world, and are sent by the ton to London, Berlin, and even to Frankfort, Amsterdam and St. Petersburg. Holland takes to them rapturously. So does Russia. . . . The demand grows with inconceivable rapidity and only stops short with the actual limits of supply."

The Detroit *Free Press* gave the house of Demorest credit for putting across the skirt that cleared the ground. This was not wholly true but it was partly true. It had been a long fight. What the voice of the people had failed to effect, the mandate of fashion had at last accomplished, and women no longer clutched frantically at their trains to keep them out of the gutter. The same paper said that Americans felt elated that they set the fashions for their English cousins and that "Paris fashions are too extravagant to suit the subjects of so domestic a queen, and here is economy united to beauty and elegance." This was true on the level of mass fashions, if it did not apply to the women well enough off to buy from Worth and other top couturiers. *Demorest's* that year had shipped three tons of patterns to Britain, a half ton to Australia, and the Russians were asking for agencies. The general Demorest agents for Europe were Wilmer, Rogers & Company, and a distributing center had been opened in Vienna as well as in Paris, London, Frankfort, Berlin and Amsterdam. Canada, Mexico and Cuba all had centers. Henry settled down happily to run the office when his parents left Paris just in time for their autumn showing. Their European business had reached such proportions that a resident director was needed. By this time Henry was corresponding enthusiastically for the family magazine and was giving his impressions of life in the French capital:

Do not suppose that the luxurious French flats of New York are French! Why, a Frenchman would almost suppose himself in heaven if in Paris he should find all our modern improvements. Combined with American enterprise, Paris would certainly be the most attractive place in the world. And, oh American girls! do not pine for Parisian life, for with it might possibly come a Parisian husband. . . . Think of the formidable Code Napoleon that awaits you should you choose one of the inconstant mates.

The New York papers observed that the Demorests had returned "loaded down with everything new and desirable in the shape of ladies' wear." They had one of their most spectacular openings, but various strategic moves were under way at this time. They had decided to drop the title *Mme. Demorest's Mirror of Fashions* from their publication, although the contents continued in the same form. They were simplifying the format and by January, 1879, they had changed the title to *Demorest's Family Magazine*, the name it would bear until it expired in October, 1899. There was no evidence that the Demorests felt the financial pinch of the times, for patterns were cheap and people who could afford little else could still buy them, but the publication field was changing drastically and competition was keen.

Mr. Demorest was greatly saddened by the death that year of his friend William Cullen Bryant. Like Greeley, he had long been a familiar figure around town, walking every day on Broadway to and from the *Evening Post* building. Mr. Demorest wrote of him: "As a man he had the simplest tastes; temperate, using neither wine nor tobacco; he went early to bed and rose early. 'Bread, water and fruit,' he used to say, 'were enough for a feast.'" The temperance note was beginning at this time to show up strongly in *Demorest's*. "Liquors are now almost entirely abandoned in the more refined circles, it being considered as partaking of the bar-room to furnish means of intoxication, and to send men reeling through the streets as against the proprieties of our advanced civilization," he wrote optimistically, if not with precision.

New forces were at work across the country, President Hayes had withdrawn the last of the Union troops from the South. The telephone, the typewriter, the phonograph, the portable camera were penetrating the social order with all their promise for the future. But the railroad strike of 1877 had had severe effects on the economy. However, the life insurance companies were flourishing, for the war had emphasized their importance. The Metropolitan Life Insurance Company, which was chartered in 1868 and began business in two small rooms at 243 Broadway, by this time had $24 million worth of insurance in force and assets of more than $2 million, so that it had to move to larger quarters at Park Place and Church Street. The New York Life Insurance Company, founded in 1845 at 26th Street and Fourth Avenue in an area still being used for truck farming, also was prospering, and Americans were making a habit of taking out life insurance.

A. T. Stewart's Hotel for Women, occupying the block from Thirty-second to Thirty-third Streets on Fourth Avenue was finished and ready for a grand opening. It had cost the merchant $2 million, and he promised that the rooms would be $5 a week with board and no more. But his altruistic plan blew up. The five hundred or more women whom he had expected to flock to his magnificent hostelry were reluctant to take the plunge, and his death intervened. St. Patrick's Cathedral was at last finished and was dedicated in 1879 by Archbishop McCloskey. Its twin Gothic spires now dominated Fifth Avenue and radically changed the look of the city. It was built throughout of American marbles, and the architecture was modified French Gothic. It was called "Hughes' Folly" when John Hughes, New York's first archbishop, dreamed of it before Fifth Avenue ran beyond Twenty-third Street. He did not live to see it completed, for he died during the Civil War. It was designed by

James Renwick, who was also responsible for Grace Church, St. Bartholomew's, the New York Stock Exchange, the Smithsonian Institution and the Corcoran Art Gallery.

With its international interests *Demorest's* more and more watched the foreign scene. It carried a detailed description in 1878 of the marriage of the Earl of Rosebery to Hannah de Rothschild, richest heiress in England. The aisle of Christ Church, Mayfair, was strewn with primroses, the Rosebery symbol. The bride leaned on the arm of Disraeli as ducal England looked on with interest. Her wedding gifts were on view for three days at the Rothschild home in Piccadilly. They included the Rosebery family jewels, a painted fan that had belonged to Marie Antoinette, a silver coffee service from August Belmont, and a painting from Sam Ward of the Earl and his bride in a gondola drawn by six swans.

A new club for the working women of London had been opened in Seymour Place. Julia Ward Howe was floating about in Europe, working with the women of Paris and lecturing in French at Florence on "Female Education." Thomas Hardy's *The Return of the Native*, which had been serialized in *Harper's Magazine*, had just come out in book form. London University had been granted a charter enabling it to confer degrees on women students, although they took separate classes from men.

Clara Barton was working desperately to interest Congress in the establishment of the Red Cross in America. Twenty-five governments had signed the Treaty of Geneva, which left American legislators cold. Mrs. Antoinette Brown Blackwell, the first ordained woman preacher, had returned to the ministry. Her sister-in-law, Dr. Emily Blackwell, along with Dr. Mary Putnam Jacobi, was trying to turn the Woman's Medical College of the New York Infirmary into a first-class medical school by enlarging its resources. Dr. Elizabeth Blackwell, its founder and the great pioneer in her field, was living quietly in Hastings, and allying herself with social service causes in her native England. Dr. Jacobi by this time had been elected a member of the New York Academy of Medicine. The first woman editor in Texas,

Mrs. Bella French, had started the *American Sketch Book* in Austin. A daily paper in Chicago owned entirely by women had been launched by Mrs. Mary B. Willard, widow of Oliver A. Willard. Frances E. Willard was the new editor and her first statement was to the point: "We intend to belong to the constructive rather than the destructive school in journalism. It is so easy to tear down—so difficult to build."

This was an important move for the Demorest family. Before long Mr. Demorest would be working enthusiastically with Miss Willard on the temperance front. Up to this point there were only mutterings on the subject in the family paper. In July, 1879, Henry, back from Paris, made his first appearance as an elocutionist before a New York audience at Chickering Hall. Good-looking, athletic, witty in his delivery, he made an excellent impression. "Each piece on the programme was almost faultlessly delivered, and awakened the most lively enthusiasm," said the New York *Telegram*. "His style is intensely dramatic, and his illustrations of humorous character very amusing and effective."

CHAPTER XII

"Ours Is a Happy Land"

THE 1880's had a promising start, with prosperity gilding the nation. Money poured into the coffers. Crops, with the exception of corn, were good. Manufacturing activities were strong and growing. Speculation was creating its own aura of external wealth. The social picture was highly varnished, the lull between the financial storms of 1873 and 1884. Entertainments reached a new magnificence. The value of American textile products in 1880, a matter of special interest to the Demorests, was $533 million, and imported dry goods were valued at $136 million. The Metropolitan Opera House opened and the literary and artistic tradition flourished. Both the flesh and the spirit were being served.

The United States had become a big consumer nation. Its population was 50 million, with approximately one Negro to every seven white men. In 1881 the Europeans who passed through Castle Garden numbered 700,000, an explosive army destined to found many of the nation's great fortunes, to enrich its culture, to diffuse through the social body their assorted traditions, hopes, ambitions and hard work. Asiatics had been banned by federal law for ten years. Mr. Demorest urged his readers to subscribe to a base for Bartholdi's statue, yet to be raised in the harbor, reminding them that "our descendants will regard this great statue of 'Liberty enlightening the world' as a modern analogue of the Colossus of Rhodes."

Europe seemed like an armed camp at the time. Britain had assumed a protectorate over Lower Egypt. Gambetta, who had led the fight against Napoleon III, had been overthrown in France. A new electoral system had been introduced in Italy. The Land Leaguers were agitating in Ireland. The Black Hand was an overhanging shadow in Spain. The Communists were busy in France, which was steadily extending its dominion over Tunis, in spite of protests from Britain, Turkey and Italy. "The great conflict in Europe today is not political, it is social," *Demorest's* commented editorially. "It is a demand by the proletariat for some alleviation of their hard lot, some more equitable distribution of the results of labor. Happy America, that has as yet no such problem to face." But Mr. Demorest thought that the soul of man was not being served. It was an engineering age, an age of railways and canals, in which not man himself but his environment was being improved. The railroad between the Caspian Sea and the Black Sea was linking Persia to Europe, and giving Russia sway over the Black Sea. Russia was a mighty power but *Demorest's* did not believe that America had anything to fear from her; rather, the time might come when "we may divide the world between us." The completed Suez and the projected Panama Canal held all manner of implications for the future.

Henry M. Stanley was opening the Congo region, establishing trading stations and building up communication lines, and in this Mr. Demorest saw the promise of civilization's push into the secret recesses of Africa. "A mighty revolution seems to be impending in the center of the dark continent," he observed. The Pope had opened the Vatican library to scholars. The transatlantic run by steamship had been reduced to six days and ten hours at the best. The Canadian government was exploring Hudson's Bay. Canon Wilberforce was calling the attention of the people of England to the great revenue that the Established Church took from its gin palaces, beer houses and other "disreputable establishments."

America lagged in shipping. The tariff, the rebel privateers of the Civil War, and the substitution of iron and steel for wooden vessels, had curbed shipbuilding to the point where the annual output at the beginning of the 1880's totaled $150 million. Silks, too, a special interest of the Demorests, were a comparatively limited field. The world's output was $400 million worth, with China and Japan producing nearly a third of the total. American imports of silk amounted to $30 million and as yet gave employment to no more than 32,000 persons. But by the close of the decade a whisper of the future was heard when a silk manufacturer in Lille spun glass fiber with cloth. It took twelve hours to produce one yard of the material. To Mr. Demorest, now a successful and wealthy man, the picture as a whole was reassuring. His spirit was always one of optimism. Looking across his own peaceful land where, nevertheless, there were still a million adults who could not read or write, he was led to exclaim:

Ours is a happy land. It has no military burdens, nor has it a navy worth mentioning, and its army is composed of only a few thousand men to keep peace on the frontiers. Our revenues are so large that we do not know how to dispose of the surplus. How fortunate that we have no power upon this continent to dispute our supremacy.

Nearly four million farms had been dug from the nation's wilderness, most of them cultivated by their owners. In the older communities the disposition now was to sell the land and move to towns and villages. The United States was mining its precious metals and importing more. In 1881 it brought in nearly $100 million in bullion and its own available mineral wealth was racing ahead of that of all the nations of the world. Half the annual output of precious metals was being mined in the United States. An army was at work prospecting in the West and Southwest. Shafts were being sunk wherever there were indications that gold or silver might lurk. This was a good omen to Mr. Demorest. "It is idle to fear any evil result from great wealth," he wrote. "It is the nations that have had the most gold and silver which have been the most progressive and in which the highest civilization has been maintained."

The assassination in 1881 of the newly elected President, James A. Garfield, smashed across the calm with deafening reverberations. "Our chief magistrate should be surrounded when he goes abroad by some sort of retinue," commented *Demorest's*. Chester A. Arthur moved smoothly into the White House to take his place, and the President whose powers were never tested soon became the forgotten man. The social scene changed dramatically in the 1880's. The divorce rate was rising fast. Maine had twenty-three to one recorded fifty years earlier. "Marriage is no longer regarded as a religious sacrament," commented Mr. Demorest. "We live in an era when discontent is rife, traveling is easy and cheap, and the temptation to seek fresh fields and pastures new is ever present." Through his magazine he condemned the current lynchings in Tennessee and applauded New York State for passing a law making it a misdemeanor for the proprietor of a hotel or public conveyance to discriminate against any person on the ground of creed, color or race. "What a shame that it should be necessary," he wrote. "The race problem is an important one in this country, and will cause many political and social disturbances in our future history." Governor Alonzo B. Cornell's veto in New York State of a bill permitting women to serve on the boards of charitable institutions—a special interest of Mme. Demorest—was condemned.

Adolphus W. Greely was establishing bases in the arctic region with an eye to discovery of the North Pole. He had found new land north of Greenland. Mr. Demorest favored the annexation of Canada but not of Mexico, two controversial considerations at the moment and an issue that aroused great indignation north of the border. The United States was beginning to spread out. It had just appointed a Minister to Korea—"a country practically unknown to the rest of the world . . . the United States is the first in the field." Mr. Demorest predicted at this point that by the end of the century every land area on the planet would be known in detail and would be in commercial communication with the leading manufacturing centers of Europe and America.

With his eye shrewdly cocked on the trade markets of the world he deplored the operations of the speculators and rated Jay Gould the most powerful man of his time, between his railroad interests and his automatic control of the telegraph lines and cables. "Aladdin's lamp was a mere toy compared with the marvelous power wielded today by this most conscienceless speculator," he commented. But much as he deplored gambling Mr. Demorest had some good words for the financier:

Gould is a strange personage. He first made his appearance at the World's Fair in New York in 1855 to dispose of a patent mousetrap. He has since accumulated a gigantic fortune by means not altogether creditable to his moral sense, but withal he is a man without any small vices. He never uses intoxicating drinks or tobacco, nor does he play cards. He has a large family, and his domestic life is a happy one. . . . He is a sickly man, is constantly under treatment and is preparing a fine mausoleum for himself.

Peter Cooper, on the other hand, "got out of life probably as much as any man who ever lived and did not wait for others to administer his benefactions but saw they were distributed himself." He had the added virtue, in Mr. Demorest's eyes, of avoiding the demoniac pipe and wineglass. "What a different world it would be if everybody was as temperate, as sensible, and as good as old Peter Cooper," he commented shortly before this philanthropic citizen died in 1883. Thousands marched in his funeral procession, proving to Mr. Demorest, as he watched approvingly, that in public appreciation "the name of the man who loves his fellow-men 'leads all the rest.' " When Emerson had died a year earlier, Louisa M. Alcott wrote of him for *Demorest's* that the "triumph of character over prejudice, ridicule, indifference and misrepresentation had seldom been more truly exemplified than in his case."

Not only did Mr. Demorest lose a number of his old friends in the first half of the 1880's but it was a significant period in his own family fortunes. Three of his children married. He reorganized his magazine and gave preliminary signs of being ready to retire from the publication field. Vienna married Dr. James M. Gano in 1880. Henry and William both were married in 1884—Henry, a graduate of Cornell University, to Annie Lawrie, and William, a graduate of Columbia University, to Alice Estella Gilbert, leaving only Evelyn at home. In 1882 the price of the magazine was reduced to $2. Its circulation had nearly doubled in the previous year but the competition was strong. A new trend was visible in its pages. For two decades it had played to the woman reader. Now the announcement was made that it would enlarge its scope and become an "epitome of the great world—its human interests and industrial activities." There would be more emphasis on current topics, on novels and stories by distinguished writers, on historical and biographical sketches.

Henry took over the direction of the art work, which had always been a distinctive feature of *Demorest's*. His professional experience abroad had made him useful in a great many ways to his father's magazine. Will had just been graduated from Columbia in 1881 and he, too, became involved in the family business. No changes were planned on the fashion end. This department would remain under the direction of Mme. Demorest, "maintaining her high standard, free from exaggeration, and striving to be both representative and accurate in statement and illustration." The Ladies Club, which by this time had been copied by most magazines and many daily papers, inaugurating the future waves of agony and advice columns, was to continue as before, but in condensed form. The maunderings of the lady correspondents of the 1870's were to be curbed. They had been running away with the field. Home and household matters would still be treated in detail. In the new line-up of writers were Julia Ward Howe, Kate Field, Martha J. Lamb, Mrs. Margaret Sangster, Thomas Wentworth Higginson and Louisa M. Alcott. *Demorest's* was bowing a little to the times, and to the array of high-powered names that stared at them from competing magazines. They could already point, however, to having run the work of Thomas Hardy, Sarah Bridges, F. S. Saltus, Edgar Allan Poe, Mrs. M. C. Hungerford, Alice Cary and Ella Wheeler. Their own Jenny June was presented as "the acknowledged woman essayist in the country." And the premiums were still good circulation getters—at the moment a bust of Benjamin Franklin, a carpet sweeper, a gold thimble, a tea set of French china, and an assortment of novelties and knickknacks. A guitar and a Bible were likely to go out together, with happy results all round.

Mr. Demorest announced all these changes at a party given at his home on his sixtieth birthday in 1882. Sixty guests as close to the age of sixty as possible were invited. The festivities began at six in the evening and lasted for six hours. Six musical numbers were presented and six souvenirs went to each guest, as all were told to enjoy themselves "like sixty," in the slang of the day. Mme. Demorest always struck an original note when parties were in the air. She was expert at decorative touches and the effective disposition of flowers. Sixty white lilies were banked in a gold hamper with six cornucopias, filled with Jacqueminot, Capucine, Maréchal Niel and Victor Verdier roses. Six musicians played under dwarf palms and each guest received six roses in different colors. The drawing room, library and dining room were all thrown open in one long vista, with ceilings frescoed to represent the seasons—a design that had been used in the family magazine and had then been adopted by Mme. Demorest for decorative purposes in her home. By this time the Demorests had picked up a great many objects of art on their travels and their house was furnished with the prevailing lush effects. A life-size Lorelei on a marble pedestal in the drawing room had been sculptured in Rome by Mrs. Emma Phinney.

New York was beginning to assume an air of sophistication in the 1880's. Architectural graces were coming to the fore, with John La Farge and Louis C. Tiffany doing opulent work to beautify clubs and public buildings. La Farge, whose stained glass and murals were achieving great distinction, did the state dining room of the Union League Club. The coats of arms with the national emblems were the work of his friend Augustus Saint-Gaudens. Tiffany supplied the lighting effects. Stanford White was just getting under way with his new architectural firm and Saint-Gaudens was working brilliantly in his New York studio until 1885, when he moved to Cornish, New Hampshire. Both men were setting their stamp on the city's buildings. Mr. Demorest, with his uncanny knack of looking into the future, predicted the coming of the glass house—"some of our young readers may live to see not one but many cities of which the houses will be mainly of glass." He had watched New York grow from a city with a population of a half million to nearly a million and a half in 1880. He had seen the practical application of steam, the telegraph, the telephone, the sewing machine, the daguerreotype, the photographic technique, the lucifer match, the use of gas for domestic purposes, the cheap postal service, and at last electricity for light. In 1882 the shop windows of New York were just beginning to gleam with the strange new radiance from this source. Mr. Demorest had observed the discovery of gold in California, a tunnel being cut under the Alps, and the completion of the Suez Canal. He had also lived through the Civil War and rejoiced in the abolition of slavery. All this was recalled on his birthday.

He had watched the thread of commerce run north until by 1882 business houses flourished intermittently up Fifth Avenue, except for the stretch below Fourteenth Street. Dry goods stores, importers, jewelers, art dealers, publishers, had settled between Thirty-fourth and Fifty-ninth Streets, and the Avenue was becoming as much a street of commerce as of homes. Electric lighting, which had its New York tryout in 1881 in a brownstone house at 65 Fifth Avenue, was on its way to being run into towns and cities all over the country. The gas officials eventually joined the new force that they could not master or keep up with; but Charles Francis Brush's arc-light system of 1880, shooting blinding rays from a 160-foot tower at Madison Square, was a sensation if not a success. People reeled back from its shattering impact. The telephone had been catching on since 1878, when the first New York telephone directory was issued with 252 subscribers. In 1880 several hundred telephones were serving the downtown area, with nearly four thousand in use all over the city. The early listings showed a preponderance of hotels, transportation companies, publishing houses and mercantile establishments.

The success of the New York elevated railroad had incited other cities to follow suit—Philadelphia, St. Louis, Chicago and Cincinnati. In 1883 more than 90 million fares were bought on the New York elevated at 10 cents a person. Horsecars in the same year carried 116,065,223 passengers. The tangle of telegraph and telephone wires in the business district began to disintegrate after 1884 when the underground conduits removed this blemish from the growing city, but it was not until the great blizzard of 1888 that the last of the poles disappeared. The William K. Vanderbilt home at Fifth Avenue and Fifty-second Street, designed by Richard M. Hunt, was finished in 1881, to stand until 1927. Cornelius Vanderbilt's house, farther up the Avenue at Fifty-seventh Street, made a substantial change in the look of the thoroughfare. The château touch was distinctive. Across the way from the William Vanderbilt home was the soaring new Cathedral, and St. Thomas's Church opened at Fifty-third Street in 1883 in a congregational shift from downtown. By this time the Easter Parade was a recognized event, gaining status and size each year as women with trailing gowns and enormous hats walked to church escorted by top-hatted husbands wearing yellow kid gloves, while the Avenue glowed with flowers and the feeling of springtime. An odd anachronism was Ye Olde Willow Cottage and Tyson's Market that flourished with a rustic air at the southeast corner of Fifth Avenue and Forty-fourth Street. The willow tree in front had been planted by Mrs. John T. Mills, the owner's wife.

Downtown, close to the Demorest holdings, the wooden spires of Grace Church were supplanted by stone ones, and Isaac H. Brown, its famous sexton, ruled his territory with unflinching spirit, coldly eying the parvenus. Enormously tall, with a ruddy face and the air of a mariner, he went swaggering down the aisle and bowed the worshipers into their seats. It was the age of Brown's majestic funerals and expert generalship at weddings. He had a hand, too, in many of the fashionable parties of the day and could always supply a likely list of men for the harassed hostess. Before Ward McAllister had drawn the lines, Brown was an unofficial prompter with a retinue of equivocal titles from Europe on hand. Near Washington Square the Church of the Ascension, designed by Richard Upjohn and the oldest church on the Avenue, acquired its rare La Farge mural in 1888, an artistic triumph that had its effect on this type of decoration in America.

Far up the Avenue the Metropolitan Museum opened its doors in 1880, having moved north from Fourteenth Street. The massive structure was designed by Calvert Vaux and its possessions in time were to range over five thousand years of art and embrace at least a million objects that would be viewed by two million visitors each year. It began downtown with a collection of 174 paintings after being incorporated in 1870. Jenny June kept track of it from the start. The obelisk had now risen in Central Park and Mr. Demorest deplored it as being singularly out of place in New York. He was more optimistic about the Washington Monument in the capital, which had reached the stage of foundation laying in 1880. "This structure will be one of the first things to impress the traveler with the splendour of our capital," he predicted with precision. The Dakota had gone up at Seventy-second Street, the marvel of its day for space, size and comfort in living quarters. Its turrets towered against the open sky with a faintly baronial air, while goats grazed in the meadows across the way from it. But the event that stirred up the public was the opening of the Brooklyn Bridge in 1883, a day of wild rejoicing. It had long been in course of construction, and New Yorkers had taken a friendly interest in each new span, delay and mishap. They had begun to doubt that it would ever be finished.

Broadway was lively from end to end in the 1880's—"like a race course, a headlong gallop under whip, spur, and halloo." Ladies Mile was a source of constant entertainment to the women of New York. Their carriages bowled from shop to shop or they strolled along in encumbering petticoats, surveying the dazzle of jewels, fabrics and novelties in the windows. Some had been up early in the morning to shop at the Washington Market but more had sent their maids to perform this function. From midnight on, Fulton Street was lined with market wagons, loaded with tempting fare from Long Island and New Jersey. The berries glistened in the brightly lighted square as their owners slept on the carts until the early morning stir began, with the hotel and club wagons rattling down for supplies. The trains brought in as much as 80,000 gallons of milk a day. When the shoppers arrived they were a study in themselves—a few of the fashionables, a great many servants, the professional buyers, and a host of housewives of average means picking over the vegetables, joints and game. Coffee houses close to the market served dishes for five cents apiece. Round about were all-night restaurants and cheap eating houses, giving a festive air to the bustling scene. These abounded on the Bowery, Chatham Square and around Printing House Square, where the hard-driven wretches of Park Row were loquacious and observant customers.

Every variety of fish, bird and fowl could be found in the Washington Market, and all the game in season. The opening of the trout and salmon season at Fulton Market on April 1 was an event that brought sightseers flocking downtown as to Les Halles in Paris. The crayfish, the turtles, the terrapin from Chesapeake Bay, the salmon from the Columbia River, the shad in season, were quickly picked up by the hotel chefs. It was current legend that any dish from any part of the world could be served at Delmonico's. New York was distinctly a man's town in the 1880's. Their mates had not yet come into the open, but the ferment was working in the social body. Food in general for the family was by no means inexpensive. Diamond-back terrapin cost $35 a dozen for those who could afford such luxuries. Canvasback duck sold in batches of three for $5. Columbia River salmon was 60 cents a pound. A saddle of lamb sold for $5. Bermuda onions were $1 and peas $2 a peck. Lettuce was 12 cents a head and strawberries fetched $5 for six quarts. Canned fruits and vegetables were coming into favor and refrigeration cars brought spring luxuries from the South. But hawkers still passed through the streets in their carts, selling vegetables and flowers. A familiar street cry was "fine sweet corn."

So many families lived in hotels and boardinghouses that catering was a well-established custom and varied in cost from the most elaborate to the simplest of effects. Breakfast and dinner were served piping hot in silver-plated dishes kept in steam-heated copper containers and conveyed by hand wagon. The better hotels prided themselves on their cuisine. Madison Square had fashion's favorites—the Fifth Avenue, Albemarle, Hoffman, St. James and Brunswick Hotels, as well as the incomparable Delmonico's, which had moved up to Twenty-sixth Street by this time. Union Square in the 1880's had the Everett, Union Place, Westmoreland and Union Square Hotels. The St. Nicholas and the Metropolitan, the Windsor and the Buckingham rounded out the list of popular hotels which, like the clubs, could ring up twelve-course dinners for the town's gourmets and were always sure to be haunted by celebrities.

The rage for apartment houses was spreading, a movement touched off by the French flats of Eighteenth Street, which were immediately rented by young married couples of Knickerbocker tradition. The building was put up by Rutherford Stuyvesant. The flats were small and dark, but a concierge gave a faintly Parisian air to this innovation. People were prone to exclaim that the new apartments in general were piled one on top of another like boxes, sometimes as many as twenty-five apartments to a building. The handsomer flats had elevators and steam heating, with well-appointed halls and garbage disposal. The fanciest kind might reach eleven stories, with balconies on the upper reaches. These sometimes had timbered ceilings, tiled fireplaces, paneled walls, deep window seats and built-in cupboards. They were considered luxury itself as they rose steadily along Madison, Lexington and Fifth Avenues, and on Seventh Avenue and Broadway.

But the independent young women who were now toying with incipient careers of one kind or another found refuge in fine old houses that had been abandoned as trade encroached. They rented their own apartments, sometimes on a co-operative basis. They enjoyed their grate fires and marble mantelpieces. They had refrigerators built into the wall and good closets. At this time they were apt to embellish their walls with Japanese hangings, to write their letters on heavy black walnut desks, to relax in rattan armchairs, to keep their knickknacks and china in hanging cabinets. Many had pianos, and they painted sunflowers, hollyhocks, buttercups and daisies on any object that would take their handiwork. They made their own breakfasts and the caterer brought them their dinners in his hand wagon. A woman cleaned, made up their fires and did their laundry. Otherwise, they were able to live free and ambitious lives without a chaperon in sight. Jenny June approved, since they were women earnestly engaged in work. Even the most modest flats had Reform stoves and dumbwaiters. Unfurnished they might cost as little as $18 a month with another $8 added for fuel, light and food, but the more expensive ones rented at $700 a year for three rooms and bathroom. Servants were available for $12 a month.

Jenny June came to the conclusion, even in the 1880's, that science and mechanical skill had reduced the work of housekeeping to a minimum. Heavy furniture, splashy carpets, overpowering tapestries and gaudy wallpaper were giving way to more artistic and harmonious combinations. Both mansion and cottage were affected to some extent. The Queen Anne touch, with its revival of the old Dutch and colonial styles, was a welcome change to Jenny June from the brownstone houses as much alike as rows of candles. It affected both architecture and interior decoration. The so-called Queen Anne house with latticed windows, massive stonework and balcony fronts, could be bought for less than $10,000.

Jenny liked to take the elevated north to Yorkville, where the line of demarcation between the city and the hamlet had disappeared and there now were uninterrupted blocks of brownstone houses, with well-paved sidewalks and large stores. The old suburban air was gone. There were still trees to be seen, however, and fresh breezes blew over the region, stirring the sails of the little boats on the East River. When she set out to show a visitor the city she invariably rode with them from Bowling Green to 125th Street on the Sixth Avenue elevated. Then she walked them along Broadway, Fifth Avenue and Madison Avenue, between Tenth and Fortieth Streets, to catch the peak of the shops. She showed them Central Park, and the newly finished Riverside Drive, with its double row of young trees along the boulevard. The big show of fashion was in the Park between three and five when society set forth for its daily outing and the equipages were a sight in themselves. The Metropolitan Museum and the Lenox Library were of major interest, although the public complained that they could not get into the library except by ticket, and they were not permitted to roam at will among such treasures as the early Bibles, the Copleys, a Rubens, a Reynolds and other famous originals.

The Museum of Natural History, rich in anthropological specimens and fossils, with models of cave dwellings, made fine fare for the young as well as their elders. The Astor Library, in its own little acreage close to Cooper Union and the Bible House, was a rich mine for the reader, and the New York Society Library, in existence since 1754, had been settled since 1856 in its own house on University Place. Some of its 35,000 volumes carried the thumbprints of such readers as George

Washington, John Adams, Aaron Burr, De Witt Clinton, Alexander Hamilton, and John Jay, who had borrowed books from its early home on Nassau Street. More recently Dickens, Thackeray, Cooper, John Jacob Astor, Alexander T. Stewart, Audubon and Melville all had used it. Emerson and Edgar Allan Poe had lectured, and Fanny Kemble and Anna Cora Mowatt had given readings in its cloistered quarters.

A special treat for Jenny, permitted her as a journalist, was a tour of William H. Vanderbilt's art gallery, where she viewed his Millets, Corots and other masters, comparing them with the Stewart collection which she knew by heart. She paused to observe the fine mosaic floors, covered with Turkish carpets, the crimson plush and tapestry of sofas and chairs, the richly bound books, the musicians' gallery, the dimly seen conservatory. She considered Tiffany's something of a museum and showed it to guests in this light. The silver in its galleries and warerooms had a world-wide reputation. The Society of Decorative Art at 28 East Twenty-first Street and the Women's Exchange on East Twentieth Street engaged her interest as having special meaning for women. Jenny knew New York by heart and in spite of her constant drive for the betterment of the poor she paused from time to time to toss a bouquet to the men who had built up the fortunes that made many of these public institutions possible:

It is the fashion now to decry rich men, to intensify vulgar hatred and prejudice against them; yet in New York, and in most of our large cities, the public owe the best they possess to their prescient wisdom. The Astor family represent the finest element in our American life. The industry, the prudence, the forethought, the judgment, the wisdom and the liberality which characterized the founder of the house have been carried along in direct line from father to son, and the women of the family are as remarkable for wise charity as the men for business enterprise and discretion.

The fashionable areas were completely deserted in the summer months. Only the Casino and the Little Church Around the

Corner stayed open all the year round. The thieves made many raids while the clergy were away, schools were closed, and the big houses were shuttered. But the work of the City Mission went on as well as the Fresh Air Fund run by the *Evening Post*. Coney Island was a nearby haven for businessmen while their families were at resorts. They could sail down in the evening, dine on a hotel piazza and listen to a band play—the never-ending brassy symphony of the late nineteenth century. But with September the liners brought New Yorkers back from Europe. The vacationers returned from Newport, Bar Harbor, Saratoga, Long Branch and all the popular resorts. Shutters came down. Dust covers were removed. The butcher, the grocer, the florist took orders. Carriages rattled up and down the avenues. Delmonico's and the hotels were jammed with diners. Schools opened. The children returned brown and sturdy from the sea and mountain air. The theaters and opera gave tingling excitement to the evenings and the city was alive again. The Demorests still went to Saratoga with some regularity, although their trips abroad now cut into their old routine.

While the Sorosis went on its quiet and modest way, the men's clubs became more and more luxurious. The financiers who fought it out in the cockpit on Wall Street during the day settled at night into their easy chairs and sipped their brandy as they planned fresh forays, while the politicians discussed the state of the nation and New York affairs in particular. The click of the telegraph was a cheerful sound through the early part of the 1880's. Railroads, grain and metals provided ceaseless excitement. Carriages bowled up to the clubs with portly figures who seemed to carry the weight of the world on their shoulders. There were approximately fifty clubs in existence by this time—political, social, sporting, literary and artistic. Since the gold scare of the late 1860's the fever of speculation had grown, not dwindled. Teams could scarcely force their way through Wall Street on heavy buying days. Messengers crowded the vestibules and aisles surrounding the Gold Room in the Stock Exchange. But where once the financiers had watched the stock board in person they now used the telegraph and runners for most of their big deals. Commodore Vanderbilt, who had no office on Wall Street, had always worked through runners. But many now enjoyed the privacy of their offices as they made swift and portentous decisions.

The powerful August Belmont, representing the Rothschild interests as well as his own, functioned in dark, low-ceilinged chambers in a dusty granite building on Wall Street. Thickset, small and lame, he wielded great power in several different worlds as well as being one of the most potent figures on the financial front. Opposite the Union League Club when the new building opened in 1880 was an old-fashioned brownstone house that had stood at Thirty-ninth Street since 1856. It belonged to the descendants of John Gottlieb Wendel, who had been John Jacob Astor's partner in the fur business in a small house on Maiden Lane. His descendants would hang on to their property tenaciously, down to the last survivor, Ella Wendel, who died in the 1930's, a recluse in what by then was known as the Mystery House of Fifth Avenue. She had preserved the $2 million site largely to make sure that her dog might have the run of the yard behind the high fence that blocked off passers-by from her secret domain. The Wendel fortune, estimated at $80 million, began with furs and mounted fabulously with real estate.

The gambling that Mr. Demorest deplored was in full swing all through the 1880's. Men of all economic levels plunged in, often with disastrous results. The mania had spread across the land and to all classes. General Grant was one of those who thought optimistically that he was making a fortune on Wall Street. He was confident of this when he crossed the continent in the summer of 1883 and watched the driving in of the golden spike that marked the completion of the Northern Pacific Railroad. Back from their trip around the world the Grants at this time were living at 3 East Sixty-sixth Street, a few blocks north of the Demorests. The General was always recognized when he set forth, grave and contemplative, to walk over to the park, to go downtown to the offices of Grant & Ward, or to meet his cronies in club or hotel. His was the most recognizable face in the entire United States, including that of the President.

When his partner, Ferdinand Ward, told him in May, 1884, that he must raise $150,000 at once in order to save the Marine Bank of Brooklyn, which handled their accounts, the General went straight to his friend, William H. Vanderbilt, and asked him if he would lend him the money for twenty-four hours. It was a Sunday but Vanderbilt did not hesitate to make out his personal check to the great war hero. However, the handsome and persuasive Ward, who had used the General's famous name to cover his own swindles, absconded with the money and Grant was in one of the tightest spots of his career. Within twenty-four hours the entire country knew that he had crashed on Wall Street and was penniless.

Vanderbilt was ready to cancel the debt. He was wholly sympathetic to Grant, but the General insisted on turning over to him all his war mementoes and real estate holdings. The next year was one of excruciating agony for him as he toiled mightily on his memoirs almost up to the moment of his death from throat cancer at Mount McGregor. The country followed his struggle breathlessly and when he died in the summer of 1885 the city showed its affection for him in a most impressive way. "Such a funeral never before occurred in America and never will again," General W. T. Sherman wrote to Mrs. Grant, who had been too shocked to attend. The General's death was treated in *Demorest's* like Lincoln's, with mourning bands, and pages of pictures of the funeral procession.

When William H. Vanderbilt retired from the presidency of his railroad properties Mr. Demorest decided that he had been roughly used by the press. "Men with great business capacity ought to be our chief rulers," he commented, "but experience shows that they cannot get the popular suffrage at the polls." Three transcontinental railroads spanned the country after President Arthur's trip to the Northwest for the opening of Yellowstone Park and the golden spike ceremony. Mr. Demorest, always alert to matters of topical interest, strongly urged Americans to explore this region, which in his eyes had the mountains of Switzerland, the geysers of Iceland, the black forests of Russia and a character of its own. "There is nothing comparable abroad to our Garden of the Gods in Colorado, the Yosemite Valley in California, and the Yellowstone Park in the northwest," he wrote. "Millions of people will yet dwell in these vast spaces where at present the inhabitants can be counted by hundreds."

Chautauqua, with its temperance links, had a heavy play in his magazine, with emphasis on its educational features. Thousands flocked at this time to Fair Point in Chautauqua County, New York, where an auditorium seating 3,000 stood in a grove surrounded by cottages, and a large tent held 1,500 more. Speakers of all nationalities poured fiery words through the still summer air. Summer courses were given for small fees. There were concerts in the afternoons and religious events as twilight fell. Many of the visitors lived in tents like Arabs, paying 15 cents a night for their quarters. Arbors, bridges and winding walks embellished the grove, and statuary gleamed white through the foliage. The devout reformers of the period found it fertile soil for their causes. One of the most popular of the lecturers was Frances Willard, small, graceful and blooming with health. She had quick movements and magnetic delivery. Her blue eyes burned with great intensity behind glasses, for she was extremely shortsighted. She was born in New York State to parents from Vermont and her youth was spent between Oberlin, Ohio, and a Wisconsin farm.

Clergymen did not always stick to their pulpits during this period of revivals and fire and brimstone preaching. The militants included Dr. T. De Witt Talmage, of the Broadway Tabernacle, a galvanic figure sometimes lampooned as a pulpit clown, who conducted unconventional services in his vast auditorium, with stupendous musical effects and oratory that left his listeners limp. His shrewd eyes surveyed the scene from beneath thick jutting brows, and a fringe of hair dangled over his forehead. Dr. C. H. Parkhurst, of the Madison Avenue Presbyterian Church, was another campaigner from time to time and roused

the criticism of his colleagues when he made personal explora-
tions of the dens of sin. Dr. Parkhurst was epigrammatic in
style and the thoughtful listened to him attentively. Dr. John
Hall, of the Fifth Avenue Church, was calm, suave and immensely popular. He avoided crusades and achieved his reputation on the strength of his sermons.

Regardless of all his other taboos Mr. Demorest fully accepted
the theater and its actors, and reported with satisfaction that
prejudice in this field had declined greatly in the preceding
twenty years. His own magazine had always paid attention to
the world of entertainment, and particularly music. The opening of the Metropolitan Opera House in 1883, with *Faust* as its
first presentation, was one of the social events of the decade
and introduced a new era. The absence of a proscenium and the
horseshoe effect excited comment. The establishment of a true
opera house was a strong clue to the fact that America was
reaching out in cultural matters. The legend spread that the
Metropolitan was built because William K. Vanderbilt wished
to uphold the status of the newer millionaires who could find
no place for themselves in the limited number of boxes in the
Academy of Music. It was easy to freeze them out of the chosen
galaxy. The horseshoe was a great equalizer for the millionaires
of the period, even if it left a wide gap between them and the
happy music lovers in the top gallery. Soon the Golden Horseshoe became legendary as the great names of the era paraded in,
flashing with jewels, wrapped in ermine, cushioned in opulence.
The leading artists of the world brought fresh distinction to the
American scene with their performances at the Metropolitan.

Except for the new opera house no theater in the 1880's was
fireproof until the Broadway Theatre was built. A succession
of fires destroyed the Park Theatre, the Union Square, the
Standard and the Fifth Avenue Theatre before the asbestos
curtain became required equipment. The Rialto had finally taken
the place of the Bowery and Union Square as the theatrical
heart of the city. The Dime Museums still displayed their freaks,
from the elastic lady to the human pincushion, but the taste for

this sort of thing was declining and the Bowery was going down-hill fast. Gilbert and Sullivan had come into vogue. The hus-band of Christine Nilsson, Mme. Demorest's old friend, had gone insane and she had returned reluctantly to the stage and sung at Albert Hall. Edwin Booth and John McCullough both were appearing in London and *Demorest's* cheerfully observed that "American plays are received with as much acceptance as those which come from Paris or London." John Drew and Ada Rehan moved about freely in social circles and were popular in all quarters.

Sarah Bernhardt drew a tremendous audience at Booth's Thea-tre when she made her American debut in 1880 as Adrienne Lécouvreur, the part that Rachel had played on her last ap-pearance on the American stage a quarter of a century earlier. Crowds mobbed the theater and paid exorbitant prices for tickets. Bernhardt stayed at the Albemarle and swung across Twenty-third Street to the theater with a queue following her. An important audience had assembled with all the elaborate trappings of the 1880's, and James G. Blaine and Charles A. Dana both watched her with critical attention. But the New York *Times* gave her a dubious review, saying she did not com-pare with Ristori or Modjeska in the role, although effective in the death scene. The critic objected to her mannerisms, and particularly to the way she rolled her eyes. He conceded, how-ever, that she was a "positively great artist." A month later Lew Wallace's *Ben Hur* made the critics and the public sit up. The reviews were tinged with skepticism but a long-lived drama had been launched on the world.

At that time Blaine was defeated by Grover Cleveland in the presidential race, and in the bitter fight that preceded the elec-tion the Rev. S. D. Burchard slipped a stinging new phrase into the language of the day. He described the Democratic party as "the party whose antecedents are Rum, Romanism and Rebel-lion." Many thought that the use of this sinister phrase went far to defeat the Plumed Knight.

CHATER XIII

Girls Go to College

IN THE SUMMER OF 1882 Mr. and Mrs. Demorest watched the dedication of the new Hôtel de Ville in Paris and attended the unveiling of Jules Michelet's monument. The military drill of an army of children from the public schools for the civic ceremony impressed them and they found the gathering at Michelet's grave comprised "all the lights and luminaries of the world of letters, and of French journalism." They had arrived in time for the midsummer fete of July 14 and watched Paris enjoy its annual holiday. Mme. Demorest thought the Fourth of July in the United States flat compared with the abandon of the French populace, and Mr. Demorest noted that holidays in France entailed less drunkenness than they did at home. "The fireworks over, dancing began in the street—on the Champs-Elysées, the Place de la Concorde, the Place Madeleine, everywhere—and kept up all night with vigor," Mme. Demorest wrote home.

They stayed at the Grand Hotel and did their usual round of

the accepted points of observation. They took in the art exhibitions and Mme. Demorest devoted considerable time to the couturiers, but much of the excitement had gone from this world with Eugénie's downfall. The Empress now was prematurely aged. Her tall figure, once so erect, was bent and drooping. Her fair locks were white and scanty. Her bluish-violet eyes, so often celebrated by admirers, were watery and dull as lead. The famous oval face was wrinkled and pallid. "It has been my lot to see other queens in exile," wrote a Demorest correspondent, "but no one so strongly aroused sympathetic sorrow as does this widowed, childless, parentless, isolated ex-Empress."

Paris was still talking about the magnificent fancy dress ball that Mrs. J. W. Mackay had recently given. She appeared herself as an Oriental Juive, wearing blue velvet embroidered with gold. Her dark hair was braided with diamonds and topped by a lilac velvet toque, with a chain of diamonds passing under her chin. One of her American guests caused lively talk when he came in evening dress with all the colors reversed. His suit was white, his shirt black linen. His tie was of black lace; his gloves were black kid. He carried a white hat. This was the year in which Oscar Wilde was visiting America, and *Demorest's* commented favorably on the fact that his eccentric attire had created a fashion at the watering places for the relaxed flannel shirt, low shoes and knee breeches for men, which spelled comfort for the wearer.

Mme. Demorest called on Mme. Boucicaut, one of her old friends. The Boucicauts owned and ran Bon Marché, and now that she was a widow she was carrying on the business by herself with great success. She had put it on a co-operative basis, giving stock to her employees. Both the men and the women had well-equipped clubhouses and took classes in music, literature and languages. She had installed a pension and benefit fund for those needing temporary relief. Mme. Boucicaut, enormously rich, contributed half her fortune to charities and half to the Bon Marché. On this occasion she was giving a concert for her employees. As usual she was magnificently turned out in mauve velvet, with bracelets set with diamonds of fantastic size. The musicians were all young clerks, educated at her expense.

While in Paris Jenny June and Mme. Demorest usually found their way into the literary salon of Mme. Edmond Adam, author and editor of the *Nouvelle Revue*, who lived on the Boulevard Poissonnière and held court after the Franco-Prussian War. Many of the artists, authors, poets, diplomats and politicians assembled in her home, which was picturesquely furnished with Persian hangings, armor, statuettes and antique lanterns. Complex and distinctive, Mme. Adam had an independence of spirit that won her American visitors. Her home was a stronghold of the Republican party. "Such a woman is an honor to her sex, and remains unspoiled by the honors freely showered upon her," *Demorest's* commented.

Another Parisian professional friend was Mlle. Guillaumin, for twenty-six years director of *La Revue des Economistes* and of a large publishing establishment. Small, alert and witty, she was adored by her staff and she often entertained them at her home. She told her American visitors that "she would be for equal rights if she had time to claim them." Her flat was in the Rue Richelieu, over her printing and publishing offices. At work she wore a muslin cap and black skirt, with a loose jacket. She would not consider the application for work of any girl whose handwriting was not completely legible.

Mme. Demorest noticed that the grisette, as such, had disappeared from the streets of Paris. Shopgirls now wore bonnets with bright-colored ribbons and artificial flowers. Men had abandoned the blouse. The dress of the Parisian workers seemed less distinctive to her on this trip. Shopping had come closer to the New York pattern, and the difference in cost was trifling except in silk hose and gloves. The cheap days of Paris shopping seemed to be at an end, and styles were as apt to be American, German or English as French, since for the moment the great designers were in eclipse. The Mother Hubbard designs, inspired by the Kate Greenaway vogue, were the only novelties of the moment. But one gratifying change detected by Mme. Demorest was the shift of emphasis from the past to the present, from "autocratic and irresponsible authority to intelligent and representative action." Always alert to the democratic touch, as well as to good business, Mr. Demorest warned his readers to take fashions more seriously, if only because of their enormous commercial importance.

The tailor-made had swept suddenly into view in America. Redfern & Company of London had a branch adjoining Delmonico's and the well-dressed women sped there for the streamlined cut, leaving some of the modistes high and dry. The tailor-made led to the shirtwaist, and the shirtwaist to the glazed sailor hat, the tight-fitting jersey, the full skirt and ultimately the towering pompadour. Lily Langtry, the Jersey lily with the statuesque form, was responsible for the Lily Langtry coiffure, the Lily Langtry hat, the Lily Langtry manner, as well as the famous jersey. Shawls were out. The garment industry was taking hold, with all its significance for the future. Many of the arrivals at Castle Garden had found their métier. High buttoned shoes went with the tailor-made, and a pearl-handled knife with buttonhook and glove buttoner became a girl's inseparable companion.

Demorest's scolded its feminine readers for using too much powder and rouge on their faces, and for making up in public. "Paint and chalk belong to the stage, and are best left to the professional beauty there; a private lady, a *lady*, should hold herself above the vulgarity of paint." Meanwhile the Ladies Club was cheerfully recommending charcoal mixed with water and honey for the complexion, and Dr. Henry Ward Beecher, in a Demorest advertisement, was advising his fellow men to wash their faces with Pears' soap. "If cleanliness is next to godliness, soap must be considered as a 'means of grace,' and a clergyman who recommends moral things should be willing to recommend Soap," ran the ad. When someone expressed surprise that he should lend himself to this sort of promotion the good divine replied with pride: "I am told that my recommendation of Pears' soap has opened for it a large sale in the United States."

Bare arms were condemned in Chicago and bangs were under fire in New York. Jeweled garters were being bought as a fad. One bride received a $1,500 garter for a wedding gift, with her monogram in pearls and a motto set in diamonds. But the average jeweled garter cost from $100 to $200 and was a conversation piece in scented parlors. Men found their own favorite article of jewelry in heavy watch chains of rolled gold, with sliding guards and pendant rings for locket or seal. They went rousting about in pearl-gray or white plug hats and brown derbies. They clung to their high hats for business and church, and in the late eighties adopted the black straw boater for summer wear. Mark Twain wore lavender kid gloves, the prevailing fad, and looked quite dudish when he attended White House receptions.

On the feminine front small bonnets had upright crowns and close brims. Kid bonnets were embossed with gold thread. Round plush hats with Tyrolean crowns, adorned with strands of Roman pearls or cut-jet beads, turned up at every tea. Widows wore small bonnets of English crepe and were allowed dull ornaments after six months but no jet or glitter for a year. Bridesmaids had switched from white to colors. The Mother Hubbard wrapper, ancestor of the sheath, had become a fashionable item not yet associated with the missionary barrel. Waists were small, panniers were ruched, basques were pointed in 1883. Muffs had shrunk to doll-like proportions. And only the woman who had ceased to care, or had her mind on loftier things, set forth in a poke bonnet. But little girls adored them. Low necks and short sleeves had been revived for full dress, and feather fans with shaded tips fluttered beneath coquettish eyes. Fichu holders were known as lace pins and large lockets added to the wistful air. It was either the tailor-made or the starry-eyed and all-feminine girl, but each had the same deadly purpose—to capture a man.

Mme. Demorest's twenty-fifth semiannual *What to Wear and How to Make It* included 120 items, from the Undine bathing suit to the Hussar jacket. This handy compendium sold for 15 cents and had the latest information on all matters of dress. In some of her showings she displayed a pale-yellow satin gown embroidered with garlands of flowers, an original that had been worn by Marie Antoinette. Kate Field at this time launched a Ladies Co-operative Dress Association with capital of $250,000 and persuaded Julia Ward Howe to become a director. Mrs. Howe was the leading spirit of the Cotton Exposition held in Louisville in 1883 and Mrs. Frank Leslie appeared in person, a strong breeze from the north. Mrs. Potter Palmer, another regal figure, sent a choice collection of her famous bric-a-brac and all the suffrage women gave Mrs. Howe their loyal support. This was followed by the World's Industrial Fair in New Orleans in 1884.

In England women were pedaling frantically on their tricycles, going on long journeys and even taking them to the Continent. For the time being it had become more popular than the horse and wagon. The royal family tried it out at Balmoral. But recreation was gaining ground. Women walked in the woods, the one thing they had always done with no fear of the big, bad wolf. They attended whist parties. They played lawn tennis but were not yet permitted to enter open tournaments lest their modesty suffer. In the United States they organized an association in 1881 and by 1883 had drummed up forty clubs with national membership. They were really leaping into space. Archery and roller skating were alternative gaieties, while the men were committed to a solemn revival of cricket. The bowling alley was getting too close to the beer garden. Billiards were more the worldly man's game.

Dancing was still a comparatively stately affair, with the Sir Roger de Coverly, quadrilles, polkas and waltzes on every program. Strauss music was universally played but the waltz was still on approbation. Mrs. William T. Sherman had written a book in which she condemned it. Mrs. Potter Palmer had not been allowed to waltz when she made her debut in Chicago, and the feeling still persisted to some extent. The 1880's was the decade of form, not eccentricity, although there were strange variations at home and abroad, in both décor and dress. But aestheticism did not sink readily into the sturdy American pattern. Fops were the exception, not the rule.

Color ran amuck for a time. The quiet spotted foulards had burst into rose patterns on apricot and strawberry grounds. Nun's veiling, percale, thin wool, cashmere, pongees and chambrays sold by the bolt. Full Highland rig showed a touch of the Victorian influence. Silks disappeared from the American sidewalk as the tailor-made took hold but the most celebrated wearer of heavy black grosgrain and moiré silk was the widow Leslie, at this time running her revived empire. She had vowed she would not dance again or wear a color after her husband's death. Within a year she had paid off his creditors by raising a loan on her diamonds. She did a spectacular publishing job on the Garfield assassination, issuing three illustrated papers in one week. Circulation rose from 30,000 to 200,000. Beneath an ultrafeminine front were solid determination and ambition. She directed the combined operations of all her properties and whisked through Park Row with a flutter of skirts and a high degree of efficiency.

Her black kid shoes were tipped with silver. She used black quills at a white oak desk. Men observed that her waist could be spanned with a necklace. There were close to 400 employees on her payroll and she paid out $125,000 a year for manuscripts from all parts of the world. Abroad she was described as "The Empress of Journalism." In time she cut down her husband's publications to two weeklies and four monthlies, concentrating on the successful *Frank Leslie's Popular Monthly*. She dropped her *Lady's Journal* in favor of her *Lady's Magazine*, all developments of great interest in the Demorest shop. Eighteen fashion magazines were being published in New York and Philadelphia in the 1880's.

Mrs. Leslie rose at seven, did the popular dumbbell exercises of the day, stirred up energy with a cold bath, had beefsteak and toast for breakfast, and set forth in her carriage in queenly style. She worked at her office until four, then drove through the Park behind her bays in the fashion parade, and paid calls. She had a box at the Metropolitan. All visiting celebrities were invited to Mrs. Leslie's. Her Thursday evenings were much discussed as, jeweled and gorgeously gowned, she entertained the famous and sometimes the infamous from all parts of the world. She rode in the Jubilee procession of 1887. Her philosophy was simple and fundamental: "A woman is young as long as she can love, laugh, and enjoy." She was a bland observer of the *Daisy Miller* vogue. She could have taught Daisy Miller a lesson. Henry James's heroine had by this time become a symbol, a public cause. His book of 1879 was dramatized in 1883 and American girls and their ways abroad became a matter of lively comment. Daisy was a conversation piece wherever the younger generation gathered. Their elders discussed her, too, and out of it all sprang the vogue for chaperoned "excursion parties." Soon well-brought-up girls were traveling under the sheltering wing of a matriarchal type who could steer them away from professional mashers, and were equally at home in the Garden of the Gods or St. Mark's Square in Venice. *Demorest's* took up the issue:

To do what she thinks is right is the American girl's gospel. She must remember, too, this handsome American girl, that she is a very conspicuous person, subject to the most painful misapprehension, particularly on the continent, and she must condescend to a degree of perfectly forgivable hypocrisy in conforming to appearances. . . . Let the American girl who travels abroad think of the propriety of a chaperone. She may not need one on the prairie, or in California, but she does need one in Paris.

The literary and art world was in a creative state on both sides of the Atlantic and the interchange of interests had become intense. Some of America's most gifted writers were working abroad, while the writings of British authors flooded the American magazines. Most of the current serials came from England. When Thomas Carlyle died in 1881 *Demorest's* drew from his life the lesson that character was of value, that the universe was made for the poet, the seer, the prophet, as well as for the dull plodder. Dante Gabriel Rossetti died in the following year. Nearby on Cheyne Walk lived the American artist, James Mc-Neill Whistler, who was fighting a battle then with brush and pen. "They have not been fair to me in my country," he observed after winning a verdict and a farthing from Ruskin, whom he had sued for slander when the author described one of his paintings as a "pot of paint thrown in the face of the public." Victor Hugo walked under the trees in the Bois and drank fresh milk from the cows on his farm. His last drama, *Torquemada*, came out in 1882, when he was eighty years old.

That same autumn a little group of literary men gathered at the fireside of a remodeled stable on East Fifteenth Street owned by Richard Watson Gilder, and there decided to organize the Authors' Club of New York. Twenty-five invitations went out and they met again at Laurence Hutton's house and founded the club. They were criticized for not admitting women but in February and March of each year they gave four afternoon receptions for ladies. Among the club members were James Russell Lowell, John Hay, Horace Porter, Theodore Roosevelt, Carl Schurz and Oscar S. Straus.

Young writers from all parts of America were converging on New York in the 1880's. With the new magazines and brisk literary stirrings it was the market place for their wares, the goal of their ambitions. The Astor House was a favorite gathering place for those who could afford it. The men met in the rotunda; the women fluttered into the side rooms assigned to them. Gail Hamilton, who had helped her cousin, James G. Blaine, to write his speeches and was a strong figure in the Press Gallery in Washington, chatted with Marion Harland, Margaret Sangster (then editing *Harper's Bazar*), or smart little Nellie Bly, who did her round-the-world dash in 1887. Mary Clemmer Ames, Gail Hamilton's old associate in Washington, who had stirred up many an issue in *The Independent,* was going blind at this time.

The Woman's National Press Association was organized in Washington in 1882 and Jenny June followed this with the New York Women's Press Club, which got off to a lively start in 1889. The Sorosis embraced so many areas that she felt the press girls needed a club of their own. One of the women Sorosis delighted to honor in the 1880's was Mrs. Martha J. Lamb, when she finished *The History of the City of New York* on which she had worked for fourteen years. It remained its own monument to her memory, and she was made a Fellow of various learned societies in Europe. Quiet, modest, with dignified bearing, Mrs. Lamb had been a familiar figure around the town for many years, prowling into the byways of the city, examining old documents, interviewing descendants of the early settlers.

Demorest's recorded with approval each fresh appointment of a woman to an educational post. The magazine hailed the opening of Bryn Mawr and praised the University of Michigan for conferring the degree of Ph.D. on Miss Alice E. Freeman, the youthful president of Wellesley. It was the first instance of this degree going to an American woman. By 1882 at least twenty-five colleges and universities were open to women, although they were curbed at the top level. The desire of women to attend college was fomenting on both sides of the Atlantic. Both Oxford and Cambridge were giving them degrees and in 1882 the girl graduates of London University appeared for the first time at the public exercises in their academic gowns. Miss Ellen Gladstone headed one of the halls of Newnham College and *Demorest's* noted that "the very élite of England's society is now thoroughly alive to the wisdom of giving young women as well as young men the very highest educational advantages." They had been notably successful in the Tripos examinations.

Mrs. Humphry Ward was appointed Spanish examiner at Oxford, a development that led a colleague to say that this choice overleaped all the barriers raised by monks, prelates, and the dons. Women had full academic rights in Norway and Sweden. From fifty to a hundred women, including a Negro, were studying medicine in Paris at this time. In St. Petersburg three hundred were chemistry and botany students at the university. The University of Zurich had thirty-one women students, twenty of whom were studying medicine. There were successful women chemists in London and a course of stenography had been started for women in Padua. Queen Margherita of Italy had a woman on her staff of personal physicians—unlike Queen Victoria, who was criticized in *Demorest's* for being unfriendly to women doctors.

The drive for higher education went on determinedly in the United States, with a strong push from the suffrage pioneers. The girls who had graduated from college spread fine reports of their experiences. Mortarboards were seen more and more on the campus as a lively debate raged on whether or not to wear cap and gown to classes. The "bluestocking" tag had not alarmed the girls whose families could afford the luxury of college. But they had another cause for worry. The census showed a great increase of women in the cities at this time. New York had nearly 25,000 more women than men, and Boston had a preponderance of 18,000. Where were those errant husbands that Jenny June upbraided to come from? Art, music and needlework were still the strong features on any agenda but Latin and Greek were having their innings, too. Charles Francis Adams, Jr., was questioning the value of classical courses in the colleges. The college presidents and professors disagreed and *Demorest's* took up the issue with the clinching conclusion that the two foremost women writers of the time—George Eliot and Elizabeth Barrett Browning—were highly rated as Greek scholars. Harvard was under fire for its tendency to make "literary dudes." The graduates were said to be self-sufficient and supercilious. The only pursuit they followed with ardor was athletics, and especially boating.

Demorest's kept a close eye on the women's colleges and Jenny June visited them regularly to see what was going on. Vassar was the most discussed in its early days and the magazine published a poem by Lizzie W. Champney that brought no comfort to conservative parents who feared that higher education would unfit their daughters "for human nature's daily food":

She'd a great and varied knowledge,
Absorbed at Vassar College,
Of quadratics, hydrostatics,
And pneumatics very vast.
She was stuffed with erudition
As you stuff a leather cushion,
All the ologies of the colleges,
And the knowledge of the past.

She knew all the mighty giants
And the master minds of science.
All the learning that was turning
In the burning mind of man.
But she couldn't prepare a dinner
For a gaunt and hungry sinner,
Or get up a decent supper
For her poor, voracious pa.

For she never was constructed
On the old domestic plan.

The girls of the period were being speciously divided into two classes—those who made good wives and those who went to Vassar. All manner of skits, jests, innuendoes were aimed in their direction, the least of which was the gibe that their bread could be cleaved with an ax. The girls were getting lessons in finance as well as in the chemistry of food, "so that a short course of study at a cooking-school or with mother's cookbook will render her a cordon bleu in a wonderfully brief space of time," was the optimistic assumption. They found time for half an hour a day of tennis and fifteen minutes of walking. They studied their parts for the next Philalethean play while setting out the pansies in the Floral Club's gardens. They dashed off editorials for the Vassar *Miscellany* while returning in the streetcar from Saturday shopping expeditions. The spirit of the institution was thought to be essentially philanthropic. Heiresses were being taught how to use their fortunes. Poor girls were learning how to make theirs by the use of their own talents. "A sisterhood is established here," said *Demorest's*, "which makes them more charitable, more loyal in after life to all women."

They shared delightful little suites of rooms with common parlors cluttered with pictures and bric-a-brac. They had chafing dish spreads at night over the alcohol lamp. They studied science in the Laboratory of Chemistry and Physics, and astronomy in the observatory made famous by Maria Mitchell. They rowed and skated on a nearby lake and explored a wide range of subjects, from harmony to Sanskrit. They had a fine assortment of societies, ranging from the Hellenic Society to the Current Topics Club and the Prohibition Club. Dr. Mary E. Allen, a young Philadelphia Quaker, was appointed professor of physiology and hygiene as well as resident physician in 1882.

On her visit to Smith Jenny June found it the only woman's college where "women were treated as rationally as men and were allowed the same freedom." It was neither a nursery nor a nunnery. Most of the students lived in homes on the college grounds. The only written rule was that lights must be out at ten o'clock. Each student received friends of both sexes as freely as in her own home. She was mistress of all her actions, except that she must show up regularly for recitations. Otherwise she could and did go walking, rowing, riding and driving, and attended musical and dramatic entertainments in town at will. In 1883 the college had a new art gallery, a department of music had been added, and a library was planned for the future.

A visit two years later to Bryn Mawr suggested to *Demorest's* correspondent as she looked at its surroundings "a handsome widow in elegant garments of gray." She was struck by the simplicity in dress, by the free air of lawn, forest and open country, by the absence of exacting social functions. The girls had tennis, archery and croquet as well as Latin and Greek. Above all, she was impressed with its scholarly standards: "Despite the growing fancy for a college education among girls of social tastes, few frivolous girls find their way through the rigid examinations which guard Bryn Mawr. Work is earnest and faithful; culture is sought for culture's sake; courses for special work in philosophy, literature, science, and history are especially strong and valuable, and are always very popular." Martha Carey Thomas was dean at the time and in 1894 became president of Bryn Mawr.

Wellesley, with its four hundred beautiful acres of land, had women heading all its departments. Each class supplied a uniformed crew for the eight-oared cedar shells with sliding seats that glided around Lake Waban. Picnics, excursions, tennis, boating, walking parties and sketching clubs were common pursuits, as well as abstruse studies. The young botanists went into the field with tin boxes, collecting specimens. The zoologists pursued frogs and bugs. Birds were studied through field glasses. Organists, pianists and vocalists visited Wellesley to give performances, and as the years went on girl students from different parts of the world arrived to study there, setting up an international tradition.

Mount Holyoke changed its seminary status in 1888 to become a woman's college and again *Demorest's* took soundings. The transition had been smoothly effected and the athletic tradition was introduced. The girls wore gym suits up to the neck, stockings and long-skirted tunics. They rowed on Lake Nonotuck. They played tennis and basketball. They founded societies and launched their magazine *Mount Holyoke*. A more relaxed spirit prevailed than in the days of the founder, Mary Lyon.

A survey made in the 1880's of the effect of concentrated mental training on the health of women provided much food for comment. This had become a live issue, with so many girls dabbling in subjects that had been reserved before for the scholar. The doubters said it would ruin their health and unfit them for motherhood. But a study of 1,400 college graduates showed that 78 per cent were in excellent health and the death rate of their children was unusually low. The girls in shops and factories who were studied could not match this record, and the final conclusion was that "idleness and novel-reading are far more likely to injure girls than active employment and sound, unexciting studies." They had no time to indulge in morbid fancies. Taking it all round, higher education was winning the day, slowly in the 1880's, faster in the 1890's.

Meanwhile, New York offered promising fare for the girl with artistic interests. The Art Students' League was busy at 38 West Fourteenth Street. Artistic anatomy was being taught by J. S. Hartley and perspective by Frederick Dillmann. An evening life class for women was under consideration in 1883. The Women's Art School had just opened at Cooper Union, with 400 applicants. The Technical Schools of the Metropolitan Museum were giving instruction. The Society of Decorative Art had classes in china painting and needlework. The Women's Institute of Technical Design was active at 124 Fifth Avenue, with designs for carpets, oilcloth, tiles, wallpaper, book covers and china painting. The Ladies' Art Association gave summer instruction to visitors from out of town. But Jenny June was scathing about all this. She was out for professionalism and technical training. She thought that much of the "daubing, hammering, sawing and painting" done in the name of decorative art was a childish waste of time. "It would be far better to acquire a useful industry than a poor and useless form of art," she wrote severely. She thought better of the Kitchen Garden Schools run by the Industrial Education Society.

Demorest's took note of every woman rancher, banker, dentist or businesswoman of any sort who came to light in a distinctive way in any part of the country. The Western women had shown themselves to be progressive and full of energy. Iowa had 955 women running farms. Here and there they managed dairy farms, owned greenhouses, ran orange groves and market gardens. They were still comparatively rare in the professions but were making headway on the educational front. By 1882 a number directed educational institutions and they were eligible to serve as school officers in most of the states. Kindergartens were gaining ground. The Peabody plan was all-pervasive. Women had never been more preoccupied with the educational opportunities of their children or had more vistas opening up for them.

A few individualists ranked with the century's financiers, like Maude St. Pierre, known as the "Southern Coal Queen," who owned 300,000 acres of land in Tennessee, Kentucky and Alabama. She overlooked 22,000 acres of mineral wealth from her mountain home in Tennessee and superintended her own workmen. There were three women bank presidents at that time and two more were directors of mining and packing companies. Aside from isolated accomplishments women were finding a solid place in the business world and a great new army of office girls was on its way with the coming of the typewriter. They were grasping at every opportunity to enter new fields. *Demorest's* noted with interest a strong drive to popularize co-operative work in millinery and dressmaking among the educated classes. As the couple traveled they always took stock of the advances made in their own flourishing field. They noted with satisfaction that by the close of the 1880's thirty-three women were studying at the Massachusetts Institute of Technology and there were 1,300 women printers in Paris.

CHAPTER XIV

❧

Bowing Out

I~N~ 1885 Mr. Demorest turned over his magazine to his sons, Henry Clay and William Curtis Demorest. He now wished to devote all his time to the temperance cause and to be free to travel at will. Two years later the retirement of Mme. Demorest from the pattern business was officially announced, although she had not been closely involved in its ramifications for a number of years. The Butterick patterns had swamped the old Demorest fame in this field. A contributing factor was Mr. Demorest's stubborn refusal to allow for ample seams in cutting. The magazine world was changing. Both *Godey's Lady's Book* and *Peterson's* were going down. *Youth's Companion* had run up a large circulation, partly by its wide distribution of premiums. More than thirty periodicals had a circulation exceeding 100,000 at this time and the *Ladies' Home Journal* was now in the field. On the fashion side the large department stores, the ready-made costume, the frequent trips to Europe by women of wealth, had all had their effect on business. America was growing up fast. Its ways were changing.

Mme. Demorest still looked remarkably young for her years. She now had three grandchildren—Walter Jennings Gano, born in 1883 to Vienna and Dr. Gano; Henry's daughter, Marie Marguerite, and Will's daughter, Alice Louise, both born in 1885. By this time Nell's philanthropies were at their peak. Her current interests included the W.C.T.U. and a movement to help discharged prisoners. She was treasurer of the New York Medical College for Women, chairman of the board of the Welcome Lodging House for Women and Children, and she had backed the Sorosis Club for nineteen years.

Jenny June paid a tribute to her old friend and employer in the June issue of 1887, emphasizing the fact that, whatever the exaggeration or caprice of the period, Mme. Demorest's influence had always been thrown on the side of the practical, the modest and the useful. Moreover, she had invariably been helpful to her colleagues. "Mme. Demorest is still a handsome woman, with a fine, commanding presence which shows few signs of her upwards of sixty years," Jenny wrote. "Her interests have always been active, her sympathies strong; and they keep her young."

The pattern business was sold to two advertising agents who formed a stock company that continued to use Mme. Demorest's name as a trade label only. It was called the Demorest Fashion and Sewing-Machine Company but the Demorests had no interest in it. When a fashion sheet went out with a liquor ad there was family indignation that Mme. Demorest's name should in any way have been associated with this infamy. The Demorests finally started an injunction suit against the agents and their company to compel them to surrender a list of names that they charged had been surreptitiously removed from their offices. The injunction was made perpetual and the defendants were forced to pay expenses.

Though the Demorests no longer sold patterns, they still distributed them. They were obtained by coupon through the magazine and were given as premiums to subscribers. Each one was made from a fresh design expressly prepared every month for that purpose by some of the old pattern workers. At the same time Mme. Demorest gave up her profitable corset business. In June, 1887, they moved their headquarters from 17 East Fourteenth Street to the adjoining building, 15 East Fourteenth Street, but the pattern business remained at No. 17, resulting in considerable confusion all round as the buyers took possession. The colored plates that had delighted subscribers for years no longer went out. Instead, excellent half-tone portraits on heavy calendar paper that could be pulled out of the magazine became a popular feature and were also incorporated in a Portrait Album. In place of the fashionable figures in tinted crinolines subscribers received, among others, portraits of Ruskin and Frances Hodgson Burnett, Mme. Patti and Louis Kossuth, Dr. Talmage and Oliver Wendell Holmes.

Immediately after the transfer of property Mr. and Mrs. Demorest and Jenny June set off for a trip to the coast, partly for business, partly for pleasure. They were impressed with the fact that San Francisco had again been rebuilt after six fires. They declared the Palace Hotel to be without rival in its size and grandeur. Mr. Demorest was skeptical of the tall talk of the land speculators. Wherever he went he found evidence of the real estate craze. "Judging from the tone of the announcements, just now is the time and the day of salvation for those who want rich investments at a small outlay of money," he commented. He was an experienced observer in this field.

They visited the great ranches and M. W. Baldwin's famous orange grove, the largest that Mr. Demorest had ever seen. They toured the beet sugar mills at Alvarado and ascended into the mountains to study with interest the lonely spot where John Brown's wife took refuge after Harpers Ferry. They viewed the sequoias in the wooded regions and observed Frémont's "Mother of the Forest." At Santa Cruz they saw more bathers than were usually on view at Newport or Long Branch, and the women seemed more fearless. The bathing masters assured Mr. Demorest that one tenth of the accidents on his beach were due to cramps from drinking. He always kept an eye on the intoxicated when they plunged in. The Demorests next took a narrow-gauge railroad running along the sides of precipitous mountains to San Jose and were impressed with the well-cultivated land and the fruit trees along the way. Mr. Demorest thought the stores, banks, hotels, schools and other public buildings superior in thrift and architectural beauty to those in the East.

At Monterey they found the pretentious Hotel del Monte, put up by the California capitalists who had built the Southern Pacific Coast Railroad, in a state of dilapidation. But it looked like an artificial palace, with its peaked roofs, pointed towers, balconies and long piazzas. The seal rocks with the "sea-monsters constantly barking, howling, and fighting" were a novel sight and Mr. Demorest studied the old cypress trees that looked like umbrellas. They collected pine cones for their grandchildren and nieces and nephews, and strolled along the beach among the pebbles of Monterey. They always remembered the small ones as they traveled, and Mr. Demorest usually carried in his pocket little rings for the children of his friends.

After leaving the San Francisco area they traveled on to Yosemite in heavily built stages, with the seats set high, so as to protect the occupants from dust. Mr. Demorest considered their visit to Yellowstone the most exciting phase of their journey west. In Los Angeles they found themselves surrounded by masses of roses and magnolias, pink lilies and palms. The leafy arcades and wind-swept foliage kept the city refreshing, even in the midst of a rush of population as real estate values rose. Eastern capital and Eastern energy, the Demorests observed, had put a new front on all of Southern California. In three years 3,000 residences and a mile of business blocks had gone up in Los Angeles. Its roads had been improved. Its pavements were laid. Electric light had been introduced, and cable cars had taken the place of the horsecars. Santa Barbara seemed like the Riviera, and Pasadena was a haven of natural beauty for the invalid or the well. There they visited Mrs. Molyneux Bell, a businesswoman who had made a fortune in real estate in New York and was now operating a vineyard. A number of the California women had succeeded as cattle dealers, ranch owners, bee farmers, dairy farmers and fruit growers, and Jenny June took notes on their accomplishments. She talked to a San Francisco schoolteacher who owned a thriving fruit farm and marketed 50,000 pounds of muscat grapes a year.

On the ride from Omaha to Chicago Mr. Demorest observed that nearly every farm along the way was supplied with cultivators, reapers and mowers. The Cyrus McCormick touch was widespread. Large herds of cattle roamed the plains. It was all a "magnificent garden of practical fertility, managed by enterprising people." On his return to New York he summed up his impressions for the benefit of his public: "One must actually see this great and growing West to have a realizing consciousness of what a splendid outlook there is for the future development of our glorious Union."

By 1886 more than 7,000 miles of new railroad had been built across the land. Most of it was west of the Mississippi. Chicago and San Francisco had been built up almost in one generation. Mining had become one of the least of the industries of the region beyond the Sierra Nevada. Grain growing, fruit raising, stock breeding were now the main sources of wealth. The growth in the East was even more dramatic. New York had just added 50,000 in a year to its population, and its expenditures for new buildings aggregated $70 million, as against $40 million in the previous year. "Surveying the whole field, no American can help feeling proud at the magnificent condition and the prosperous prospects of the land of his birth," said Mr. Demorest.

Free Britain and democratic America led the rest of the world in ultrarich men at this time. Outside of the Rothschilds and the Krupp family, there were few millionaires abroad, while the United States had its Goulds, Vanderbilts, Astors, Stanfords, Huntingtons, Sages and others in the 1880's. The Rockefellers and Carnegie were rapidly climbing to the top. But much of the wealth of America was in the hands of its women. The unmarried women of Massachusetts had $29 million on deposit in the savings banks of their state. The wealthiest women of the day were listed as Mrs. William Astor, Mrs. Bloomfield Moore, Mrs. Margaret Crocker, Mrs. Robert Goelet, Mrs. Bradley Martin, Mrs. Edwin Stevens, Mrs. M. W. Baldwin, Mrs. Levi P. Morton, Mrs. M. Bates and Mrs. A. T. Stewart, who had recently given Long Island a cathedral, school and bishop's palace as a memorial to her husband. Miss Nellie Gould, Jay Gould's daughter, had $6 million and she worked for many charities, among them summer homes for sick babies and impoverished women. The Drexel girls of Philadelphia were the three wealthiest young unmarried women in the country. Their aggregate fortune amounted to $13 million. They, too, worked for church and charities.

But Mrs. Hetty Green led them all, with an inherited fortune augmented by her own shrewd operations. In 1888 she lived in a cheap lodging house in Chicago and rode to business in the streetcar, while she had $32 million neatly tucked away. Later, in New York, she became a well-known figure on Wall Street, scuttling around in dingy black with an unbecoming bonnet but outsmarting the cleverest of the financiers. Mrs. Green won the approval of the Demorests because she endowed churches and schools and gave considerable thought to benevolence. Hetty was believed to have married Edward Henry Green because his tailoring bill, which reached her by mistake instead of a valentine, was a model of rigid economy.

Shortly after their return from the West the Demorests and Jenny June visited Washington and were glad to see the Washington Monument finished at last. Now only the marshy grounds around it needed draining. The city seemed by degrees to be ridding itself of its marshes and the miasmatic conditions that once had been pestilential. Mrs. Grover Cleveland received the little party of three in the Red Room. The walls at the moment were Pompeian, the ceiling was in old gold, the furniture was ebony and gilt upholstered in crimson plush. The various shades on view were cherry, terra cotta and maroon. On each side of the mantelpiece was a case of faïence. A handsome lamp on a massive brass standard, bought for the White House by Mrs. Cleveland, was an object of interest. Frances Folsom had been married to President Cleveland in the Blue Room.

As her visitors rose she moved smoothly into the Red Room, tall, self-possessed, with dark, curling hair and deep blue eyes matching the blue of her gown. Her air was serious and attentive, and it seemed to Jenny June that she talked with freedom from affectation, but with judgment and good sense, selecting her topics in a manner that suggested an intuitive sense of fitness, and also a habit of "right thinking and conscientious aspiration." Mrs. Cleveland remarked that her whole previous life seemed to have been a preparation for the position she now filled. She paid tribute to Wells College, which she had attended. In leaving, the Demorests thanked God for the free republican institutions which brought the chief magistrate so close to the people and which endowed the President's wife with influence and power for good, yet without involving her in any way in politics.

Mr. Demorest looked down sagely from the Congressional gallery and counted heads on those who had temperance leanings. There were not too many. John Sherman was the presiding officer and all was dignity and repose on the day he paid his visit there. They had a livelier time in the Supreme Court, where the Bell Telephone case involving $150 million was being heard. There they had a chance to study Alexander Graham Bell, a tall man with iron-gray hair, dark-blue eyes and a "very striking, intelligent and cultivated face."

While Mr. Demorest called on politicians his two companions took in a number of social events and studied the charity institutions. Jenny wrote tactfully of the politicians "brought in from the freshness of a rougher life, whose natural aptitude prevents them from being long at fault." The official life in the capital demanded a code of its own, since the greenhorn was constantly being drawn to the head of the table by virtue of his political position. She did not think that this represented the best life in the capital, and she turned with relief to the literary and

scientific figures then exercising wide influence in Washington.
The famous Hundred Literary Lights still met occasionally at
the home of Mrs. Horatio King.

A number of writers lived in the neighborhood of Capitol
Hill at that time. Mary Clemmer Ames, Grace Greenwood and
Mrs. Emily Edson Briggs (Olivia), all Press Gallery veterans,
lived in the area east of Fourteenth Street. Mrs. Mary E. Nealy,
poet and journalist, and the well-known Frances Hodgson Burnett were in the general vicinity. Mrs. F. H. Southworth's home
for many years was in Georgetown, where she worked busily in
a simple brown timber cottage. She was besieged by visiting
writers and all who saw her were surprised to find so gentle a
woman pouring out such spirited books. Mrs. Jean Davenport
Lander, the tragedienne, had moved to the capital and remodeled
a house for herself. Mme. Demorest was on good terms with
Mrs. Lander, who was as well known for her charities and
philanthropy as for her acting. Nell made a point of visiting the
Louise Home in Washington, established by W. W. Corcoran
for elderly women—mostly those who had lost all their possessions in the South. Fine new hotels were rising in Washington
but the Demorests found the Willard still the best.

The magazine changed subtly after the Demorest sons took
over. More attention was paid to the news of the world. The
oil fields in the Caspian Sea region were causing talk. One near
Baku was reported to be producing more oil than all the wells of
America. Europe had four million men under arms. The statesmen of France and Germany were glaring at each other over
their respective frontiers. "The feeling is very general that were
a great war to take place in Europe, the United States could not
avoid some sort of entanglement," said *Demorest's.* "Hence the
appropriations passed by Congress for guns, forts, torpedo-boats
and fortifications. The people do not want to fight, and are reluctant to spend vast sums of money on armaments which they
hope never to use."

This was an old theme of Mr. Demorest's. He still kept close
to the magazine and wrote for it on the temperance cause.

When in town he went to the office as if nothing had changed. By this time he owned twenty buildings around Union Square. While he was traveling in the West, H. Rider Haggard's *Allan Quartermain* was running in the family magazine. *She* in *Harper's* had provided considerable excitement for the reading public and was later presented by William Gillette as a play in Niblo's Garden. Its mixture of magic and cannibalism, of pagan philosophy and horror gave a strong jolt to those who could take such robust reading. Or so it seemed in the 1880's.

In 1886 Robert Louis Stevenson's *Dr. Jekyll and Mr. Hyde* took the town by storm. Richard Mansfield later played the role. Julia Marlowe spent a glowing evening on the stage in October, 1887, with the *Times* critic predicting "Julia Marlowe; remember her name, for you will hear of her again." The play was *Ingomar*. Later she became part of the team of Sothern and Marlowe. Lily Langtry was appearing at the Fifth Avenue Theatre at the same time and the reviewer noted that "she never looked handsomer, she never wore such gorgeous costumes, she never received so many floral gifts." The echoes of her affair with Prince Edward followed her wherever she appeared. That same autumn young Josef Hofmann brought a Metropolitan Opera House audience to its feet with shouts of applause as he finished Beethoven's First Concerto. He was eleven and had already been hailed as a musical genius in his native Poland.

Sorosis gave Mary Anderson a complimentary breakfast at the close of her New York engagement that year and Mme. Demorest sat between her and Mrs. James Brown Potter. Miss Anderson, a Sacramento girl who had found fame on the stage, was twenty-eight at the time. Clara Morris was then living in The Pines, an old manorial residence at Riverdale. She was in her late thirties, a woman of delicate physique with expressive gray eyes. Visitors found her a good storyteller, with a sharp sense of humor. But she did not mingle with her fellow professionals as Mary Anderson did. Mme. Ristori was writing her memoirs and Marie Corelli was coming into view in England as a novelist.

By 1887 another cable had spun its way under the ocean, this

time linking Vancouver with Hong Kong. The immigrants landing at Castle Garden in 1887 numbered 133,000—40,000 more
than the year before. They saw the city of hope stretch before
them, with its modest spires and towers. Many of the Hungar-
ians and Italians had been brought over by the railroads. The
half-day holiday law had just gone into effect in New York. At
first businessmen opposed it but all complied with the require-
ments. "In this country," commented *Demorest's*, "we have too
few holidays. We are such 'workers after wealth' that we
hardly find time for any recreation." The labor organizations
had pushed the measure. The family magazine viewed the rise
in labor power with some apprehension in 1887 and set forth
its case:

Many of the views put forward by its leaders are impractical, if
not wild and dangerous. But the Labor Party is helping to destroy
the Democratic organization, as the Prohibition movement is dis-
rupting the Republican party. We do not attach very much importance to the appearance of the laboring man in politics, for we
do not think it possible to found a great party on class distinctions.
Political organizations, to be permanent, must appeal to a wide
variety of interests. A nation controlled by the poor alone, or by the
rich alone, would not be worth living in.

The sudden death of Henry Ward Beecher from a cerebral
hemorrhage on a March day in 1887 was big news across the
country. He had asked that no crape be used or any of the other
customary emblems of mourning. His house was kept brilliantly
lighted at night, and flowers were distributed about the rooms
as if for a festive occasion. Dickens, too, had forbidden his family to wear mourning. Mr. Demorest's final comment on his old
friend Beecher was a halfhearted tribute to one who had
broken the code and brought shame on his house: "Henry Ward
Beecher was a great man in his generation, but will he live as
one of the first-class men of his century? . . . He was not a
creative genius. He leaves no successor, he founded no church,
he is identified with no creed . . . his influence was disintegrating,

not formative. Hence, like Theodore Parker, if he exists at all in the future, it will be as a memory, not a force in human affairs."

New Yorkers were going abroad that summer in great numbers for the Jubilee of Queen Victoria. For weeks the papers and magazines were filled with extensive details on her life. *Demorest's* likened the pageant to the Field of the Cloth of Gold. James G. Blaine was invited to sit in the Abbey. Queen Victoria rode in an open carriage drawn by eight cream-colored horses, each with a footman in scarlet and gold, amid an unprecedented blaze of pageantry and a historic gathering of crowned heads. She wore black satin covered with lace in which the rose, shamrock and thistle were woven. On her head was a circlet of black velvet and Alençon lace, studded with precious stones, finished off with an aigrette. In New York there were fireworks in the bay and bursts of oratory to celebrate the Jubilee. "A Woman that Feareth the Lord, she shall be praised," was the text of the sermon preached in her honor at Trinity Church, a stone's throw from the money marts of America. But the Demorest forces felt that Queen Victoria had not done much to help her sex.

CHAPTER XV

Temperance Crusade

M R. DEMOREST went into full-scale action on the temperance front in 1885 with the establishment of the National Prohibition Bureau. He had joined forces with Frances Willard to drive what he considered its greatest scourge from the land. None of his friends was surprised. All the temperance pronouncements in his magazines over a period of years had been leading logically to this development. It was one strong reason why he was ready to turn over the reins of his publishing empire to his sons. His convictions on the subject were so intense that his writings and speeches now took on a fanatical note. Mme. Demorest backed him up in her own reserved way.

In 1884 he had worked for the election of Governor John St. John of Kansas, who ran for President as the Prohibition candidate. When Grover Cleveland was elected, James G. Blaine was not the only man wounded in spirit. St. John's campaign had been a small flame in a big conflagration, but it symbolized a new drive in national affairs. Out of more than 10 million voters, 150,000 had cast their ballots for the Governor. Prohibition had become a political issue and it had come to stay. In the course of the campaign Mr. Demorest urged work clubs for workingmen and -women to keep them out of the saloon, since the rumshop had been called the poor man's club.

Within a year of the national election the Prohibition party held its convention at Syracuse in September, 1885, and the names of H. Clay Bascom and W. Jennings Demorest were submitted for the governorship of New York State. Mr. Demorest promptly bowed out in favor of Mr. Bascom and was immediately nominated for Lieutenant Governor. This time he accepted and made a fiery speech:

The evils of the liquor traffic are so conspicuous that we need have no fear of exaggerating them. It cannot be portrayed in too glaring colors when it destroys one hundred thousand lives annually, manufactures 100,000 drunkards, squanders billions of dollars worth of property, causes nine-tenths of the crime and pauperism of our country, desolates our homes, debauches our political machinery and corrupts our judiciary. We ought not to parley any longer with this monster evil.

Once the tocsin had been sounded, things moved fast. Mr. Demorest had the money and influence to promote his own campaign. At the ratification meeting held later at Chickering Hall the women decorated the platform with flags and palms. In accepting, Mr. Demorest spoke of the Hydra-headed monster that could not be destroyed by ordinary means. It was not temperance he sought but total prohibition, annihilation of the liquor traffic. Because of the attitude of the two political parties toward the subject he could see nothing for it but the creation of a third party that would embrace "all the good and true men of both parties." The liquor interests had money, social advantages and the political machinery of the country under their control, all of which they would use to destroy the new party, Mr. Demorest predicted, as he closed on an exclamatory note: "We have the remedy. It is a simple one—Prohibition. Let it ring through the land. Proclaim it from every hilltop. Prohibition must be our watchword and our motto must be, 'Prohibition, our high Ambition.'"

In the campaign that followed, Mr. Demorest was presented in the dual role of editor and real estate operator. He had made a fortune with his real estate operations in the Fourteenth Street area, in addition to his magazines and the fashion and pattern business. The J. J. Little Company, in which he held a partnership, had printed General Grant's memoirs, a book that at the moment was selling in great volume. He belonged to the Congregational Church and for thirty years had taught in Sunday school. That summer he had entertained 450 children at the farm in Saratoga. He contributed liberally to all benevolent causes. Mme. Demorest's philanthropies were extolled at the same time. The campaign moved on but Mr. Demorest met with defeat, although he ran up the largest vote ever given a Prohibition candidate in the state.

By that time he had organized the National Prohibition Bureau, later the Constitutional League, to test the constitutionality of liquor licenses and the liquor tax law. Headquarters were at 32 East Fourteenth Street, one of the Demorest properties. From this focus volunteer lecturers stumped the country, with Frances Willard, Mrs. Sallie F. Chapin and Mrs. Mary T. Lathrap prominent among them. The movement was national in scope and they had carte blanche to be "educational and agitational." They worked first in the South, armed with the Demorest circular, distributed at a dollar a thousand. It summed up their aims:

No temporary or half-way measures
No delusive panacea to silence conscience
No legalized monopoly
No legalized sanction of the crime
No attempt to bolster up the business by making it respectable
No justification of the rum-seller
No grant of a license or indulgence for his criminal and death-
    dealing traffic
No bribery or concession for a money consideration

No political barter of our rights and privileges
No debauchery of the people or our country's best interest
No concession to the rum-seller
No choosing between two evils when you have an alternative, but
    the immediate and utter annihilation of the business of rum-
    selling by Prohibition.

Mr. Demorest battered away at the "satanic" idea of licensing liquor. It could no more be regulated than cholera or smallpox, he argued. Miss Willard was his most effective witness and she turned all her dynamic drive to bear on this matter so close to her heart. Her own temperance campaign was soon world-wide and Mr. Demorest gladly poured much of his own fortune into promoting the cause as a whole. The Democratic party was committed to the saloon, said Miss Willard, and the Republicans to the beer interests because of their German support. Neither of the old parties could afford to sponsor prohibition. But the *people* could afford to try it. *Demorest's* published this speech of Miss Willard's in tract form and it went traveling around in the same lively fashion as the patterns had in the past. Mr. Demorest's own pronouncements had the prevailing clarion ring: "Up with the home, down with the saloon! Prohibition the dawn of the millennium! Prohibition first and last—now, always and forever."

Swinging his arms, his beard now streaked with silver, his steel-gray eyes burning with enthusiasm, he swayed large crowds as he pounded at them with statistics, with denunciation, with all the intensity of his vigorous nature. His interest in the cause dated back to his boyhood days when he heard his first temperance lecture in Brighton. On his way home he wrote on the coalbox of a grocer who sold liquor: "Hell fire sold here." After repeating this over and over he signed the pledge, and from that time on was a temperance enthusiast.

Every issue of the magazine now ran detailed news of small prohibition victories, as well as articles by Mr. Demorest, not in his old contemplative manner but laced with fervor. It was all in the style of the day. He had used the same technique against slavery during the Civil War. He found signs of hope in South Carolina, Mississippi, Florida, Georgia and Rhode Island. Maine was far in the vanguard but the Empire State was deaf to it all. "The liquor saloon graduates wife beaters, thieves, murderers," he said in December, 1885. "Yet you vote to keep them open. Was there ever such madness as this?" He predicted that the liquor trade would be sunk beyond resurrection. All that summer he kept the flag flying, insisting that there could be no halfway measures. He took the clergy to task for not being more enthusiastic in backing the temperance drive, although some were out on the hustings with him, and Dr. Talmage spoke in much the same tone of voice.

At that time Mr. Demorest organized and was president of the Anti-Nuisance League. He started actions against some of the leading hotels to break up liquor selling under a Supreme Court ruling that "no legislature can bargain away the public health or the public morals." He was denounced and ridiculed in the press when he followed this unpopular line, but he pursued the work relentlessly. Nevertheless, he was credited with having contributed perhaps as much as any one man to pushing the cause of prohibition at that time in America and he soon became known around the world for his advocacy of temperance.

"Touch not, taste not, handle not, for at last it biteth like a serpent and stingeth like an adder," he warned the young as he launched his Medal Contest in May, 1886, the most effective move of his campaign. Before his death he had distributed more than 40,000 silver, gold and diamond medals to young people around the world, the prize winners in elocution contests based on temperance tracts sent out from his bureau. The contest became immensely popular with growing boys and girls as well as with their parents. Schools and Sunday schools took it up. Mr. Demorest came to be known for his medals as his wife had been known for her patterns.

The first contest was held in the Bedford Street Methodist Church in New York. In the summer of 1887 the work was introduced on the Pacific coast when Mr. and Mrs. Demorest were visiting there. From that point on it went around like wild-fire and in 1888 contests were being held by the Bands of Hope of London and Glasgow. Missionaries tried it out in their lonely fields, doing their own translations, so that eventually Mr. Demorest's medals turned up in Australia, Hawaii, South Africa, China, India, Bulgaria, Tasmania and Norway. A hundred and ten contests were conducted in New York in churches of all denominations. The plan was directed from 10 East Fourteenth Street, another of Mr. Demorest's properties. From five to ten children under the age of twenty-one competed in each instance. The recitation book was supplied and it was a temperance tract in itself. The underlying idea was the indoctrination of the young in temperance principles. The secondary aims were training in oratory and the public interest stirred up in communities where the contests were held.

"All young people should be taught to read well, and declamatory exercises are useful not only in cultivating the voice but in improving taste in belles-lettres," said Mr. Demorest. "The ability to express emotion by voice should not be neglected in the training of the young." His own family had always done it on both the public and the private level. Their mother sat on the platform in Chickering Hall at the first public anniversary of the National Prohibition Bureau.

Tales of drunkards' wives and other domestic horrors ran in the family magazine during this period of concentrated activity by Mr. Demorest. There was plenty of fuel to stoke this fire in the woeful spectacle presented by the slums. The public was getting it on all sides—from Frances Willard, from Dr. Talmage, from W. Jennings Demorest, from speakers all over the nation. In 1890 Carry Nation would break loose with her hatchet in Kansas, but she was a lone wolf. Meanwhile, leaflets poured out from headquarters, a paper storm that the Demorest interests knew well how to handle. Ten million of what the founder called his Prohibition Bombs were distributed in 1886. This time the lecturers on their rounds lined up compact groups to fight for representation and Mr. Demorest again sounded the battle cry:

One more river, And that is Prohibition, One more river to cross. Shall we, the free and enlightened, Christian, law-abiding people of America, justify the horrible death-dealing, home-destroying, crime-producing, pauperizing liquor traffic by a legal sanction? We say no! A Thousand times no!! Never!!! Never!!!

At the same time Mr. Demorest and his associates did much valuable work for the temperance cause. They assessed the situation in the various states, compiled statistics, drew the attention of those who would listen to their best-grounded arguments and backed a number of successful nominees. In learning their recitations by heart children became aware of the dangers of the saloon. Mr. Demorest toured the Southern, Western and South-western states, studying conditions at first hand and talking to the men who might work for his cause.

But all this did not help the family magazine. Its editorial tone had always been temperate and balanced. It had never indulged in the abuse and ridicule that characterized many publications of the time and it had avoided extremes until Mr. Demorest embarked on this campaign and plainly used the magazine to promote his views. He was not alone in this. Personal journalism was riding high. The old Demorest features went on as before. Improvements were made in the scope and look of the magazine but the propaganda note grew shrill. Most publications avoided the temperance issue altogether, although it was one of the big reform movements of the day. Divorce, spelling reform, and cruelty to animals also were in the limelight. But strong articles on prohibition ran in *Harper's Monthly*, the *Atlantic Monthly*, *The Galaxy* and *Putnam's*. *Arthur's Home Magazine* was completely committed to the temperance cause and had a department called "The Reformer." In 1886 no fewer than 134 temperance periodicals were in the field, twenty-eight new ones reaching the market as the Demorest campaign got under way. The Prohibition party had newspaper backing, too, and gained strength in certain states. The W.C.T.U. was the mainspring of the whole movement and Frances Willard was the star White Ribboner, much admired by both of the Demorests.

By this time Miss Willard was president of the W.C.T.U., which had moved its headquarters from Chicago to New York. The organization had given the White House a life-size portrait of Mrs. Rutherford B. Hayes, popularly known as "Lemonade Lucy," for her abstemious regime and temperance principles. The temperance women of Britain had just declared war against those who gave liquor licenses to confectioners and other dealers whose customers were mostly women and children. They were getting up a Jubilee memorial for Queen Victoria urging that bars be closed on Sunday and they had picked up nearly 750,000 signatures.

Mme. Demorest's pet charity had been founded in 1885. It was directly linked with the liquor situation and was designed to help the women and children thrown out of their homes or neglected because of drunken fathers and husbands. She felt that no provision was made anywhere for this particular class. The institution was known as the Welcome Lodging House for Women and Children. Those who could afford it paid a small sum for the sake of their self-respect. They were clothed as well as housed, for they often arrived in a seminaked condition. It was quite the fashion in the slums for a drunken man to throw his wife out into the gutter in the middle of the night.

The tastes of great men in relation to liquor made a breezy article in the *Tribune* on April 24, 1887, which was deplored by Mr. Demorest, who thought that Greeley would not have approved. Whiskey was the winning drink with most of the war heroes. The authority quoted was Francis Moore, a Vermonter who had served as bartender for years at the Fifth Avenue Hotel and had had ample opportunity to observe the ways of his customers. General Sherman had stuck to one brand of whiskey for so long that others had come to ask for it as Sherman whiskey. He took a good stiff drink but not too often. General Philip Sheridan enjoyed a square drink of whiskey and needed no water to wash it down. General Grant used to come in occasionally in the last year of his life and drink a bottle of Bass's ale at the bar. Both Edwin Booth and Lawrence Barrett chose whiskey.

Robert Ingersoll favored beer. James G. Blaine stopped in at the hotel but never went near the bar. P. T. Barnum poured down one glass of gin after another, and no glass was ever large enough for the lusty showman. President Hayes was so well indoctrinated that he would not take a glass of lemonade at the bar lest it had been stirred with a spoon contaminated by firewater.

As he toured the country campaigning Mr. Demorest observed that labor was giving trouble on several fronts. The eight-hour day was being discussed, with employers dead set against it. The Knights of Labor he called the men who were agitating at that time and he predicted, with one of his sure looks into the future, that if the working people organized for political and social ends they would be all-powerful. Europe swarmed with unemployed and prices had been falling steadily since 1870. All kinds of manufactured goods as well as raw materials commanded less in the markets than at any time in a hundred years. England was losing ground commercially to the Germans, and in Mr. Demorest's estimation the only really prosperous country was the United States, helped along by its silver coinage. The influx of immigrants was raising the population rate at unprecedented speed. Employers were doing so well in America that they could afford to raise wages. At the end of 1886 Mr. Demorest wrote:

We are growing marvellously in population and wealth. We number now about six million people in New York State and about $45,000,000 was spent last year in the city of New York on new structures. In no era of the world has wealth been created so rapidly as during the last thirty years. . . . All over the country will be found rich men who have made their fortunes in corporate investments, such as the telephone companies.

With his temperance campaign well under way Mr. Demorest set off for Europe with his wife, Jenny June and Evelyn. They were entertained in London by Edward John Phelps, the Minister who had succeeded James Russell Lowell. They visited Lady Wilde, for Evelyn wished to see if "Oscar brought up his mother or his mother brought up Oscar." After meeting Lady Wilde, she decided that his mother had brought up Oscar. Lady Wilde was living then in a small house in Mayfair, too small and crowded for her large person and flamboyant dress. Jenny thought her prose and verse quite good, and she noticed that matrimony seemed to have improved Oscar. He had given up some of his peculiarities of dress and manner, had grown stout and was anything but handsome. His elder brother Willie, who would marry Mrs. Leslie, was even taller than he and with their mother they made a curious trio, all looking singularly like one another.

That evening the Demorest party saw Henry Irving in the *Vicar of Wakefield* and thought Ellen Terry poor in the role of Olivia. They met Robert Browning at a dinner. He was then working on *Asolando*, his final effort, but his powers were failing. Mme. Demorest instinctively took note of the fashions wherever she went—a summer blend of straw bonnets, feathers, lace and flowers. Jenny was more interested in a conversazione of the Art Society at the South Kensington Museum and Mr. Demorest in the London Inventions Exhibition, where he wandered eagerly through a maze of electrical apparatus, studying new methods of heating, lighting and driving power. They toured the galleries, visited the shops, studied gloves, hosiery, laces and fabrics of all descriptions. They found the Liberty shops, which had grown in ten years from one floor on Regent Street to massive buildings, something new in the field of merchandising. They decided that English clothes had improved and particularly commended the tailor-made suits, tea gowns, ulsters, walking boots and luggage.

While they were there Britain was convulsed with a struggle between the Liberals and the Tories. Two million new voters were ready to cast their ballots at the next election. Tories did best in foreign affairs but great reforms sprang from the Liberals, said Jenny, as Gladstone held the fort on the Liberal side. She decided that the new democracy coming to the fore in Europe was more radical and revolutionary than any program in America. She and Mme. Demorest closely studied the women's advances in Europe. They thought that in industry and the professions they were making more headway than in America. Of more limited but quite personal interest was their discovery that Mme. Isabel, a famous Bond Street milliner, was a graduate of Girton, and another successful milliner in the 1880's was Lady Granville Gordon. A number of titled women were going into trade, and female superintendents of fashionable dressmaking establishments made more than lawyers and doctors at that time.

Englishwomen were busy in the arts. They did unconventional things in a thoroughly conventional way. A few had made money. Some had acquired fame. In Paris the travelers decided that among the best-educated girls were the daughters of modistes and market women. They were struck by the opportunities American women had to study art in France. The charred ruins of the Tuileries still lay in full view, with the twisted chandeliers showing against fragments of frescoed walls. Flower booths bloomed at Porte Saint-Martin, so recently the scene of carnage. They watched the feast of the lanterns on the Seine and observed Turkish goods at every little shop on the Place de la Concorde. Worth's business had fallen off noticeably. He employed only a tenth as many workers as before.

On her return to America Mme. Demorest found that Gainsborough hats, covered with lace and clusters of plumes, were sweeping the field in the coaching parade and at the races. The ostrich tips were cardinal, yellow or shrimp pink, and long tan or gray gloves picked up a contrasting note of color. Mme. Demorest considered these costumes too ornate for the occasion but she always enjoyed Jerome Park, with its terraces of deep green and the grandstand bright with color and animation. It was a yellow year, with golden tints in gowns, straws, braids and gauze; golden thistles, golden leaves, golden buckles, gold thread and gold lace, the symbol of the times. White flannel was catching on for summer wear and the angular figure had apparently had its day. Grand proportions were coming in for admiration, with Lillian Russell leading the field.

Plush, satin and tinsel brocades were the fashionable materials for winter wedding dresses, with plush and tinsel sashes. White moiré was second choice, cut princess style rather than with basque. Bridesmaids wore delicate colors with their Gainsborough hats. Long ostrich plumes arched over the crown and drooped toward the shoulder from high-crowned hats. It was noticed at the spring openings in 1886 that many of the choicest dress materials were made on foreign looms from American designs. Astrakhan and bouclé had been abandoned by the fashionable trade but wool laces were popular. Cottons were thin and sheer, with batiste and surah in the running. The sweet sixteen effect was convincingly carried out with garden hats of mull and lace with ribbon bows, or the regular sailor with rows of narrow ribbon round the crown and long streamers down the back. Newport ties were catching on. Bronze shoes with lacelike openwork over the foot were used for full dress wear, and bronze hose came into view, creating a craze for combinations of bronze and salmon pink.

The Newmarket and Norfolk jackets for shopping were worn with plain dresses, and long raglan cloaks were made up in cheviot, tweed and Irish friezes—the "stable cloths" deplored by Worth, as he surveyed cumbersome bison cloth and other heavy suitings. Sarah Bernhardt's favorite twelve-button gloves had created a fashion and black kid was worn dramatically with white gowns. Jersey silk gloves and pearl and point lace fans went partying together. Women were beginning to wear paste diamonds instead of their authentic jewels. A number of jewel robberies had led to this practice. When Mrs. Vanderbilt, wearing her true jewels, took them off at night not even her personal maid knew where she kept them. The more fashionable women wrote their letters on Marcus Ward's linen paper. They liked rough parchment with deckle edges and used crests, initials or tiny representations of gates, lodges or doorways—all presumably linked to their estates. The use of sealing wax had been revived. White was used for weddings, purple for mourning, lavender for condolence. Dinner invitations were sealed with chocolate-colored wax.

Children's clothes no longer closely resembled those of their elders. At the age of five boys went into short pants and shirt waists for summer and pants with sack coats for winter—a routine that tided them over until they reached the age of ten, when their fathers took them to their own tailors. Jockey and polo caps were worn by small boys and a few were pushed kicking and screaming into Little Lord Fauntleroy suits, an English fashion that did not take root in America. Girls wore fetching little coats of cream wool with borders of wool lace, and Turkey-red cotton frocks with tucked and gathered skirts. On parade they often were decked with Valenciennes lace over strawberry or old gold satin. Their seaside dresses were apt to be poppy-red velveteen or wool.

The tennis girl's costume was more a matter of underwear than of top wear. She was seriously advised to wear a thick wool vest and drawers, with a tight waist of strong linen. Her dress was of light flannel suiting with a box-plaited skirt and a belt fastened with an antique clasp, matching those that clipped her collar and cuffs. The linen collar inside her outer rolling collar was attached to her chemise, the idea being to keep her all in one piece when she leaped at the net. Her wrap was a scarf of wool lace. Her hat was of shirred mull with upright bows fastened with small silver pins. But in 1886 roller skating was the big craze and *Demorest's* noted that it was interfering with all other forms of public amusement—theaters, concerts, lectures. The oracles of the magazine considered walking better exercise and expressed the view that even dancing was more healthful, as well as being decidely more graceful.

Red umbrellas brightened up rainy days but the parasols were lacier than ever. They now had steel tips to jab at the insolent or to serve as walking sticks. The yum-yum umbrella of India or China silk had fine plaiting to the tips of the ribs. Black stockings were worn with light dresses, but special imported hose had pink and brown stripes to match summer gowns. A wrangle was brewing over the aesthetic effect of a black stocking with a pink tulle dress. Ecru was the popular color and black lace gowns over tinted slips created seductive effects. Hats of black Spanish lace, their brims faced with velvet, had loops of ribbon, pompons or ostrich aigrettes.

In the middle of her husband's temperance campaign in 1886 Mme. Demorest's brother Edwin was killed in a railroad accident on his way to Saratoga, when his train was derailed at Greenwood, Mississippi. His sister was to have met him in New York and to have gone with him to Saratoga. She hurried south to Staunton as soon as she heard of the accident. Two years earlier her father, Henry Curtis, had died at Saratoga at the age of eighty-six. He was keen and vigorous to the end, tramping about his place, keeping up with the news, reading his daily paper—an old custom with him, for he had helped to get out the first newspaper printed in Schuylerville. His widow, Electa, was eighty-one at the time of his death and she, too, was an active old lady, seasoned, wise and thoughtful.

Mme. Demorest kept in touch with both her parents while they lived and her mother came close to the century mark. All her sisters except Kate had married by this time, and her nieces and nephews were always welcome visitors at her home. A particular favorite was Anna's son, Henry Curtis Morris, who attended in turn Peekskill Academy, the New York Military Academy and Massachusetts Institute of Technology. His sister, Ethel Morris, a frequent visitor at Saratoga, married Dr. William Goodell, of Springfield, Massachusetts. Matilda was married first to E. C. Gamble. Their son Charles was accidentally blinded and for the rest of her life she and her family were deeply interested in the welfare of the blind. After Mr. Gamble's death she married William Ziegler, and soon started the *Matilda Ziegler Magazine For the Blind*, a publication that circulated in forty countries as well as in the United States. Mr. Ziegler had large business interests and was the founder of the Royal Baking Powder Company. William Curtis Demorest, son of the crusader, was associated with him both in this company and in extensive real estate operations. It was they who developed Malba, Long Island.

Like the Demorests, the Zieglers frequently visited the farm at Saratoga and helped to improve the property. Their city home was at the southwest corner of Fifth Avenue and Fiftieth Street. The farm was run by Ed and Nellie Barker, a brother and sister who were companions to Mrs. Curtis in her old age. After her death the family turned over the property to Kate, who for years had been a tower of strength in the Demorest fashion empire.

CHAPTER XVI

The Last Trumpet

WILLIAM JENNINGS DEMOREST and Cardinal Manning stood side by side in the Crystal Palace in 1889 while the American condemned the churches for failing to act strongly and firmly on the temperance issue. He was addressing the Legion of the Cross and said:

The Church is almost omnipotent in this good work when she chooses to do her duty. Give me the influence of the Catholic Church, and we could have Prohibition within one year; or let the women of the Catholic Church combine, and nothing could withstand them.

Mr. Demorest was touring Britain in a whirlwind campaign for his cause, and statesmen and clergymen turned out to listen to him. The United Kingdom Alliance sponsored his tour and he spoke in London, Glasgow and Manchester, where he had many manufacturing friends. The British papers gave columns of comment to the temperance leader from America and his wife. The medal contests had whipped up public interest abroad. A fete and temperance demonstration was staged in the grounds of Fulham Palace by permission of the Bishop of London. Bands of Hope, temperance societies, and thousands of curious spectators flowed into the grounds on an August day, while choirs sang the temperance hymns and bands thundered salvation. The gathering had the air of a great revival meeting.

In Glasgow Mme. Demorest, who shrank from making speeches, got up and accused the church of being indifferent to the temperance cause. She plunged boldly on and said that it had been the bulwark of the traffic all along, even though temperance workers had a certain degree of church support on their side. Her audience laughed and cheered when she gravely announced that she was not accustomed to speaking, either before or after dinner, and that she and her husband were workers rather than talkers for the temperance cause. They had long ceased to believe that talking did much good. The fashionably dressed Mme. Demorest, whose patterns had found their way to the Clyde, was quite a success as she talked in her calm and measured way. But the battle-rouser followed and brought his audience to its feet as he attacked the "despicable selfishness of these teachers who by their silence or duplicity apologize for those execrable monsters of iniquity, the liquor dealers."

Before the Demorests left Britain Canon William Barker, Chaplain to Queen Victoria, told them that the United States could better afford to try advanced experiments in temperance than Britain. However, he conceded that the temperance movement had done more to unite religious factions in England than any other force. Mme. Demorest and Lady Somerset, president of the British Woman's Temperance Association, became firm friends at this time and Nell entertained the Englishwoman later at her New York home. Lady Somerset was the Frances Willard of England and in a single year held 115 meetings, attended 27 conferences, traveled over 8,000 miles and spoke in 20 countries.

On his return to America Mr. Demorest was feted at Martinelli's and the New York *Herald* described this banquet for the "cold water men." He told them that the United States was far ahead of England in the Prohibition movement, but that Scotland was showing interest and was putting its parliamentary candidates through a stiff catechism on their temperance views. Mr. Demorest's triumphal tour abroad had established him more than ever as a widely known figure.

In 1888 the temperance women gathered for the first time in New York to celebrate the fifteenth birthday of the W.C.T.U. They filled the Metropolitan Opera House. No star of the dramatic or musical world was present on this occasion. They were mostly middle-aged women, plainly dressed, clutching satchels, their hair not coiffed in the manner of the hour, their costumes not stemming from Mme. Demorest's, but Jenny June reflected on the "strong and earnest purpose in their thoughtful eyes and in the lines of their intelligent faces." Mme. Demorest was chairman of the committee on decorations, and eighty-four draped flags with the shields of different states clung to the Golden Horseshoe. Every gallery was packed and delegates filled the orchestra seats. The banners of the W.C.T.U. hung across the stage and no opera star ever received a greater ovation than Miss Willard did when she walked into view. Jenny June described her on this occasion as "unquestionably the greatest woman organizer of this age of organization."

Clara Barton, the pioneer of the Red Cross who had poured liquor down the throats of dying men on the battlefield, was there in her best black silk, her homely face alight with interest. Governor St. John, who had run for the Presidency, General Clinton B. Fisk and Mr. Demorest were honored guests. The Chautauqua salute was given them by the slow lifting and lowering of the handkerchiefs of the assembled members of the W.C.T.U. Miss Willard read the Crusade Psalm and gave one of her more stirring addresses, calling the W.C.T.U. "the strongest and most successful society in Christendom." She was re-elected president, while women wept and waved their handkerchiefs and men cheered wildly. The day wound up with a reception given by Mme. Demorest at her home for Miss Willard and the newly elected officers of the national organization. The W.C.T.U. leader was her guest throughout the convention.

That same year the International Council of Women met in Washington under the auspices of the National Suffrage Association with delegates from all parts of the world present. They gathered in Albaugh's Opera House and had eight days of meetings, speeches and receptions. They discussed education, philanthropy, temperance, politics, social purity, legal, industrial and professional problems. Again the veterans were on view. Clara Barton spoke for the Red Cross and Frances Willard for temperance. Susan B. Anthony, Elizabeth Cady Stanton, Lucy Stone, Antoinette Brown Blackwell, Julia Ward Howe, Jenny June, all were vital figures in the gathering. A permanent international council was formed, with Mrs. Millicent Fawcett as honorary president. The resolutions passed by the assembled women covered a wide range: an identical standard of personal purity and morality for men and women, equal wages for equal work, full opportunities for industrial education, and the opening to women of all educational institutions, including schools of theology, law and medicine. Another strong blow had been struck in the campaign for equality, and this time it was international.

The Centennial of Washington's inauguration in New York kept the city in a state of excitement in 1889. President Harrison landed at Elizabethport and embarked on a steamer before being officially escorted into New York. A reception was given at City Hall. The Centennial Ball was held in the Metropolitan Opera House, and the scene of the first inauguration was re-enacted on the steps of the Sub-Treasury, with Chauncey Depew delivering the oration, and the President addressing the throngs who squeezed their way into the narrow thoroughfares. The route originally planned for the procession was up Broadway to Waverly Place, through to Fifth Avenue and then up to Fifty-seventh Street. But Mr. Demorest was the prime mover in having the route changed to bring it through Fourteenth Street and around Union Square, where the statues of Lincoln, Lafayette and George Washington stood. An industrial parade was held on the following day. The arch at Washington Square was officially dedicated as part of the Centennial celebration.

Two Presidents' wives died that year—Mrs. Rutherford Hayes and Mrs. John Tyler. The doings of Lucy Webb Hayes had always been of interest to the Demorests, who approved of her religious, temperance and philanthropic principles. "Mrs. Hayes will always be remembered as the lady who kept wine from the White House table throughout the administration," said Mr. Demorest. The W.C.T.U. had the Daniel Huntington portrait of her that hung in the White House reproduced in miniature for circulation among its members as an example to all. Dark-haired, graceful, with large gray eyes and a face full of purpose, Mrs. Hayes had made a strong impression on the public. She dressed in a quiet way and believed in a higher mission for women than the study of Paris fashions. Julia Gardiner Tyler, on the other hand, was a White House belle who gave much thought to her attire. Maria Mitchell, one of the true pioneers, also died in 1889.

Things were going well for women as the decade closed. Sorosis members, meeting in March of that year, laid plans to celebrate their twenty-first anniversary in 1890 with a great gathering of club representatives from all parts of the country. Mrs. Croly sent out a call to ninety-four clubs, and sixty-one sent delegates to the epochal convention held in Madison Square Garden that led to the establishment of the General Federation of Women's Clubs. The founders of Sorosis were aging visibly now. But brains and beauty, style and earnest purpose were combined as three hundred women, some of them the most gifted of their day, dined first in Delmonico's, according to tradition, but now under the harsh and unfamiliar electric lights.

Jenny June viewed the gathering as the revelation of a new force let loose in the country, a social revolution accomplished in the quietest way, by the simplest means. Mrs. Ella Dietz Clymer, a tiny woman with soft brown eyes, who was a niece of Mrs. Robert Dale Owen, closed her address with the words:

"We look for unity, but unity in diversity." Jenny quickly picked up this thought and Unity in Diversity became the Federation motto, engraved on the first membership pin in 1893.

The Federation was organized in the Scottish Rite Hall in New York after the convention of 1890 ended, with an advisory board made up of Mrs. Croly, Mrs. Clymer, Mrs. M. Louise Thomas, Mrs. Sophia C. Hoffman, Mrs. Mary R. Hall, Mrs. Amelia K. Wing and Mrs. Charlotte Emerson Brown. The New England Woman's Club, powerful and individualistic under the direction of Julia Ward Howe, stayed aloof at first but finally came into the fold. It was as old as Sorosis and had met first in the home of Dr. Harriot K. Hunt in Boston. Within a year the Sorosis of Bombay had applied for membership, followed by clubs in Ceylon and Australia. The power of the Federation became apparent at the Columbian Exposition in Chicago in 1893 when 210 women's congresses were held, representing women around the world. By 1896 the Federation was ready for concerted action in education. It took the lead in establishing free libraries. It promoted scholarships, and as the years went on engaged in war work, conservation, civics and social economics, fine arts, legislative action, international projects, work for the handicapped, national defense and community effort of various kinds.

The states continued to organize federations until 505 clubs in twenty-four states were tied to the central body by 1897. The small and isolated clubs which had left faint echoes in different parts of the country long before Sorosis was founded had pointed the way to the great consolidation that now linked women together in different parts of the world. By the 1960's the General Federation, with headquarters in Washington, was an international body with membership in fifty countries. In the United States alone 15,500 clubs with a total of 850,000 members represented a mighty wave of feminine influence. All agreed that Sorosis had established lasting bonds of unity among women and had given them new power. The tendrils nurtured by Jenny June had taken root. The birth of the General Federation had fomented organization and the world of women's clubs was firmly established before the turn of the century.

By this time women had found sporadic openings in industry, in the professions, in trade. Strong efforts were made to fight child mortality and to push public health and hygiene. Of every million children born in the 1890's 150,000 died in the first, 53,000 in the second, and 28,000 in the third year of their lives. International consciousness was slowly awakening. The colleges were stirring up zest for higher education. The Woman's University Club of New York was incorporated in 1891. Absorbed as Mme. Demorest was in all these developments there was no cause in which she showed more interest than the good of the small child. She stirred up many of New York's richer women on the subject and found Mrs. William Astor a true benefactor in this field. These women could afford to think in terms of philanthropic gestures. Their husbands grew ever richer. By the 1890's the membership of the Stock Exchange had risen from 400 to 1,100. As much as $34,000 was now paid for a seat. There were telegraph and telephone offices in the building and the gallery around three sides of the board room was open to the public.

Grand Central Station was roofed with glass and under it were restaurants, waiting and baggage rooms, a police station, a barbershop and many utilities instead of the barren waste of the 1870's. By 1889 it was estimated that 95 million trips had been made across Brooklyn Bridge since the day of dedication. It was still regarded as the wonder sight of the city, and young people made it a regular promenading ground. The two new giants of Park Row who had succeeded Horace Greeley and the elder Bennett were locked in mortal combat—tense, vivid, red-bearded Joseph Pulitzer, running the *World* from wherever he happened to be, and William Randolph Hearst, whose explosive touch was rocking the established foundations of journalism. With the younger Bennett also in the field a formidable triumvirate whipped up public excitement at will. The *Tribune* plied a quieter course with Whitelaw Reid in charge. Since Greeley's death it had concentrated on news and no longer championed causes.

New York had approximately 500 churches at that time and most of them were filled for all services. The Sunday quiet of the city was marked. Lower Broadway was almost like a country road in 1889, although plenty of life was visible around the hotels farther up. The New York Bible Society, the New York Tract Society and the City Mission all were active in their various ways. The City Mission had a corps of women making house-to-house visits to needy families, and trained nurses to do tenement-house work. The Y.M.C.A. had eleven branches at strategic points. Chauncey Depew and Cornelius Vanderbilt were actively interested in the one at Grand Central Station.

All the Demorest family stood enthusiastically behind the head of the house when he ran for mayor in 1890, a forlorn hope but one that kept the temperance cause in the public eye. His defeat by Hugh J. Grant did not dismay him. He rarely showed ill-humor over failure or abuse. In spite of his vigorous campaigning Mr. Demorest was a mild man in his private life and genial in disposition. That year another grandchild was born and was named for him—William Jennings Demorest. He was the son of Henry Clay Demorest and Annie Lawrie and was destined to graduate from Columbia University, serve in the First World War and become a prominent figure in the real estate world—a particular interest of his grandfather's.

With the mayoralty contest behind him Mr. Demorest set off in the spring of 1891 with Nell and Evelyn for Mexico to spread the temperance message there. He told the Mexicans that a large proportion of the children of Maine, Iowa, Kansas and the Dakotas had never seen a drunken man, in contrast with the "devastation, crime, and wretchedness which prevail in the city of New York, and which are almost entirely caused by drink." Again the medals and tracts were scattered. Again a group was organized to work for temperance.

Evelyn was married to Alexander Garretson Rea of Philadelphia in May, 1892, and three months later the family home on

Fifty-seventh Street was again crowded for the birthday celebration of Mr. Demorest. This time it was his seventieth, and many of the old faces were gone, but his sons, his two daughters, with their husbands, and Matilda, now Mrs. William Ziegler, all were there. The White Ribboners sent a basket of seventy white roses. The temperance campaign gave the Demorests little time now for the Curtis country home at Saratoga. Mr. Demorest was tense, hard-working, picking up any thread of hope as he went along. To keep in touch with his many interests while in the country he had rigged up a homemade telephone from one farmhouse to another, with wire and two cigar boxes. He was greatly pleased with it, for it carried music thirty feet to another room when the organ was played. His taste for invention had not diminished.

The race track was alive with sharpers and raffish gamblers. Richard Canfield was setting a high pace with the bogus as well as the bona fide. He dressed in white tie and tails and wore a corset after he became stout. His Club House was rated the most luxurious gambling establishment in America and fortunes were made and lost as at Monte Carlo. Saratoga had ten gambling establishments in 1894, and 40,000 visitors settled in the resort for August. Diamond Jim Brady and Lillian Russell were in and out of the Club House. Brady swaggered about with diamond rings and enormous shirt studs of diamonds and rubies. Lillian drove along Broadway in her victoria, with black horses and the pigskin harness and white doeskin reins made for her by Mark Cross. Flo Ziegfeld hung over the gaming tables and was a canny plunger. William K. Vanderbilt stopped in for an unfortunate moment and lost a fortune. John W. Gates, better known as Bet-a-Million Gates, was a regular visitor, and two famous lawyers, John Graham and Abe Hummel, were marked figures at the spa. Berry Wall brought his bride to Saratoga. All this had little to do with life on the Curtis farm, where White Ribboners came and went, hymns were sung, and a network of international communication was in operation. But everyone turned out for the floral fete of

1894, when 50,000 persons watched a promenade of carriages and floats. Governor Levi P. Morton rode at the head of the pageant, and bicycles smothered in flowers wheeled along behind him.

The country was still in its gala mood from the Columbian Exposition of 1893 in Chicago, which had quickened appreciation of man's creative talents. The Fair as a whole had given stimulus to the artistic life of the nation and had affected its architecture in a permanent way. It was rated another big step forward for women, as they gathered from all nations under the firm directing hand of Mrs. Potter Palmer. The Woman's Pavilion, like the rest of the Fair, was much discussed for its effect on the arts. And through Mrs. Palmer the French Impressionists came strongly into view and were studied by visitors from all over the country.

By this time the Statue of Liberty was in place in New York harbor, a statue to Horace Greeley stood in front of the *Tribune* building, and the Players had been organized in Gramercy Park by Edwin Booth. Barnum was dead and the elegance of the 1880's had merged into the splendor of the 1890's. The great fortunes amassed in the two preceding decades were now being spent in lordly fashion. Oil wells, mines, railroads were discussed in the Windsor and St. Nicholas Hotels, in Delmonico's and the clubs. The homes on Fifth Avenue had their own private ballrooms. Their art collections were being assembled on expert advice. Jewelers, furriers and modistes were kept busy supplying the feminine demand, and imports poured in from Paris. Newport, Narragansett and Bar Harbor were the summer haunts, with their ocean sweep and spreading villas. The Berkshire Hills and the White Mountains drew many. There was coaching in the Catskills, bathing at Atlantic City, Asbury Park, Ocean Grove and Long Beach. Martha's Vineyard and Nantucket cast their own particular spell on many vacationists.

The opera was in its heyday with tiaras as common as field daisies. But the boxes were no longer decorated with masses of flowers. Only one bouquet, usually of violets, was carried in the white-gloved hand. Or lilies of the valley were worn on shimmering black evening gowns. Footmen opened carriage doors as box holders moved out of the opera house in their shining cloaks, jewels flashing, aigrettes tossing, their faces slightly dreamy from the singing of Nordica, Calvé, Melba, the de Reszkes, Plancon or Maurel. Philanthropy had become the stepsister of opulence. Ward McAllister had issued his edict about the Four Hundred and had founded The Patriarchs, the final test of social acceptance. The annual trip to Europe, yachting at Newport, the races at Saratoga, were essential entries on the social calendar. Dinners were stately and interminable, with ten to a dozen courses. Favors were costly and bizarre. Social rivalry was a blistering reality, with Mrs. William Astor directing the field. There was no denying the supremacy of dark-haired Caroline Schermerhorn Astor, cold and queenly in bearing, immune to social pressures. Her house at Fifth Avenue and Thirty-fourth Street, her villa at Newport, her country place at Rhinebeck, were the inviolable ramparts of social eminence. She yielded only reluctantly to the upstart Vanderbilts from Staten Island when Mrs. William K. Vanderbilt, the vivacious, chestnut-haired young matron from Mobile, Alabama, gave a costume party in 1883 in her new château on Fifth Avenue that even Mrs. Astor could not afford to ignore. But the Four Hundred was firmly defined by the time she gave her own last ball in 1892 at her old home at Thirty-fourth Street before following the tide of fashion uptown.

Anglomania was spreading in American social circles, spurred on by international marriages. The first and most significant to history was the marriage of Jennie Jerome and Lord Randolph Churchill in 1874 and the son they bore—Winston Churchill. Consuelo Yznaga came next. She married Lord Mandeville in 1876 and subsequently became the Duchess of Manchester. In 1895 Anna Gould married Count Boniface de Castellani, and then Consuelo, daughter of the William K. Vanderbilts, married the Duke of Marlborough in St. Thomas's under pressure from her mother. The social pace was fast. "How long can this last for American fathers and daughters?" asked Charles Dana Gibson in 1894 as he sketched his famous girls:

The pace for the father will last as long as daughter loves him, and for the daughter as long as Dad's money holds out . . . The pace of the American girl in society can never last long until she learns to take it easier. . . . Too much of everything—too many dinners, too long dancing, too late suppers, too much shopping, too many dressmakers, too many visits and calls, too many bowling, fencing, tennis and riding clubs, all too much.

In the Four Hundred were the "horsy set," who followed hounds, drove coaches, discussed the sales at Tattersall's and knew what they were talking about; the charity set, who stitched, visited, taught and saved, and were always on the wing from one committee meeting to another; the literary set, a small but flourishing class who had taken up belles-lettres and went in for poetry evenings. A few society girls modeled for the sketch artists. This was a new fad and they showed up readily in their Virot hats and Pingat coats, making 75 cents an hour and giving it to charity. One enterprising girl went to Paris, consulted Worth, Doucet, Raudnitz, Félix and the other top designers, and came back with gowns for the stay-at-homes.

Brides who could not afford to hoard their wedding gowns sent them to Lewando's French dyeing and cleaning establishment at Fourteenth Street and Fifth Avenue and made them serve other purposes. Personal maids abounded and a whole corridor was set aside for them in one Newport villa. Repoussé silver adorned most fashionable dressing tables and matinee stools were used in carriages. The flower show had come to stay and the fast and springy three-four time of the Redowa was carrying girls off their feet. The five-step waltz was hectic, too, but "dancing in the barn" was considered nothing short of a romp. Adolescents enjoyed themselves in dancing class with the military schottische, the cadet polka, the heel-and-toe polka, the Knickerbocker and the Berlin. All ages had gone overboard for baseball. The Polo Grounds swallowed up larger crowds of amusement seekers than any other stop between the Battery and Harlem Bridge.

Kate Field estimated that American women were spending $62 million a year for cosmetics at the beginning of the 1890's and women had begun to worry about their weight. The outdoor life was having its effect. "The fragile and delicate women are in a very small minority," *Demorest's* noted. "Artificial, made-up faces are absent; and bright ones with the rosy bloom of health abound . . . they rather proclaim the benefits of physical culture and healthful living . . . and give hints of daily constitutionals in the Park and long country rides." But the girls did not like it. How to lose weight became an absorbing topic. William Banting's system, which was simply starvation, had fallen from grace and the new trick was to eat lean, nonfattening food. "No bread, no sweets, no grease allowed," said the official advisers. The tailor-made drew attention to nature's curves. Dr. Dinsmore, Mme. Demorest's ally, tackled the question medically and went in for reducing her patients by scientific measures. She considered obesity a disease, not an indulgence. But Lily Langtry had learned how to keep her celebrated shape and preserve her complexion, too. Twice a week she retired to a lounge and covered her face with thin strips of veal, an old Persian trick to demolish wrinkles.

In the winter of 1894 all the girls were in and out of gyms, taking muscle development exercises. The Berkeley Ladies Athletic Club, an offshoot of a similar club for men, occupied the adjoining clubhouse and was stampeded with votaries. They had a gymnasium with their own instructor and attending physician. Downstairs they had three bowling alleys, a swimming pool, and facilities for tennis, badminton, fencing, whist and chess. The reception room was done in Louis XVI style and the club had 250 blue-blooded members. The less ambitious had equipment at home—dumbbells, trapeze, punching bag and Indian clubs. With the outdoor life had come an acute consciousness of their flabby muscles. At the same time they took lectures on cooking, poetry and pronunciation, and kept Maltese,

THE LAST TRUMPET (269)

Angora or Persian cats, talking birds or a variety of dogs. Some girls led packs of from five to eight dogs and carried malacca sticks with silver knobs to manage their restless charges. Matrons flocked to take the electric cure. In wrappers and Turkish slippers they fought their headaches and nerves with electric trickles on the soles of their feet or the tops of their heads. There were many parlors where they could have this sort of treatment to enable them to face one more ball. Russian bath parties were the 1890's version of the Turkish bath.

Other diversions were "dove" coaching parties and Beatrice luncheons for brides-to-be before the age of the shower. The "Cranford" tea was a novelty, with the guests playing Elizabeth Gaskell's characters. Hostesses wrapped everything, even the breadsticks at luncheons, with ribbons and bows. Pansies and violets showed up regularly at their functions. The violet was the flower of the hour in 1894. *Trilby* had just come out. There were Trilby stickpins, Trilby shoes, Trilby spoons, Trilby hats made entirely of violets, and a million Trilby corsages. The most up-to-date young men sent their girls bunches of violets, or one stately American Beauty rose in a slender vase of Austrian glass or a Dresden china holder.

The more daring girls went slumming occasionally, eating twenty-cent lunches in little Italian restaurants and giving the hypothetical difference to charity. They favored bizarre entertainments in the Bowery quarter and wore their shabbiest clothes. The debs and bachelors who plied this game called themselves the Flitter Mice and the Buccaneers. Amateur groups such as the Plantation Warblers, or the Mandolin and Guitar Club, composed of twelve young women in Greek tunics, gave musicales for charity. For luck girls carried small brownies made of enamel and gold, studded with diamonds. Their enamel watches hung from their necks on black satin ribbon or else were thrust into their belts. They liked quotation parties and confession albums. Who is your favorite author? What is your favorite flower? What is your dream of happiness? They learned to write with Parker pens and their desks were a clutter of silver accessories, from stamp boxes to paper knives. Red morocco desk fittings with silver monograms were considered dashing. Book plates were a new fad, and many girls now had bookcases of their own in their homes—a Chippendale on delicate legs, a Louis XVI cabinet, a colonial cupboard, or a home-made device to hold their morocco-bound poets.

The twelve most read books in 1894, according to a national survey, were: *David Copperfield, Ivanhoe, The Scarlet Letter, Uncle Tom's Cabin, Ben Hur, Adam Bede, Vanity Fair, Jane Eyre, Last Days of Pompeii, John Halifax, Gentleman, Les Misérables,* and *Little Women.* There were innumerable reading clubs across the country and some young women earned their living as readers for these clubs, selecting the books and arranging the material. The push toward culture was disturbing the dovecotes. It was much discussed in the men's clubs. They blamed it all on the colleges. Would these learned girls make good wives? That was the question that found a variety of answers in practice. They need not have worried. Few of the girls had gone true "bluestocking." In odd moments the more frivolous ones still trapped butterflies in their flower gardens, looking picturesque with their colored silk nets on lacquered sticks and tin-lined boxes with chloroform. Canopies and striped awnings enlivened countless lawns at the summer resorts and country homes. Breakfast was apt to be served outdoors with spirit lamp, alcohol egg boiler and chafing dish close to the white wicker furniture and glowing flower beds. Strawberry teas followed tennis and croquet matches. Lawn parties were in high esteem. Hammocks swung from trees. Rugs were laid on the grass to keep out the damp. Japanese lanterns rustled in the branches at night and blancmange and frozen peach custard were served ad infinitum. Mandolins, guitars and aeolian harps made strumming music for boating parties on moonlit evenings. Country fairs for charity were popular events, with offerings ranging from pullets to preserves. These usually ended up with rustic dances and messy lawns.

The suffrage question was monopolizing tea table gossip

in the 1890's. Mothers no longer pestered their daughters' beaux for subscriptions to charity but for their signatures to some monster petition. "The young men look upon the suffrage movement as a great institution," *Demorest's* noted. "They are asked to the best dinners, coddled, humored, and flattered with consummate tact, all for their signatures." The Four Hundred were deeply involved. Even the Sorosis Club of Bombay had adopted for its motto "The world was made for women also." A debate at Bryn Mawr on woman suffrage in 1894 aroused more excitement in that conservative institution than any subject that had come up since its opening. The vote was a tie.

But all other interests paled before the bicycle craze that had succeeded the tandem and the earlier velocipede. By 1895 there were 40,000 women cyclists in the United States, with New England and New York claiming the greatest number. The nation's full bicycle army was estimated at 2 million. Business grew slack at the riding academies. Croquet sets and roller skates were consigned to the attic. The girls wore little caps, or hats with perky birds' wings and upstanding quills that added to their air of flight and speed. Their long jackets went billowing out behind them. Their leg-of-mutton sleeves ballooned. They usually wore gaiters and equestrian tights or well-fitted knickerbockers. *Demorest's* advised against "tossing plumes and flying ribbons, or fluffy ruffs and boas or chiffon blouses." The well-groomed cyclist must be strictly tailor-made, with pongee blouse, a blazer or jacket, and leggings to match. Soft felt hats with a protecting brim for the eyes were recommended. The editors viewed the new sport as a "democratic leveler of people and classes" as well as a healthful sport.

All ages joined in the fun, but one clergyman, outraged by Sunday bicycling, issued a solemn warning: "You cannot serve God and skylark on a bicycle." There were bicycling breakfasts and bicycling luncheons, summer and winter, with bicycle bells sometimes summoning the guests to table. The Newport Bicycle Club gave expert instruction to the gilded set. In New York the same young people haunted the Michaux Club on

Fifty-third Street, close to Broadway. Frances Willard and the Rev. Phebe A. Hanaford both took to their wheels. The Queen of Italy and several European princesses were ardent cyclists. But Lillian Russell was the true eye-catcher. Superbly poised in white serge she rode twice daily around the reservoir on a gold-plated bicycle with mother-of-pearl handle bars studded with jewels. Diamond Jim Brady often rode by her side, the silvered spokes of his gold-plated bicycle gleaming in the sun.

The young Demorests were enthusiastic cyclists, and Madame encouraged them in this sport. On their Sunday trips to Claremont they were sometimes caught in the middle of the bicycle parade. A favorite route for the younger generation was up Riverside Drive past Grant's Tomb and on to the Claremont Inn, where they could dine out of doors with Japanese lanterns swaying overhead and music floating out into the night. But by 1896 the "horseless carriage" had made its appearance and by the close of the century this new fad had taken possession, with all its promise for the future.

The final word in bicycle chic was polo played with long-handled tennis rackets and rubber balls. These bicycle polo tournaments were held at Newport, Narragansett Pier and Bar Harbor. Girls were taking up golf by this time, too, and moved with ambivalence from white duck sailor suits in the morning to gauzy ruffles by night. But Edward Bok in the *Ladies' Home Journal* impressed on them that the "vast and overwhelming majority of women . . . prefer to be womanly, and dress tastefully and prettily, as God intended women should dress." *Puck* commented in August, 1895, that the bicycle makers had accomplished more for dress reform in two years than the preachers of that cult had effected since clothes had come into use. The Rainy Day skirt came next, clearing the ground by five inches. By this time Amelia Bloomer was disclaiming her own fame, insisting that Elizabeth Smith Miller, daughter of Gerrit Smith, the abolitionist, was first responsible for the divided skirt. The huge sleeves of the 1890's had become a curse and an embarrassment second only to the crinoline. When the girls went sleighing in the midst of a blizzard, with streetcar gongs clanging and yellow headlights blazing their trail, there was scarcely room for their escorts to bundle them tighter in their buffalo robes. Hands off, said the monster epaulets.

Somehow they achieved the happy mean when they got to sea in their yachts. There they were feminine, wind-swept and sportsmanlike all at the same time. And some had a say in the designs of the family yachts. "The American woman wants her yacht to be her summer home; and when she gives her order to the builder, comfort, not speed, is her requisite," said Demorest's. "A big white schooner, very broad, and very smart, and neat with her rail fringes, glittering brass, snowy decks, and deck furniture in white whicker. . . . The great aft cabin, for Madame the owner."

Mrs. Lucy C. Carnegie was the first woman member of the New York Yacht Club. She was permitted to fly the club burgee, enter races but not to use the clubhouse. Meanwhile, the sparkling Mrs. John Jacob Astor IV practiced pistol shooting in her spare moments and Mrs. Potter Palmer of Chicago became expert on the moors and at knocking down clay pigeons. The fashionable set wore sturdy calfskin walking boots, or clumsy light tan shoes for golf, skating or bicycling. Overshoes were pointed in the 1890's. Carriage shoes were lined with fur. Dress shoes were of satin, suède or patent leather. And in their boudoirs women lounged about in scarlet Turkish slippers, fur-bordered pantoufles or satin mules.

The Demorests watched each fad come and go with philosophical detachment as they grew older. Mr. Demorest continued on his vigorous way until he came down with pneumonia in the spring of 1895. He was ill only a short time and died at his city home on April 9, 1895. He was seventy-three and had been turning out his temperance talks to the end. His last piece, finished just before his death, was on "The Great War of the Nineteenth Century" and the war, of course, was the temperance war. When he learned that he was dying he said he was ready to go. The morning after his death a message arrived from his friends in England: "We mourn a leader passed from Contest to Conquest." It was signed "Willard—Somerset—Gordon."

His funeral was held on April 12 at the Reformed Church, Madison Avenue and Fifty-seventh Street, not a stone's throw from his home. Mme. Demorest, who, like all her sisters, had turned to Christian Science in her later years, selected the flowers—white roses, orchids and lilies of the valley in the chancel, a pall of violets and lilies of the valley on the coffin. A memorial service was held at Chickering Hall, where Mr. Demorest had appeared so often, as Vienna's proud father, as a public man who followed the more important lectures and sponsored many causes. John St. John and Professor Samuel Dickie, chairman of the National Prohibition Committee, both spoke, and the choir of the American Temperance Union sang the editor's favorite hymns. "Mr. Demorest," said Professor Dickie, "was a man who had the strength of his convictions. He thought it better to be with the minority when he knew it was right than to be with a majority which he thought was wrong."

Mme. Demorest did not survive her husband for any length of time. She was already an invalid at the time of his death. She gave up the house as too much of a burden and moved into the Hotel Renaissance at 4 West Forty-third Street, which later became the Columbia University Club. She died there on August 10, 1898, at the age of seventy-four. Burial was in Kensico Cemetery. The Spanish-American War was raging at the time and the century was nearing a close. The Bradley Martin ball held at the Waldorf in 1897, with its historical pageant and footmen in blue and gold, was the last great social function of the decade and the outcry over its extravagance was such that the Martins fled to France to escape further censure. The Demorest magazine had followed the trend of the times. In the year of Nell's death it was taken over by the Arkell Publishing Company, publishers of *Puck* and *Judge*, and it expired a year later. *Godey's Lady's Book, Peterson's* and *Arthur's* all succumbed in 1898. They belonged to another generation. The *Ladies' Home Journal* and the *Delineator* had cut heavily into the fashion trade. *Good Housekeeping* was showing promise. *Harper's Bazaar* was in difficulties but would recover. The *Woman's Cycle*, which was founded and edited by Jenny June as the official organ of the General Federation of Women's Clubs, was quickly absorbed by Marion Harland's monthly *The Homemaker*. Butterick withdrew from his many publications in 1899 but his patterns continued to flourish. The Demorest name was dead in the publishing world after a long and honorable history but Demorest patterns and the dress-cutting system continued to show up in different parts of the world for years to come.

In the year that Mme. Demorest died Jenny June fell in her home and fractured her hip. Within a few months her husband David was dead. After these two misfortunes her health declined and she passed most of her time abroad, traveling in Germany, France and Switzerland, and resting for long periods at Ambleside and Oberammergau. She helped her daughter, Mrs. Vida Croly Sidney, to organize the Society of American Women in London. By this time she had finished her 1,183-page *History of the Woman's Club Movement in America*, rounding out a lifetime of prodigious effort. On her seventieth birthday the Woman's Press Club gave her a diamond-studded lorgnette with the inscription: "Having eyes, she has seen; having ears, she has heard; and, having a tongue, she has spoken in behalf of all women." It was a satisfaction to her to see her son Herbert started in the editorial field.

Jenny had recently returned from Europe when she died suddenly two days before Christmas, 1901, at the age of seventy-two. Services were held for her at the Little Church Around the Corner and she was buried at Lakewood, New Jersey. Both she and Mme. Demorest had lived to see much of their work take root. The new century dawned and fashions and crusades went on in the deathless tradition of woman's wish to look her best, and of man's need to chart new horizons.

Bibliography

BOOKS

AMORY, CLEVELAND. *The Last Resorts.* New York: Harper & Brothers, 1952.
————. *The Proper Bostonians.* New York: E. P. Dutton, 1947.
————. *Who Killed Society?* New York: Harper & Brothers, 1960.
ALLEN, DR. R. L., *Hand Book of Saratoga.* New York: W. H. Arthur & Company, 1859.
Appleton's Journal of Literature, Science and Art. New York: D. Appleton & Company, 1869.
BIGELOW, JOHN. *Retrospections of an Active Life.* Garden City, N.Y.: Doubleday, Page & Company, 1913.
BRADLEY, HUGH. *Such Was Saratoga.* New York: Doubleday, Doran & Company, 1940.
BRANDOW, JOHN HENRY. *The Story of Old Saratoga.* Albany: Brandow Printing Company, 1900.
BROWN, HENRY COLLINS. *Brownstone Fronts and Saratoga Trunks.* New York: E. P. Dutton & Company, 1935.
————. *In the Golden Nineties,* Vols. 11 and 12. Hastings-on-Hudson, N.Y.: Valentine's Manual Inc., 1928.
————. *Valentine's Manual of Old New York.* Hastings-on-Hudson, N.Y., 1927.
BRYANT, WILLIAM CULLEN (ed.). *Picturesque America,* Vol. 2. New York: D. Appleton & Company, 1894.
BURKE, WILLIAM JEREMIAH, and HOWE, WILL D. *American Authors and Books, 1640-1940.* New York: Gramercy Publishing Company, 1943.
CAMPBELL, HELEN (STUART). *Darkness and Daylight.* Hartford, Conn.: A. D. Worthington & Company, 1891.
CROLY, MRS. JANE C. (JENNY JUNE). *The History of the Woman's Club*

Movement in America. New York: Henry G. Allen & Company, 1898.

CUNNINGHAM, JOHN. *Memories of Jane C. Croly, Jenny June.* New York: G. P. Putnam's Sons, 1904.

DEPEW, CHAUNCEY M. (ed.). *One Hundred Years of American Commerce.* 2 vols. New York: D. O. Haynes & Company, 1895.

DEMAREST, MARY A. and WILLIAM H. S., *The Demarest Family.* New Brunswick, N.J.: Thatcher-Anderson Company, 1938.

DUNCAN, WILLIAM CARY. *The Amazing Madame Jumel.* New York: Frederick A. Stokes, 1935.

EARHART, MARY. *Frances Willard: from Prayers to Politics.* Chicago: University of Chicago Press, 1944.

EGGLESTON, GEORGE CARY. *Recollections of a Varied Life.* New York: Henry Holt & Company, 1910.

FAITHFULL, EMILY. *Three Visits to America.* New York: Fowler & Wells, 1884.

Fifty Years on Fifth. New York: Fifth Avenue Association. Printed by International Press, 1957.

FINLEY, RUTH. *The Lady of Godey's, Sarah Josepha Hale.* Philadelphia: J. B. Lippincott Company, 1931.

FURMAN, BESS. *White House Profile.* Indianapolis: The Bobbs-Merrill Company, 1951.

Historical and Biographical Sketch of the Demarest and Demorest Families. Washington, D.C.: Colonial Research Bureau.

History of Saratoga County. Some of its Prominent Men and Pioneers. Philadelphia: Everts and Ensign, 1878.

JENKINS, STEPHEN. *The Greatest Street in the World: The Story of Broadway.* New York: G. P. Putnam's Sons, 1911.

KNOWLES, HORACE (ed.). *Gentlemen, Scholars and Scoundrels.* New York: Harper & Brothers, 1959.

KOUVENHOVEN, JOHN ATLEE. *Adventures of America; 1857-1900.* New York: Harper & Brothers, 1900.

LAMB, MARTHA J. *History of the City of New York: Its Origin, Rise and Progress.* 5 vols. New York: A. S. Barnes & Company, 1877.

LONGLEY, MARJORIE, SILVERSTEIN, LOUIS, and TOWER, SAMUEL A. *America's Taste 1851-1959.* New York: Simon & Schuster, 1960.

LUTZ, ALMA. *Susan B. Anthony.* Boston: Beacon Press, 1959.

LYNES, RUSSELL. *The Tastemakers.* New York: Harper & Brothers, 1954.

MACK, EDWARD CLARENCE. *Peter Cooper, Citizen of New York.* New York: Duell, Sloan & Pearce, 1949.

MORRIS, LLOYD. *Incredible New York.* New York: Random House, 1951.

MOTT, FRANK LUTHER. *A History of American Magazines,* Vols. 3 and 4. Cambridge, Mass.: Harvard University Press, 1938.

MOULTON, CHARLES WELLS. *Frances Elizabeth Willard. A Woman of the Century.* Buffalo: Moulton Publishing Company, 1893.

NEVINS, ALLAN. *Abram S. Hewitt: with some account of Peter Cooper.* New York: Harper & Brothers, 1935.

OSBORNE, DUFFIELD. *The Authors Club*. New York: The Knickerbocker Press, 1913.

ROGERS, AGNES. *Women Are Here to Stay*. New York: Harper & Brothers, 1949.

ROSS, ISHBEL. *Ladies of the Press*. New York: Harper & Brothers, 1936.

SACHS, EMANIE LOUISE. *The Terrible Siren, Victoria Woodhull, 1838-1927*. New York: Harper & Brothers, 1928.

SCHLESINGER, ELIZABETH BANCROFT. *The Nineteenth Century Woman's Dilemma and Jennie June*. Reprinted from the *New York History*, October, 1961.

SHAPLEN, ROBERT. *Free Love and Heavenly Sinners; the story of the great Henry Ward Beecher scandal*. New York: A. A. Knopf, 1954.

SMITH, JOSEPH. *Reminiscences of Saratoga*. New York: The Knickerbocker Press, 1897.

SMITH, MATTHEW HALE. *Sunlight and Shadow in New York*. Hartford, Conn.: J. B. Burr & Company, 1869.

———. *Successful Folks. How They Live*. Hartford, Conn.: American Publishing Company, 1878.

SPARKES, BOYDEN, and MOORE, SAMUEL TAYLOR. *Hetty Green, A Woman Who Loved Money*. New York: Doubleday, Doran & Company, 1930.

STERN, MADELEINE B. *Purple Passage*. Norman: University of Oklahoma Press, 1953.

STODDARD, HENRY LUTHER. *Horace Greeley*. New York: G. P. Putnam's Sons, 1946.

STONE, WILLIAM L. *Reminiscences of Saratoga and Ballston*. New York: Virtue & Yorston, 1875.

SYLVESTER, NATHANIEL BARTLETT. *History of Saratoga County*. Richmond, Ind.: Gresham Publishing Company, 1898.

WHARTON, EDITH N. *The Age of Innocence*. New York: D. Appleton & Company, 1920.

———. *A Backward Glance*. New York: D. Appleton-Century Company, 1934.

Women of the Century. Boston: B. B. Russell, 1877.

NEWSPAPERS

Detroit *Free Press*
New York *Commercial Advertiser*
New York *Daily Graphic*
New York *Daily Times*
New York *Dispatch*
New York *Evening Mail*
New York *Evening Post*
New York *Herald*
New York *Sun*

New York *Sunday Times and Noah's Weekly Messenger*
New York *Times*
New York *Tribune*
New York *World*
Ohio *State Journal*
Philadelphia *Ledger*
Philadelphia *Press*
Saratoga *Daily Democrat*
Saratoga *Eagle*
Saratoga *Republican*
Saratoga *Sentinel*
Saratoga *Whig*
Saratogian
Schuylerville *Herald*
Schuylerville *News*
Springfield *Republican*
Troy *Budget*
Troy *Daily Whig*
Troy *Sentinel*
Troy *Times*

Index

McAllister, Ward, 202, 266
McCloskey, Archbishop, 190
McCutcheon's, 14
McMillan, Alexander, 77
Medal contests, 245-46, 256
Merriman, Mrs. Emilie J., 64
Metropolitan, 50
Metropolitan Life Insurance Company, 190
Metropolitan Museum of Art, New York City, 203, 206, 228
Metropolitan Opera House, New York City, 193, 212, 238, 258, 259
Metternich, Princess von, 109
Mexico, 173, 263
Michigan University, 223
Miller, Elizabeth Smith, 272
Mills, Mrs. John T., 202
Miniature Magazine, 146
Mirror of Fashions, Mme. Demorest's, 21-22, 27, 28-29, 30, 31, 32, 33, 35, 36-37, 39, 43, 51, 111, 142
Mitchell, Maria, 105, 226, 260
Monterey, California, 233
Montez, Lola, 162
Moon, C. B., 68
Moore, Mrs. Bloomfield, 235
Moore, Francis, 248
Morris, Clara, 238
Morris, Ethel, 254
Morris, Henry Curtis, 254
Morrisey, John, 66, 68, 125
Morton, Levi P., 91, 265
Morton, Mrs. Levi P., 235
Mount Holyoke College, 227
Mowatt, Anna Cora, 207

Napoleon III, Emperor, of France, 194
Narragansett, Rhode Island, 265
Nast, Thomas, 62, 88, 167
Nathan, Benjamin, 88
Nation, Carry, 246
National Conference of Charities and Correction, 171
National Prohibition Bureau, 241, 243, 246
National Woman Suffrage Association, 101, 166, 259
Natural History Museum, New York City, 206
Nealy, Mary E., 237

New England Women's Club, 261
Newnham College, 223
Newport, Rhode Island, 69, 122, 123, 265
New York, New York, 8-9, 10-18, 19, 26, 41-42, 65-67, 75-78, 87-88, 168-170, 190-91, 200-10, 224, 228, 262-263, 264-73
New York Academy of Medicine, 191
New York Club, 91
New York *Democrat*, 123, 132, 138, 139
New York *Dispatch*, 58
New York *Evening Mail*, 71
New York *Evening Post*, 143, 189, 208
New York *Globe*, 132
New York *Graphic*, 160, 188
New York *Herald*, 58, 112, 113, 118, 143, 257
New York *Illustrated News*, 43
New York *Independent*, 60, 165
New York Life Insurance Company, 190
New York Medical College for Women, 231
New York *Mercury*, 33
New York *Star*, 114
New York *Sun*, 129, 132
New York *Telegram*, 123, 140, 192
New York *Times*, 53, 72, 147, 167, 213, 238
New York *Tribune*, 10, 42, 53, 72, 143, 248
New York Women's Press Club, 223, 275
New York *World*, 53, 90, 102, 159
New York Yacht Club, 273
Nilsson, Christine, 117-18, 173, 213
Noble, Agnes, 94
Northern Pacific Railroad, 158, 209
Nouvelle Revue, 216

Olmstead, Frederick Law, 169
Opdyke, George, 12, 15, 29, 42
Orchard Lawn Grove, Saratoga, 125-26
Otis, Mrs. Harrison Gray, 3
Ottarson, Mrs. F. J., 91
Owen, Mary C., 102
Owen, Robert Dale, 94
Oxford University, 223